THE LONELY SHIPS

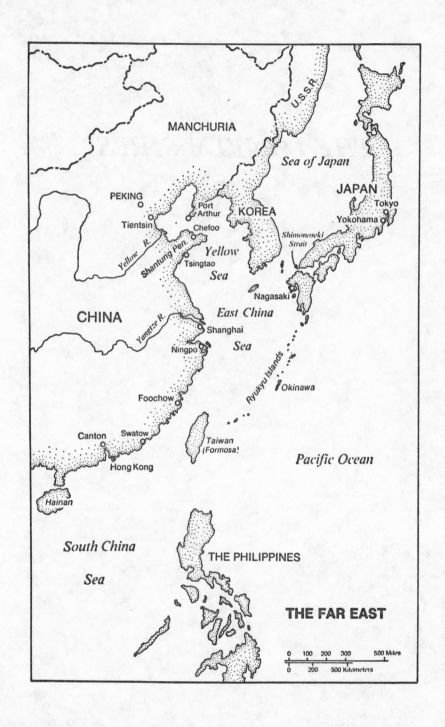

The Lonely Ships

The Life and Death of the U.S. Asiatic Fleet

Edwin P. Hoyt

David McKay Company, Inc.
New York

Copyright © 1976 by Edwin P. Hoyt

MANUFACTURED IN THE UNITED STATES OF AMERICA

Author's Note

I am indebted to Rear Admiral Ernest M. Eller, the former director of Naval History, for encouragement in the writing of this book, and also to Vice-Admiral Edwin Hooper, present director of Naval History, for the same reason. Admiral Arleigh Burke and I talked over certain aspects of it a long time ago, and I owe him a vote of thanks for his cogent observations. The late Admiral Thomas C. Hart was helpful by correspondence and in an interview. I am also in debt to various librarians at the U.S. Navy Library, the Classified Archives Division of the Navy History Division, and the U.S. Naval Academy for the use of much material. The ships' history section of the Naval History Division was also helpful. I also used the facilities of the Rutland Free Library, the Nantucket Atheneum, and Yale University's Sterling Library.

Nantucket
November 1975

Contents

10   *Contents*

Introduction

The United States Asiatic Fleet was born in the 1850s to protect American interests in the Far East. It died under Japanese attacks in the Philippines and the East Indies in March 1942.

Between those dates it wrote a history of action in many parts of the Far East—in the ports and on the rivers of China, where it "showed the flag" and took occasional potshots at troublesome warlords; in Manila Bay, where it destroyed a Spanish fleet in 1898; and again in the Philippines and in the East Indies in the early days of World War II, where, with pitiable forces and ill-equipped allies, it took the full brunt of the Japanese military juggernaut.

The saga of the Asiatic Fleet begins in the turmoil of nineteenth-century Manchu China, when the Western powers and Japan were in a race for trade and privileges in China. As the foreign businessmen moved in, first to the ports and then deep into the interior along the rivers, the gunboats—British, American, Japanese, French, German, and others—followed.

It was a period when the foreign powers, backed by their navies, were tearing China apart. In 1840-42 the British defeated China in the Opium War, obtaining the cession of Hong Kong and the opening for trade of five "treaty ports"—Canton, Amoy, Foochow, Ningpo, and Shanghai. These were the first of numerous treaty ports opened by China in response to demands by the Western powers, where the Westerners conducted trade with China on terms they imposed.

It was the era of "extraterritoriality" in China, during which foreigners obtained, and sometimes abused, rights of jurisdiction over the Chinese. In this period, by war, threats, or skulduggery, Japan seized Formosa and Britain took Kowloon (opposite Hong Kong), and Britain, France, Russia, and Germany all occupied strategic ports or other areas of coastal China under grants of leaseholds. Foreign settlements or "concessions" were established in many Chinese cities, including

French, British, and American concessions in Shanghai, the latter two became known as the International Settlement.

The encroachments of foreigners and the presence of their warships in Chinese waters led to constant friction with the Imperial Chinese government as well as various nationalist groups. In 1900 Chinese resentment against the foreigners exploded in the Boxer Rebellion. To quell this revolt, eight foreign nations, including the United States, sent troops to China. In the vanguard of these forces, in a rare shift from sea to land duty, were men of the Asiatic Fleet.

As the twentieth century progressed, the shadow of Japan spread ever deeper over the Asian mainland. Annexation of Korea in 1910 was followed by territorial gains in China in World War I. The invasion of Manchuria in 1931, and attacks on Shanghai and the conquest of much of the Chinese heartland in the later 1930s.

Japanese arrogance in China caused mounting tensions between Tokyo and the Western powers, whose warships were in the area. These tensions reached a summit in December 1937 when Japanese warplanes sank the U.S. gunboat *Panay* in the Yangtze River, sending a tremor around the world as the two Pacific powers maintained a collision course.

Shortly before the Japanese assault on Pearl Harbor in December 1941, the Asiatic Fleet moved most of its ships from China to the Philippines. From there, after the Japanese attacked, it made a fighting retreat to the islands of the Malay Barrier, guarding the Indian Ocean from Malaya to New Guinea.

With a handful of aging cruisers and destroyers, a small fleet of submarines, and virtually no air support or hope of reinforcement, the Asiatic Fleet fought gallantly against impossible odds in defense of the Dutch East Indies. Its submarines harried the enemy in a dozen seas. Its "expendables" expired in the smoke of Bataan and Corregidor.

Finally, battered in East Indian waters and bombed into sinking hulks in the Philippines, it ceased to exist—a few of its ships and men did manage to escape to Australia.

The story of the Asiatic Fleet forms one of the most fascinating, stirring, and least-known chapters of U.S. naval history. It is a saga of a Cinderella fleet in a prestigious U.S. naval establishment, of lonely ships in far-off places, of strange encounters in the mysterious Orient; and, as it fought to its death in those first few months of World War II, of valorous actions in victory and defeat. It is, also, a story of extraordinary personal heroism.

Here is that story.

Part One

THE RISE OF
THE ASIATIC FLEET

I

Gunboat on the Yangtze

They would call it an "incident" when it was all over, for that was the language of the day used to indicate a confrontation between two unfriendly nations when the clash did not quite provoke a war, but fell just short of it.

That was the case on December 12, 1937, when Japanese warplanes bombed and sank the U.S. gunboat *Panay* on the Yangtze River in China. It was the first great confrontation between the United States and Japan. Barely a month earlier the Japanese had captured Shanghai after a bloody battle. Now they were about to grab another glittering prize—the new Chinese capital of Nanking, 150 miles west of Shanghai.

As the Japanese neared Nanking, many Western residents, including Americans, prepared to flee the city. And the little twin-stacked U.S.S. *Panay*, trim in her white and buff paint and lavishly bedecked with the Stars and Stripes, moved downriver toward Nanking. Inside the beleaguered city the atmosphere was tense. The Japanese had already warned the foreign diplomats to leave, for their lives were in peril.

An ominous series of events preceded the coming explosion on the Yangtze. For years, following their conquest of Manchuria in 1931, the Japanese had been plotting further aggressions against China. Then, in July 1937, they struck in force. After a trumped up incident at the Marco Polo Bridge near Peking, the Chinese capital, the Japanese invaded China proper. Within a month the capital fell.

The next blow struck Shanghai. There, backed by a massive fleet, the Japanese landed troops on August 11. The battle for the great port began. Three days later the Chinese air force attempted to bomb the Japanese warships in the harbor. Their principal target was the *Idzumo*, flagship of the Japanese fleet, moored off the bund at Hangchow. In-

stead of hitting the *Idzumo*, the Chinese bombs landed in the middle
of the International Settlement, between the Palace and Cathay hotels,
killing more than twelve hundred people, mostly Chinese.

As the bombs fell, Admiral Henry Yarnell, commander of the U.S.
Asiatic Fleet, neared Shanghai in his flagship, the cruiser *Augusta*. At
flank speed and through rough weather, the ship had sped south from
Tsingtao, on China's northeast coast, following news of the Japanese assault on Shanghai.

Yarnell had spent a typical fleet summer—or had tried to. He had left
the Philippines in the winter, spent a week in Shanghai, the next few
weeks at Vladivostok, and then moved on to Tsingtao. But now he
steamed back into battle-torn Shanghai, arriving at 4:40 in the afternoon of August 14, or "Bloody Saturday." The *Augusta* was promptly
bombed by the Chinese air force, which mistook her for a Japanese
cruiser. No one was hurt—the bombs missed and managed only to
shower the *Augusta* with fragments.

As the Battle of Shanghai raged, *Augusta* remained off the bund, and
was under fire nearly every day by either Japanese or Chinese. On August 20, as evening fell and the men of the ship gathered to watch
movies, a shell burst on the well deck. Shrapnel killed Seaman First
Class F.J. Falgout and wounded seventeen other men.

During the next five months the Yangtze was filled with the warships
of the Western powers—far more American than any others. *Augusta*
stayed in place and was joined by the cruiser *Marblehead*; a dozen destroyers were in and out, and many other vessels came to bring supplies
or pay calls. Of the gunboat fleet of the Yangtze Patrol, the flagship
Isabel roamed the river, *Panay* was far upstream, while *Tulsa*, *Sacramento*, and *Oahu* were often in Shanghai.

The Japanese attack brought reinforcements for all the fleets of the
foreign powers. Soon there were nearly nine thousand Western troops
and sailors in Shanghai—British, American, and French for the most
part.

The U.S. Navy, wanting to put a stop to Japanese expansion by a
show of force, called for the reinforcement of the fleet in these waters by
four heavy cruisers. But in Washington the Department of State decided it was too risky.

From his perch aboard the *Augusta*, Admiral Yarnell had little doubt
concerning Japanese intentions: They were determined to make a colony of China—the largest and most populous country in the world.
Such an ambition, Yarnell felt, should be resisted. But here again he
was opposed by a State Department that was unwilling to antagonize

the Japanese. It didn't seem to matter if the Japanese bombed American ships, so long as American ships didn't shoot back. One day a Japanese bomb wounded a radioman standing next to the admiral on the flagship's bridge. Yarnell took this personally, and announced that now he would shoot back. The State Department protested to the Navy Department that the admiral was making inflammatory statements.

The war escalated. The Soviet Union sent a number of planes and pilots to China to fight the Japanese around Nanking, but the Japanese were not halted. In mid-September, with Nanking subject to bombing attacks, Ambassador Nelson Johnson moved out into the Yangtze aboard the gunboat *Luzon*; in late November he and the *Luzon* moved up to Hankow, six hundred miles inland on the Yangtze. And downriver came the gunboat *Panay*, to stand by at Nanking, ready to evacuate the Americans.

Panay's captain was Lieutenant Commander James Joseph Hughes, a graduate of the U.S. Naval Academy, who had held command of the gunboat for about a year and knew her well. Just thirty-nine years old, he celebrated his birthday in November, when the Sino-Japanese war began to get serious from the American point of view. While he steamed downriver to Nanking, his wife was on her way to Canton, for American service families were being removed from the trouble that almost everyone knew was coming.

Hughes' executive officer was Lieutenant Arthur F. Anders, another career navy man and a Texan, whose wife was also in China and was also moving to Canton. *Panay* had three other officers, Lieutenant (j.g.) John W. Geist, Ensign Harry Biwerse, and Lieutenant Clark Grazier of the Navy Medical Corps, the ship's doctor.

The ship also carried some fifty enlisted men and petty officers, and a Chinese crew of about a dozen, who did most of the hard work and in addition waited on the enlisted men and the officers. Four of these Chinese—Far Ze ("Fuzzy") Wong, Ducey Ting, King Fong Sung, and Yuan Te Erh—were enlisted in the U.S. Navy as mess attendants. The rest were local people, and might leave the ship when she moved away from their home city, to be replaced by others by the gunboat's comprador, or Chinese business agent. A small fleet of Chinese sampans also subsisted on the Americans' leavings and by running their errands.

On December 8, as *Panay* lay at anchor off Nanking, Generalissimo Chiang Kai-shek, the Chinese president and commander-in-chief, left Nanking with his wife and headed upriver, realizing that he could no longer manage the government of China from the threatened city.

Most Americans had left the city, too, but the embassy still had a small staff there to safeguard the interests of the some twenty citizens who remained. George Atcheson, the Second Secretary, was in charge of the embassy staff. The plan called for Atcheson and his people to round up all the Americans the moment it became apparent the Japanese were going to take the city, and to move them aboard the *Panay*. There might be some difficulty—the Americans still there stubbornly insisted that they would be all right: the businessmen believed in business as usual; the missionaries felt the hand of God would protect them from any enemies. Then there were the foreign correspondents, who felt the war was their job; these included Norman Alley, a cameraman for Universal Newsreels.

On December 9 the Japanese in Shanghai asked the Americans remaining in Nanking to please leave the city as they might be injured in the fighting, but the hard core hung on—which meant the embassy staff stayed, and the gunboat remained in the river.

By December 11, the only exit from Nanking through which people could move without fighting the Japanese was the Hsiakuan Gate, and General T'ang Sheng-chih, the Chinese commander, said he did not know how much longer he could keep that gate open. The Japanese were upon him in overwhelming strength, and he was fighting a rearguard action with bravery but without hope.

That day was a Saturday. Secretary Atcheson could see that the end of Nanking's resistance was near as he made the rounds of the city, asking all Americans to come aboard the *Panay*. Most decided the time had come to do so.

They went to the bund, and found a launch waiting there to take them to *Panay*, anchored off the San Chia Ho section of the city. Almost immediately Captain Hughes decided it would be best to move his anchorage as Japanese shells were falling around the area. He, a number of freighters and a British gunboat did weigh anchor.

The evacuation began.

Panay steamed upriver twelve miles that afternoon, and then anchored, as was the custom on the river when dusk approached. She was traveling in consort with three Standard Oil river tankers, and was anchored then at the southwest end of a little island in the river. The night was quiet, although they could hear the sounds of war from the city and the area beyond it.

Next morning the quiet was shattered. The Japanese opened fire on the river, sinking a dozen junks anchored only half a mile astern of the *Panay* and the tankers. Now the real worry was the Japanese artillery, for purposely or not, the gunners could be very poor shots. So Captain Hughes decided to move farther upriver.

At nine o'clock that morning anchors came up and the convoy headed upstream—the 450-ton, 191-foot gunboat in the lead, and the three tankers, *Mei Ping, Mei An,* and *Mei Hsia,* all larger than *Panay,* in her wake.

It was not long before a Japanese army signalman on shore began wigwagging to *Panay,* calling attention to a Japanese fieldpiece that was being trained on the river. So *Panay* stopped, and the Japanese sent an army lieutenant aboard with a small detachment. This aggressive action made Hughes furious, but he restrained himself because he did not want to be the one to initiate trouble. The Japanese lieutenant—in broken English or in writing or by sign—asked questions about the Chinese, which Hughes refused to answer. He also wanted to inspect the ships. Hughes refused. He then told the Japanese to get off his deck.

They did, and *Panay* moved on.

At eleven o'clock that morning, Hughes reached a point in the river known as the Hohsien cutoff, twenty-seven miles above the Nanking customs jetty. There was no sign of military activity even though the Nanking-Wuhu railroad ran nearby on the west side of the river. So Captain Hughes ordered the anchor dropped. It came to the bottom in some forty-five feet of water and stuck nicely. The tankers came up and anchored—*Mei Hsia* above the gunboat, *Mei An* astern, and *Mei Ping* alongside, for the *Panay* had been invited to send a party aboard the *Mei Ping* for some relaxation.

After the little fleet had anchored, Secretary Atcheson used the radio to send messages to Shanghai and Hankow telling where *Panay* was and instructing his listeners to inform the Japanese so there would be no trouble.

The plan was to remain in the area, out of harm's way, and to move back to Nanking as soon as possible to make contact with the handful of Americans who had elected to stay. No one knew quite what was going to happen—Secretary Atcheson spoke wistfully of "resuming" his functions ashore, not understanding that never again would Nanking be the same, nor China for that matter.

Since the day was Sunday, it called for a big noon dinner aboard the *Panay,* and the presence of so many guests made it an even more festive occasion. The only drawback, under the U.S. Navy's strict no-liquor regulation, was the absence of alcoholic refreshments—a lack that was felt particularly by Luigi Barzini and Sandro Sandri, Italian war correspondents. After the meal a pair of chief petty officers took a party of enlisted men over to the *Mei Ping* for a few beers. Since the tanker was a commercial Standard Oil vessel, this was perfectly legal—only on American warships was the no-liquor law invoked. The officers and the rest of the crew either went about their duty like the passengers, walked the deck to ease the effects of a large dinner, wrote letters, or settled down for an afternoon nap.

At 1:35 that afternoon, a spotter on the bridge of the gunboat reported to the captain that strange aircraft were in sight at high altitude, coming in from the southeast.

Captain Hughes picked up his cap and headed for the bridge. When he got there with Chief Quartermaster John Lang, the spotter reported a flight of three bombers, at high altitude, so far away he could not make out any insignia.

Because of the dangers of the river and the number of vessels moving about, American gunboats had, for several weeks, been sporting two huge American flags painted on the awnings that covered the upper deck. In addition *Panay* was flying her largest ensign from the mizzenmast. There could be no doubt by anyone who really looked that this was an American vessel.

When Captain Hughes reached the pilothouse and got his glasses, he moved to the companionway, which led to the open bridge above, and scanned the sky. He saw six aircraft, strung out in a line as they made an approach on *Panay*. They were coming in fast. As Hughes watched through the glasses, the leading three planes seemed to lose altitude very suddenly and head right for the ship.

They were in bombing formation!

2

The Rising Sun Pilots

On this December 12 morning, the Japanese forces around Nanking were elated. The battle seemed nearly over, and Chinese troops, almost all disorganized and without weapons, were fleeing the city in every direction. On the east were Prince Asaka's troops, coming from Shanghai. On the south were General Yanagawa's men, who had landed at Hangchow Bay, southwest of Shanghai, and worked their way inland. This was a combined operation, and the naval air forces under command of Rear Admiral Teizo Mitsunami were covering the advance of the Japanese ships up the Yangtze. They were also seeking targets, particularly ships, for the naval airmen, trained for the purpose, were much more highly qualified to bomb shipping than the army air forces, which had no such training.

Admiral Mitsunami knew very well that a number of foreign gunboats and foreign-owned merchant ships traversed the Yangtze regularly. The Japanese were not so much concerned about the inviolability of the foreign passenger and freight vessels—these ships were, after all, engaged in commerce in China, and it could be argued that they were helping the Chinese war effort. Whether or not this was the case, the Japanese could always raise a smokescreen with such a charge. And they knew it would find an immediate sympathetic response in the pacifist and anti-involvement circles of the West, particularly in the United States.

But to bomb a foreign warship in the Yangtze was another matter, and the Japanese government at home had warned that such an act would create an international problem. It would also most certainly sway public opinion in the country involved against Japan. In Tokyo the foreign ministry had made strong representations to the military to be careful. Foreign diplomats had also kept the Japanese informed of the movements of the river gunboats and other warships in China.

At this time, the Japanese navy command knew that the gunboat *Panay* had gone upstream from Nanking. Secretary Atcheson's report to Shanghai had been received. But the Third Fleet, who had the information, did not transmit it to the Second Combined Air Group of the combat forces. And Admiral Mitsunami, the air force commander, did not know where *Panay* or other Western gunboats were. He did not care either, it seemed, for he made no inquiries.

His major concern this morning at his headquarters in Shanghai was to be sure that the Second Combined Air Group was properly represented at the formal march into Nanking. It was not every day that the Imperial forces captured a foreign capital, not every day that China fell to Japan, so the admiral wanted the naval air forces to have their moment of glory along with the army and the fleet.

On this same morning of December 12 Lieutenant Commander Takeshi Aoki, at army headquarters outside Nanking, telephoned army headquarters at Changchow, an advance base to the east. There he reached Lieutenant Commander Motoharu Okamura, an intelligence officer. Aoki had information that seven merchant ships had loaded Chinese troops during the night at Nanking and were now fleeing upriver. They must be stopped, and the Changchow forces were ordered to stop them. Headquarters regarded this as a priority mission, and all planes, navy and army, were to be used. But Okamura knew that this would be strictly a navy task—the only army aircraft available were about a dozen planes used almost entirely for infantry reconnaissance and artillery spotting. So the bombing of the ships would be the responsibility of the naval forces that were split between Shanghai and Changchow.

On receipt of Aoki's information, Lieutenant Commander Okamura moved swiftly. He called for a staff car and headed for the airfield. Telephone communications were not working properly and, in any case, would not be secure enough for this important matter.

Okamura had almost reached the airfield when he saw another staff car coming toward him, and deduced that it must be an air officer coming for instructions. He stopped, got out, and flagged down the other car. In it was Lieutenant Masatake Okumiya, commander of a dive-bombing squadron of the 13th Naval Air Group.

Okamura took no time for explanations. He ordered the lieutenant to turn around and follow him back to the airfield. Once there, he called together the pilots of half a dozen Mitsubishi-96 medium level bombers.

An advance army unit, Okamura told them, had discovered seven large merchant ships and three smaller ones fleeing up the Yangtze loaded with Chinese troops. They were about twenty miles upriver from Nanking. It seemed impossible for any army units to get at them, so here was a mission designed perfectly for the naval air arm. They all knew, he said, the importance of this action. Further, if they did their job well it meant much glory and perhaps a citation for their unit.

Apparently the stolid army lieutenant who had forced himself aboard the *Panay* that day, and who had tried to extract information from Captain Hughes despite the language problems, had gotten his report through to headquarters. Not being able to ascertain the facts, he had made them up. And now several Japanese air units were being committed to an attack.

In the true sense, the pilots had no briefing. They were simply told that the enemy was out there on the river in ships, and they were to go get him.

They went. Lieutenant Okumiya got into his single-engine biplane dive bomber, which had been bomb-loaded and gassed up. Lieutenant Shigeharu Murata got into his big Mitsubishi with his crew. The other fliers jumped into their planes. Soon six dive bombers of the 13th Naval Air Group and six level bombers were in the air. As soon as Aoki could get the information to leaders of similar squadrons of the 12th Naval Air Group, they too took to the air. Now twenty-four planes—dive bombers, fighters, and level bombers—were hunting those ships in the mistaken belief that thousands of Chinese soldiers were escaping upriver. Chinese who would fight again and disrupt the time table of the Imperial forces—unless they were stopped.

Away they went, one after the other, circling and heading west to cover the one hundred miles that separates Changchow and the Yangtze. Finding the river, Lieutenant Murata headed upstream, flying high as was the fashion of the Mitsubishis. Then, suddenly, about forty minutes out, he spotted four ships. They were too far away to be seen clearly. What he could see were small boats moving between the ships, which indicated that these were troopships transferring soldiers.

Lieutenant Okumiya came up alongside with his dive bomber, passed, and led his squadron on. He saw the ships, and waggled his wings at his squadron mates to call their attention to the scene below in case any of them were daydreaming. He craned his neck and scanned the horizon in an automatic search for enemy aircraft. There was nothing in the air but his dive bombers, the fighters, and the big bombers. He signaled for an attack, and for himself selected the second ship in line. Following a prescribed plan, his squadron mates lined up in single column behind him, each man selecting the ship he preferred, and they prepared to head down—even as Lieutenant Murata's medium bombers leveled off to make their flat runs.

The level bombers, each carrying six 120-pound bombs, came in slowly and carefully, each flying to approach at a slight angle across the group of ships. They watched as the bombs fell, and they saw two hits on one ship. They circled then and moved off to give the dive bombers their chance. They had dropped only half their bombs and would return as soon as the dive bombers had made their attack.

Seeing them, Okumiya waited impatiently until they had finished their attack. Then he nosed over into a 60-degree dive and headed down to 3,300 feet. There he concentrated on the yellow water of the river and his target ship, until the ship overflowed the circle of the bombsight. Then he released his bomb—a 500-pounder—and with a shudder pulled out of the dive. His altimeter read 1,500 feet.

He looked back over his shoulder as he pulled away and was dismayed to see a big circle in the water behind one of the ships.

He had missed!

So had his squadron mates, he saw, as each of them went into his dive and pulled up to drop his bomb short of the target.

Another six dive bombers under Lieutenant Ichiro Komaki came in from a different angle and made their attack. They could not recall seeing any hits. They did come back and strafe, and the level bombers came back to attack again. But their recollection was only of seeing men in black suits rushing across the decks of the ships. Meanwhile the fighters flashed down from the sky, strafing the ships in a series of runs. Then the Japanese left, feeling that their attack was hardly a success. They had damaged two of the vessels, and, as far as they could see, the others were heading for the bank to ground. They set off for Changchow to refuel, remap, and then return and finish the job.

The time was 1340. The afternoon had a long, long way to go.

When the squadrons began landing at Changchow, Lieutenant Okumiya, one of the first to arrive, went in to report that they had hit two of the four ships, but that two seemed undamaged. He secured permission to return with his squadron and attack once more. Soon five of the dive bombers were in the air. On the river, leading his squadron, Okumiya saw nothing at all—not a single ship was in the channel. He

3

"Abandon Ship!"

Aboard the *Panay*, when Chief Quartermaster Lang spotted the level bombers coming in, he shouted: "They're letting go bombs. Get under cover!" And he and Captain Hughes ducked as the long shapes detached themselves from the airplanes above and began to whistle down.

Most of the passengers of the ship were on the rail, staring up into the sun. Army Captain Frank Roberts was focusing his field glasses for a better view. Just then one of the bombs struck *Panay* and another hit in the water off to port. The radio mast sagged, a tremendous blast knocked those at the rail off their feet, and everyone on deck was deluged with water and in danger from falling debris. The planes had struck hard.

Ensign Biwerse was knocked off his feet, his whole uniform was stripped from his body, and his shirt hung around his neck in rags. The bomb had smashed the 3-inch gun in the bow. It had wrecked the pilothouse, where it wounded the captain and damaged the radio.

This bomb and several near misses came from the level bombers flying at 11,000 feet. Cameraman Alley got on his feet, grabbed his newsreel camera, and began cranking away as the dive bombers came in out of the sun.

The crew began to recover from the first shock. Chief Lang, who had been wounded in the arm by fragments, helped Captain Hughes down to the main deck. Chief Machinist Mate Peter Klumpers, down in the engine room, awoke from a nap to find himself in darkness and began stumbling around in his attempt to raise steam.

Radioman First Class Andy Wisler came on deck to help get the captain to safety where he could be treated for his wounds. Wisler saw a seaman and passed the word to bring the doctor. Executive Officer swung south toward Wuhu, and then north and east, and finally he found two ships in the river, and attacked.

Only when Okumiya was in the midst of his screaming dive did he look carefully and see that the ship he was attacking bore very clearly the red, white, and blue of the British Union Jack. His bomb had narrowly missed H.M.S. *Cricket* and H.M.S. *Scarab*, a pair of British gunboats that were just upriver from Nanking. He signaled his comrades to cease the attack.

At that moment Lieutenant Okumiya began to wonder what ship it was that they had attacked a few hours before.

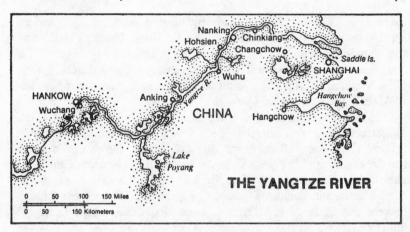

Anders, now in command, came up from below, even though he was so severely wounded in the throat that he could not talk. Wisler asked for permission to man the machine guns and it was given—Anders could still nod his head. So Wisler rushed topside and began firing, with others passing him ammunition. The angle was bad, and he was not hitting anything, but he kept firing until the cases of shells piled up around his ankles.

One of his ammunition passers was Speed Adams, a radioman and a veteran of the Yangtze Patrol. Soon another bomb wounded Adams in five places—none of them vital. Fireman First Class Robert Hebard was wounded in the right buttock. But that did not keep him from manning another machine gun and firing at the Japanese as they came.

It was unbelievable that the Japanese did not see the American flags —three of them—on the *Panay*, those two painted on the topdeck awning covers, and the huge banner waving from the mizzenmast. The Stars and Stripes looked nothing like the Chinese Nationalist flag with its big fields of blue and red. Cameraman Alley, now recording the whole adventure, was watching and close enough to know that there could *not* be a mistake.

The bombs were aimed at the tankers, too, and one bomb went straight through the wardroom ceiling of the *Mei An*, killing the captain and everyone else in the room. But the main target was the *Panay*, and if the Japanese could not tell that they were bombing Americans, the Americans could certainly recognize the red balls of the Rising Sun on the wings and tails of the enemy aircraft.

As the attack continued, the wounded were assembled aft on the main deck. The captain's wounds included a fractured leg. Anders' throat was bubbling with blood and breath. Emile Gassie, a clerk from the Nanking embassy, also had a broken leg, Engineering Officer Geist was wounded in the leg but could still stump around. Fireman First Class William A. McCabe was hit in the shoulder, and so was Machinist Mate Second Class Karl Johnson.

One shell fragment had struck the main fuel line of the *Panay*. Chief Watertender Emery Fisher had been below and had taken a bath in fuel oil when the stuff came spraying out at him. He stumbled up to the deck, rubbing his eyes, and others helped him clean up. Chief Machinist Mate Klumpers still fumbled around in the dark down in the engine room, but could not get anything started. He soon enough discovered the ruptured fuel line and knew that *Panay* would never get under way.

By this time three flights of Japanese had swarmed down on *Panay* and the tankers, and in pulling out, the dive bombers had several times passed by so closely that the men of the gunboat could distinguish the features of the pilots. Not see the American flags? Not very likely.

The two Italian journalists, Sandri and Barzini, were scuttling to get below to avoid this third attack when Sandri was hit by a machine-gun bullet from a strafing Japanese plane. Barzini later found he had several holes in his coat, although he was not wounded.

It was apparent that the most dangerous place on the ship was the sick bay, aft, which had big windows and was almost totally exposed to fire. So Dr. Grazier had his wounded moved down into the upper part of the boiler room, where thick steel plates protected the interior from those buzzing Japanese machine-gun bullets and cracking bombs.

On deck Wisler and others were still manning the machine guns. The trouble was that the guns were fixed for firing at objects along the river banks, and although they could elevate vertically, they did not traverse across the ship or even to her center line the way antiaircraft guns should. So the field of fire was very limited. Nevertheless Ensign Biwerse said he was sure he saw Wisler score hits on at least one of the Japanese planes. That was satisfying.

The whole battle was small scale. *Panay*, after all, was only about the size of a large tugboat, and the bombs the Japanese were using were mostly of 50 kilograms, or about 120 pounds. But the effect of a 50-kilogram bomb on a vessel less than two hundred feet long could be, and was, devastating. Twenty minutes after the first bomb fell, there was a foot and a half of water below decks, and the pumps, once started, were unable to stem the flow. She was taking water fast, and she was in danger of sinking. Her engines could not be started, and there was not a chance in the world that she could be gotten moving except by slipping anchor and putting her into the current of the Yangtze. That way she might capsize and drown them all, or she almost certainly would sink in deep water.

The captain was still dazed because of his wounds. Executive Officer Anders called for damage reports, and the answers he got were ominous.

Topside, the gunners were manning the guns, and the Japanese now could not help but know that the ship on which they were concentrating their fire was an armed vessel—it could not be a merchantman. The leader of the gunners was now Swede Mahlmann, a chief petty officer who had come up on deck so fast he had not had time to put on his pants. But although they fired until the guns were hot and they nearly exhausted the .30-caliber ammunition, they did not bring down any Japanese planes. And the water below was rising fast.

Lieutenant Anders could not talk, so he communicated by writing. The blood ran down and spotted his messages, making them hard to read.

Lieutenant Geist was deciphering them and trying to carry out orders. It was not yet two o'clock in the afternoon, but it was time to get going if the men were to be saved.

"Can we run the ship aground?" asked Anders in his scribbled message. "If not, abandon ship."

The answer to the question was No. No power.

So Geist began to pass the word: "Abandon ship!"

The Japanese were gone for the moment, and whether or not they would attack again remained to be seen, but the men of *Panay* had no time to wait. They must take the chance of being machine gunned in the river as they headed for the shore. Otherwise they would sink with their ship.

So the preparations began. The *Panay*'s two launches were pulled alongside, and Dr. Grazier began collecting medical supplies to aid the wounded, for he did not know when they would have professional help other than his own. Lieutenant Geist headed for the wardroom and the ship's office, where some $40,000 in cash and vouchers was stored. But the safes in both places were jammed from bomb concussion, so near had the hits been to these areas of *Panay*.

Across the water, the tankers saw the gunboat men getting ready to abandon ship and they took their own measures. Captain Mender of *Mei Hsia* had steam up—she had been only slightly damaged by the

Japanese. He headed into shore—to ground and get his passengers off before the Japanese could return and kill them all.

Mei Ping had suffered heavily from the bombing, and was heading for the south bank, to get her passengers off. *Mei An* grounded on the opposite bank.

Mei Hsia came alongside *Panay*, in order to give some help, but was waved away by frantic men on the gunboat. There was a good reason: Up above the Japanese could be seen re-forming for another attack, and the tanker, loaded with gasoline and oil, was a bomb waiting for a fuse. If she caught fire and drifted down on *Panay*, that would be far worse than no help at all.

So Captain Mender turned away, and the men of *Panay* hastened to abandon their sinking vessel before the Japanese could hit them again.

The boats went off on the first long, long six-hundred-yard voyage to the shore, then came back and picked up a second load, low in the water because they had been holed by Japanese bullets in the strafing attacks. Several trips by each boat were needed to evacuate everyone from the *Panay*. During the process Japanese planes strafed the boats, wounding more of the men. Lieutenant Anders and Ensign Biwerse waited for the last boat, as did Radioman Wisler, Chief Lang, and a few others. Finally, at 3:05 in the afternoon, the boat was alongside, and the men went aboard.

Panay was abandoned to the Yangtze. She was very nearly sinking.

4

It Was All a "Mistake"

The attack on *Panay* interrupted her radio transmissions in mid-message to headquarters, Yangtze Patrol, in Shanghai. Two hours later the flagship *Augusta* was querying the commander of the Yangtze Patrol for news of the gunboat. Admiral Yarnell was concerned—long experience with Japanese arrogance convinced him that any of his ships could become involved in an "incident" at any time.

The commander of the Yangtze Patrol replied that he had had no word from *Panay* since 1335, when a message she was sending was suddenly broken off. (He did not know it then, but the message was cut off when that first Japanese bomb destroyed the radio shack.)

Yangtze Patrol said that the British had the only ships in the area, but they were downstream from *Panay*, nearer Nanking, and that as soon as possible they would try to discover what had happened.

As these messages were being exchanged, the men of the *Panay* were making their way to shore, under fire from Japanese planes and land parties. "Fuzzy" Wong and the other Chinese from the ships helped get the wounded ashore and into the thick growth of reeds that would hide them from the Japanese. Sixteen of the *Panay* people had been wounded, and Dr. Grazier tended to them as best he could as they lay in the mud among the ten-foot-high reeds. Two men were dying: Seaman Ensminger and Sandri.

Soon after the men got ashore, two Japanese patrol boats headed downriver toward *Panay* and machine gunned her. Some of the Japanese boarded the ship but left very quickly and went slowly back upriver. They managed to get off shortly before the *Panay* rolled over to starboard and sank to the bottom of the Yangtze.

Thus when Okumiya's bomber pilots had refueled and returned to the scene of the action, they saw nothing. *Panay* had sunk and the three tankers had all run aground, away from the channel.

Meanwhile the "errors" of Japanese army and navy men continued to endanger the Americans. When the soldiers on the banks saw the Japanese planes bombing and strafing a ship, they decided the vessel was the enemy—Chinese—so they set out in their patrol boats and machine gunned the *Panay*. Their boats were spotted on the river by other Japanese planes which concluded that Chinese soldiers were escaping in them. So the Japanese planes roamed the river banks, shooting indiscriminately. Luckily they did not find the Americans hidden among the reeds. Finally they flew away.

The action was over. The repercussions were about to begin.

By late afternoon word was around in Shanghai of the attacks on the two British gunboats farther down the river, and concern heightened over the fate of the *Panay*. The hours dragged on.

A party from the *Panay* reached Hohsien, a little town eight miles upriver, where a telephone call, relayed in Chinese by local operators, was made. Eventually the call got through to Yangtze Patrol headquarters in Hangchow, bringing the first news of the sinking to the outside world.

Hangchow flashed an URGENT message to Admiral Yarnell aboard the *Augusta* in Shanghai, informing him that the *Panay* had been bombed and sunk above Nanking and that the British gunboat *Bee* was going upriver in search of survivors. The news hit Shanghai like a bombshell.

At Japanese headquarters in Shanghai night had fallen before the combat reports came down from Changchow with the news that the naval air forces had been tangling with several ships on the Yangtze. Already the United States naval command had been asking the Japanese for information about the missing *Panay*. Now the Japanese naval command was getting worried. Admiral Mitsunami ordered all naval pilots who had been operating over the Yangtze that day to report to the flagship *Idzumo* in Shanghai next morning. And he announced plans to fly to Changchow himself.

The tired Japanese pilots, not entirely happy with their success in battering the ships on the Yangtze, were hardly in bed that night when they were shaken rudely into wakefulness. This time there was a message from Vice-Admiral Kiyoshi Hasegawa, commander-in-chief of Japanese naval forces in China waters. It ordered the squadron leaders who had attacked ships on the Yangtze that day to report to *Idzumo* next morning. The terse command puzzled them. There was something ominous about it. Yet they still hoped it might mean they were about to get the citation they believed they deserved. For the rest of the night, they slept uneasily.

Next morning the four lieutenants who commanded the air units flew down to Shanghai and boarded the *Idzumo* on Battleship Row. They were met by a grim lieutenant commander who informed them they had sunk an American gunboat and had killed a number of men on three American tankers. They were not aboard *Idzumo* for any unit citation. The lieutenant commander told them all he knew about the affair, then bowed deeply to them—a gesture often accorded in Japan to a condemned man.

Then the pilots went before a group of high naval officers headed by a frowning Admiral Hasegawa. They were grilled on the previous day's events, then sent back to base. Later they were given severe written reprimands by Admiral Mitsuma Yonai, the navy minister, chastising them for attacking American and British ships without identifying their targets and warning them to "henceforth exercise greater care."

Meanwhile Admiral Hasegawa went to the *Augusta* to meet with Admiral Yarnell and express Japan's apologies for the terrible "mistake" that had been made.

But words did not make any difference—the dirty work had been done, and no one in the rest of the world would believe that the bombing was not deliberate.

In both Japan and America the effect was electric. Ambassador Joseph Grew in Tokyo half expected war. The *Dallas Morning News* was among American newspapers that just about called for it. But Japanese officials outdid themselves in offering apologies and expressing readiness to make amends. Admiral Mitsunami was recalled to Japan in disgrace. The Japanese attitude helped calm American anger. So did the news that the men of *Panay* and the three tankers had been picked up safely by the British gunboats *Bee* and *Ladybird* and the American gunboat *Oahu*.

Inquiries and diplomacy went into high gear. A U.S. naval command investigation on the *Augusta* found it was "utterly inconceivable" that the dive bombers coming within six hundred feet of the ships could have failed to identify them. This conclusion was amply supported by the newsreels.

When these reached the United States they were screened by both newsreel executives and a representative of the President of the United States. President Franklin D. Roosevelt had heard from the beginning that the Japanese planes had come in so low that it was impossible they could not know they were striking an American ship. Now cameraman

Alley's film showed Japanese planes pulling out of their dives at so low an altitude that the viewer could see the expression on the pilots' faces.

Roosevelt was worried. The United States had no desire whatsoever to get into a war with Japan. But the President knew that public opinion would never square the Japanese official statements with the pilots' faces. The White House asked the newsreel executives to cut out the revealing close-ups of the planes, and they did so. The footage that might have caused a war was eliminated.

On December 13 President Roosevelt sent a note to the Japanese ambassador in Washington demanding a complete apology and full reparations. The Japanese, torn between embarrassment and habitual truculence, took their time. Just before Christmas they gave their answer. The sinking of the *Panay*, they insisted, was all a mistake—the fliers had mistaken the vessels for Chinese ships. Various excuses, from mixed-up intelligence reports to poor visibility, were offered to support this contention. But the Japanese met the American demands in full. Later they paid an indemnity of $2,214,007 for the loss of the ships, a seaman and a tanker captain, and injuries to seventy-four other people.

The crisis was over, but the portent remained—a portent that foreshadowed the outbreak of war between the United States and Japan less than four years later, when the Japanese attacked Pearl Harbor on December 7, 1941.

But many a person wondered: How could such a crisis have occurred anyhow? Why should an American gunboat be operating deep within China, a neutral in the midst of a raging war, a sitting duck for any trouble that might develop?

The answer lay in events going back more than a century—to the early maritime trading contacts between Western merchants and the mysterious, reclusive East in the first half of the nineteenth century.

For out of those contacts came the military presence of the Western powers—including the United States and its Asiatic Fleet—in a weak, exploited China.

5

The First U.S. Warships in the Far East

The *Panay* incident was only one—grander in scope, perhaps, more dramatic in detail, more far-reaching in its repercussions—of the scores of confrontations between our Asian fleet and the nations of the East and those who claimed colonies there. The history of these ships is fraught with military danger and diplomatic drama, individual heroism and human ineptitude, superhuman perseverance and stubborn wrongheadedness. Often the conflict of will between nations and between the men whose careers included a tour in Asia raged as fiercely as the turbulent Asian seas.

This is the story of these struggles and of the ships and men that fought them. It is a story of loneliness, for they were indeed lonely ships on lonely assignment, but it is a story of challenge and adventure as well. It is a tale of men who won acclaim and power and those who met untimely death and even disgrace in foreign seas, of ships that claimed great victories and those that remained in wreckage beneath the Asian waters. It is a long story, but one that must not be permitted to pass from memory. Too many American lives, too many hopes and dreams have spent themselves in the Asiatic Fleet for it to ever be forgotten.

One fine September day in 1867 the bright new sidewheel gunboat *Monocacy* sailed out from the blue waters of Hong Kong, bound for Shanghai, on the muddy Whangpoo River. There she would show the American colors and prove to both the foreign community and the Chinese the superiority of an American-built gunboat of the most modern design. For *Monocacy* was just that, a "double ender"—with bows fore and aft—a great stack in the middle, tall masts, half a dozen sleek boats and barges, and that huge wheel amidships with the decorative white fretwork hiding the working parts. She was, indeed, the pride of the Americans on Asiatic Station and her presence comforted traders and made the Chinese realize that the United States was a power of importance in the world.

Hong Kong was then the headquarters of Rear Admiral H.H. Bell, the commander of the U.S. Asiatic Squadron. *Monocacy* and the admiral's other ships were ubiquitous. They called in at Shanghai, steamed far up the Yangtze River to Hankow, then raced back downriver to go outside into the East China Sea and run up to Chefoo, the American summer station. Thence a ship might cross the Gulf of Chihli to Port Arthur, a Chinese port leased to the Russians, or over to Korean or Japanese waters, all the while delivering messages, checking on the treatment of American merchants, succoring American sailors, and, above all, showing the flag. It was all a part of the diplomacy of the period, and every nation in the world took the exercises seriously. There was a fine protocol to be observed. There were rules for calling on the local dignitaries and a camaraderie of the Westerners that led them to consider themselves, except in times of national frictions, just one great happy group.

Monocacy's voyage that September was strictly routine. It was one of those regular changes of station that made life in the Asiatic Squadron so pleasant that some American sailors were asking for the duty. Indeed some officers even gave up the chance of promotion rather than leave this world where a rich man was a king with all that money could buy, and foreigners, by virtue of the exchange system, were automatically rich men.

On this September morning *Monocacy*, under Commander F.H. Carter, sailed off from Hong Kong without a care in the world. Yet this was a voyage her crew would never forget. For soon *Monocacy* ran into a storm. She was battened down and then hove to under storm sails that night, but the wind kept rising, and the seas followed in ever towering rows. By eight o'clock the next morning the gale had become a typhoon with winds blowing at hurricane force. The men of *Monocacy* came to appreciate the violence of the storm when the steering gear carried away.

Although she was a steam-driven sidewheeler, she carried sail to assist her in her progress when needed. This day, if she could have made any progress beyond just keeping afloat, it would be deemed something of a miracle.

The wind roared on as the "eye" of the hurricane moved closer to the *Monocacy*. By noon it was almost impossible to stand on the deck of the ship. At 1:30 the forestaysail blew away—one minute it was there and the next it had ripped loose and went kiting off into the maw of the storm, never to be seen again. The men then set up the storm staysail, but the officers quickly realized that it, too, would soon tear loose and go the way of the other sail unless something was done to save it. So the sail was hauled down, leaving the ship even more to the mercy of the winds.

Two hours later the second and third cutters were lifted out of their davits and carried away, but the storm mainsail was set and the ship rode more easily.

The eye of the storm neared, and the wind moderated at about five o'clock that afternoon. The old hands knew that the end was not in sight—they would have to go through it all over again as the other half of the storm hit them. The wind had varied from north-northeast to southeast; it switched around that evening and blew toward the southwest. That did it for the fourth cutter, as the waves swept across the ship and cut it loose. Fortunately *Monocacy* was buoyant and seaworthy, and she bobbed back like a cork from each ducking. But the seas grew far heavier on this other side of the storm.

Just before seven o'clock that evening, the ship's launch was lost to an especially vigorous sea, and the fact that it was hooked to its davits made not a penny's worth of difference. The davits were smashed and one was carried away with the boat. Seas of increasing intensity also took the fore-topmast and the main-topmast, and broke the fore-topsail yard in two. The storm mainsail was lost in these few minutes, blown overboard and carried away in the spume.

Commander Carter was appalled by the damage but cheered by the strong way his ship continued to ride in the worst storm he had ever witnessed. Vividly he described the scene: "The fury of the storm from that hour until 9:00 P.M. exceeded in violence anything I had ever conceived, and seemed to strike the vessel with the force of a heavy, solid body, and it was a matter of wonder that anything could resist its terrible force."

At about this time, the guys that wired up the smokestack began to give, and the tall stack creaked and swayed in the wind. Two hours of this strain were too much—the guys began to snap and the stack went over the side, noticeably decreasing speed of the engines and thus the maneuverability of the ship as the draft to the fireboxes was lost.

There was only one answer: The ship must raise sail if she could not

raise steam. The old salts must get out on the main yard and hoist the
head of the mainsail at least enough to give them way. It was done at
fearful cost in energy, by men who fought against the raging wind to
bring that sail head up inch by inch until it caught and held.

Two hours later, at 11:30, it was all over. The wind whisked away,
leaving a residue of breeze and a moderately heavy sea. Before dawn the
horizon began to grow bright, and Commander Carter knew he had
weathered the blow. Cautiously he took soundings, and when he discovered they were in thirteen fathoms of water he ordered the hook
dropped, and they anchored. Thus the *Monocacy* had her baptism in
the waters of the Chinese sea devils. For the next thirty-five years and
more she would weather the storms of these seas as she did her job
along the China coast and in Japan, in many ways the symbol of American might and the American presence in the Orient.

The need for that presence was first felt in America in the middle
1820s, after mariners from Boston, Salem, Baltimore, New York, Philadelphia, and a dozen other ports began trading around the world. Simultaneously American vessels were setting out for Calcutta and Java
and Hong Kong to trade for spices and ivory and tea, and even to traffic
in opium along the way. In the prosperity that was emerging after the
War of 1812, shipowners and captains were suddenly discovering the
immense fortunes to be earned in the Far East trade. But there were
complications. China and Japan were not entirely pleased to be invaded
by this rapacious horde of foreign seekers of wealth. As for China, the
British arrived first, and they sent parts of their powerful navy to the
Asiatic Station to prevent incidents. However, American traders were
usually able to duck under the Union Jack in the waters off Amoy and
Canton. But American official interest in the Far East and its trade was
on the rise, and in 1822 the navy formed a Pacific Squadron, rechris-
tened a few years later the Far East India Squadron. The title shows
how Americans considered the Far East in the early nineteenth century
—as an adjunct to India!

The new naval arm, consisting of both steamers and sailing ships—
although the steamers also carried sail in the manner of the day—had
little to do for several years. But events were taking shape in the Orient
that would soon change that.

In the summer of 1821 Captain George Gardner in the whaling ship
Globe, out of Nantucket, discovered off the shore of the Japanese islands a whole new whaling field hitherto unknown to the Western
world. He was so successful that in less than two years he came home to
his misty island with more than two thousand barrels of sperm oil, set-

ting a new world record. Thereafter a whole succession of American whaling captains sought out the Japanese grounds, even though they knew the emperor of Japan permitted virtually no commercial intercourse between his subjects and the flat-eyed foreigners from the Western world.

The American whaling activities resulted in serious conflict. American ships were fired on or captured by the Japanese. American sailors who were unlucky enough to be shipwrecked were often imprisoned, tortured and at times murdered.

In 1837 an American trading firm in Canton dispatched the ship *Morrison* in an attempt to make commercial contacts with the Japanese and open the way for Christian missionaries. The *Morrison* carried seven shipwrecked Japanese sailors bound for repatriation—but this did not prevent the Japanese from firing on the vessel and trying to capture or sink her in the Ryukyus, where she first stopped, and again in the port of Kagoshima on Kyushu Island. The *Morrison* retreated without even unloading her castaways.

Several years passed. The navy then sent Commodore James Biddle, of the Philadelphia Biddles, to try to open trade with Japan. Arriving in 1846 on the *Columbus*, Biddle tried a friendly approach to the Japanese but was sharply rebuffed and told, in no uncertain terms, to leave— which he did. Six years later the United States decided to take another crack at the Japanese trade barrier. This time the job was put in the hands of Matthew Calbraith Perry, commander of the East India Squadron, and a man with more than forty years' experience in the navy.

Commodore Perry set out for Japan in November 1852, arriving the following summer in Tokyo Bay with the warships *Susquehanna* and *Mississippi*, each towing a sailing ship. By a judicious combination of friendship and toughness, Perry at last overcame Japanese obstinacy; and the following year—when he steamed into Tokyo Bay with a formidable eight-ship fleet—a treaty was signed. Japan was open to trade with the West.

In the interim Perry visited Shanghai, Canton, and Hong Kong to encourage good treatment of American ships and traders there, too. After his visit to Canton, Perry chartered a British steamer, the *Queen*, armed her with American sailors and marines, and left her to protect American interests. That was the first "permanent" American warship in Oriental waters. At the same time the sloop *Plymouth* was sent up to Shanghai and the *Susquehanna* to Hong Kong for the same purpose.

Even though there was not yet an Asiatic Fleet, its functions were being performed in these canny actions by Commodore Perry. By the middle of 1854, the protective power of the American flag in the Far East was already swelling the influx of traders and missionaries to China. And in Shanghai, American and British forces had already shown what they could do in consort if trouble came.

They did so in the spring of 1854 as the T'ai P'ing rebellion—a revolt of the peasants against the Manchu dynasty and the foreign intruders—was stirring all China. The Imperial troops had the effrontery to camp on the Shanghai race course, which interfered with the pleasures of the Europeans. Troops of *Plymouth*, H.M.S. *Encounter*, and H.M.S. *Grecian* were landed and together they drove the Chinese off the course. It was no joke—three men of the landing party were killed and several wounded. But the might of the foreigner was established.

Commodore Perry returned from his trip to the Far East convinced that the United States ought to occupy Okinawa, a strategic island south of Japan, in addition to several other islands. But Franklin Pierce's administration was not interested in putting a coaling station and fortress there just to preserve American influence. Consequently, there was no extension of the Perry visit except for the establishment of consular and trade relations. Townsend Harris, the first American consul, got a cold reception when he went to Japan in the late 1850s. However, he eventually succeeded in negotiating a commercial treaty, and conditions seemed to be improving when, in 1860, a Japanese mission was dispatched to America.

But with civil war raging in Japan there still were unpleasant incidents. And again the Western powers showed a readiness to help each other in emergencies. For example, one day in the summer of 1863 a local potentate fired on the U.S.S. *Wyoming* in Shimonoseki Strait. The *Wyoming* fired back, but it was a French force that landed in the strait and destroyed the batteries.

The advent of the young Emperor Meiji in 1868 brought about the end of the old shogunate and the bureaucracy that was essentially antiforeign. Japan began to embrace modern Western ways, which included all the trade that anyone could want. As a result, the work of the foreign naval forces in Asian waters was then diverted from Japan—at once very modern in outlook and very independent and nationalistic—toward other parts of Asia.

American trading activity overseas during this period was widespread. The high-water mark of the American merchant marine was reached in the 1850s. In 1852 alone, some sixty-six clipper ships were built in American yards, and the American flag was seen in every port in the world. But this was the golden era of the American merchant fleet. With the discovery of gold in California in the late 1840s, America's interest soon turned toward developments on the western seaboard rather than toward her maritime affairs. That change of focus, plus the panic of 1857, brought an end to a mercantile expansion that might have made America the power that Britain was to become on the high seas.

The Civil War consumed all of America's energies until 1865. The next year an Asiatic Squadron was formed to tour the China seas. By this time, the Yangtze was the home of many American shipping interests, and *Monocacy*, with her fearless presence on the rivers and in Shanghai Bay, was a comforting sight for Americans.

Change came to the Asiatic Squadron almost immediately following the typhoon that *Monocacy* survived so well. Admiral Bell, who was drowned in an accident at Osaka, Japan, when his boat swamped crossing the inner harbor bar, was replaced by Rear Admiral S.C. Rowan, who showed an uncanny ability to infuriate the British. It all started down in Hong Kong that same autumn of 1867, when an American officer aboard the U.S.S. *Supply* quarreled with a Chinese comprador and in the ensuing argument a local boatsman was injured. The high and mighty Vice-Admiral Sir Henry Keppel, chief of the British forces in China, held the position that the right and wrong of things were his to adjudge, and ordered the Americans to pay compensation. In the argument over jurisdictions, Admiral Rowan and Admiral Keppel grew so heated they would not salute each other's presence.

Then in 1869 the Shanghai Chamber of Commerce suggested that the Yangtze be opened to foreign commerce as far up as Szechwan Province, which meant Chungking, 1,400 miles upriver. By fast action the British easily froze the Americans out of that endeavor. But it was as much the fault of Congress as anyone else. Admiral Rowan did not have a vessel capable of going through the dangerous Yangtze gorges, and Congress was not about to give him one. In the meantime Admiral Keppel took his flagship up—the fact that he went high and dry on a bank at Hangchow did not long delay him. Consequently, the British got the jump on the upper Yangtze, just as they had down south in Canton and Amoy.

For a time official Anglo-American relations in China continued to be difficult. Yet both forces were there to stay: The American colony in China was growing steadily and by 1871 numbered in the thousands. There were 145 Americans in residence at Hankow on the Yangtze, and many more in Chefoo, Canton, Shanghai, and other trade ports. The

China Station now was augmented by newer vessels: the steam tug *Palos* and the ship *Benicia*.

The Orient was interesting to American officers and men of the squadron because of its strangeness, but it had not yet become the place for the "soft life" where the Chinese did all the ships' dirty work. The men of the American vessels were mustered at dawn by a reveille gun and drums. Until eight bells, or eight o'clock, they holystoned the decks and swabbed them down. Then they were called to breakfast, which included a spirit allowance of rum or whisky. At two bells on the day watch, which was nine o'clock in the morning, they were turned-to in dress uniform; an hour later they were inspected. Then it was workaday—except on Sundays, when the chaplain took over for the morning and the men loafed in the afternoon. During the rest of the week the officers found plenty to keep them busy in shifting supplies, painting, chipping, and all the housekeeping tasks of making sure that the ship was ready for action.

In the next few years Americans, like other foreigners, explored China waters extensively—sometimes with the approval of the Chinese and sometimes not. In 1874, Commander E.O. Matthews took the gunboat *Ashuelot* a thousand miles up the Yangtze from Shanghai to Ichang. That same year American sailors landed at Shanghai to protect fellow countrymen when the local Chinese rioted against foreigners. This time the trouble arose over French desecration of a Chinese graveyard which occurred when the French increased their famous concession in the city.

By this time Admiral Rowan had been replaced by Rear Admiral A.M. Pennock. A far better relationship with the other foreigners was in the offing, and the beginning of a new, settled life for foreigners in Asia was at hand.

In the summer of 1876 Lieutenant Commander Albert S. Barker arrived in China to take command of the *Palos*, which by now had been completely fitted out as a gunboat. Barker's experiences in the Asiatic Squadron were typical of the everyday life of the navy in these far-distant waters.

In Canton, accompanied by the American consul and vice-consul, Barker set out to make a formal call on the viceroy, who represented the Dragon Throne there. It took them an hour to thread their way through the city by sedan chair. At the residence, an interpreter translated their names into Chinese and wrote them on pieces of red paper nine inches long by five inches wide—these big "visiting cards" indicated their high rank. In the courtyard, a salute of three guns was fired in honor of the consul and another in honor of the lieutenant commander. Then they were led in a procession of sedan chairs to a great hall where the viceroy came forth with a number of attendants. All then walked in to a smaller hall where a meal was spread with Chinese delicacies, preserves, and sweetmeats, with a cup of tea at each plate.

They talked, they sipped wine, they drank tea, they nibbled at sweetmeats—and then they went away. That was the end of the reception. As they left the courtyard, they were ushered out with additional three-gun salutes.

A few days later the viceroy came to call on the lieutenant commander aboard the *Palos*, and Barker did his very best to match the air of ceremony. Luckily, he could pipe the viceroy's retinue over the side, have his men at attention with weapons, and fire a salute for the visitors. It was the first of many, many such ceremonial occasions for the men of *Palos*, for this was China and this was how things were done.

Still, the reason for being on station was not simply to pay honor to the government of China but to represent American interests in a country where the central government at Peking had relatively little control over the far-flung corners of the empire. And that summer of 1867 the squadron command was worried about bandits and political troubles in various parts of the country. So Commanders Barker in *Palos* and Matthews in *Ashuelot* were ordered to make a tour—to call at Macao, the Portuguese settlement on the coast near Canton, and at Hong Kong and all the treaty ports. They also traveled to Swatow, up the coast from Hong Kong, and anchored in Tong Sang Harbor, off Thunder Head, where they conducted target practice to sharpen the shooting eyes of the men. They went to Amoy and visited the foreign residents to see that all was well. Of course they called on the Chinese authorities, too; it was part of the game, to let them know that the Americans were alive, well, and present in force.

The dangers of the day were well illustrated by Matthews' experience in *Ashuelot*. He ran aground on unmarked rocks in Haitan Strait, en route to Foochow, but got off without injury. Such occurrences were not uncommon along the rock-strewn coasts of China, as the Americans and other foreigners were just beginning to chart the shores. Fortunately, the shallow-draft, sturdy gunboats were ideal for the task, for they could get off shoals without serious damage to their bottoms.

Then it was into the Min River, and to Pagoda Anchorage, fifteen miles downstream from Foochow, where the foreign trading vessels came. There were calls back and forth among sea captains, exchanges with men-of-war of other lands, and many parties.

On the Fourth of July Lieutenant Commander Matthews was forced to make a speech at the American consulate party in Foochow. Red in the face, pulling at his collar, having practiced all afternoon long, Matthews rose.

"Ladies and gentlemen," he said. "History tells us of but one naval officer who was an orator, the celebrated Mark Antony. . . ."

Then came a long pause as Matthews fiddled with his collar and grew redder. His mind was a total blank.

Finally . . .

". . . and—ladies and gentlemen—you see that I am not an exception to the rule. . . ."

Whereupon the lieutenant commander sat down to thunderous applause. Next day the foreign language press remarked on the "appropriateness" of the senior American naval officer's speech.

In these days before travel agents, men such as Commanders Matthews and Barker were the travel writers of America and the world. They came home from their voyages and wrote stories of faraway places in which they had lived and worked; they were the "foreign correspondents" and the eyes and ears of America as well as its defenders. And by and large they wrote interestingly and faithfully of their adventures, in the language of the day, with the attitudes of the times. Thus, their accounts included careful, detailed discussions of the beds they slept in, the people they met, and strange foreign customs, such as the highly ritualized tea-purchasing system of the south.

The primary purpose of these naval men, however, was not to entertain but to learn and to protect the interests of their nations. They never forgot that.

This particular voyage took the two gunboats to Pootoo and then to Ningpo, south of Shanghai, where they stopped. Here the commanders rode sedan chairs into the interior, and then boats and then more chairs to Shidowza, a famous monastery. They were gone four nights.

From Ningpo the gunboats traveled to Shanghai, which Lieutenant Commander Barker found full of missionaries and traders. After two weeks in Shanghai, they headed north into waters where trouble might be brewing—everyone in the south was talking about possible war between the British and the Chinese over new trade concessions. The destination was Chefoo, on the Santung Peninsula, where they found a British squadron lying nervously at anchor in the harbor, plus the whole diplomatic colony from Peking which had come down to the coastal coolness to avoid the scorching heat of the interior. George Seward, the American minister, was among those sunbathing on the beaches that summer.

From Chefoo Lieutenant Commander Barker took *Palos* up to Taku Bar, a silt barrier in the Pei Ho River estuary below Tientsin. There he anchored within sight of the forts that guarded the estuary against foreign incursions. These waters, he knew, had a special "political" significance, since Peking, site of the Imperial Chinese government, lay only some eighty miles northwest from Tientsin.

The tension over the trade negotiations also compelled the British to send a full house of ships to the area. By a show of force, they were putting all the pressure they could on the Peking government. This pressure carried the day. A new treaty between Britain and China was signed, and the foreign ships—British, French, Russian, and American—stood outside the forts and gave nineteen-gun salutes to Li Hung Chang, Chinese viceroy at Tientsin.

At Tientsin, Lieutenant Commander Barker's job consisted largely of going out to dinner, shooting, hunting, and riding trips into the interior. He made an overland trip to Peking from Tungchow, a port on the river that could be reached by boat from Tientsin. Barker saw the sights of Peking, walked the city's great protective walls, visited the Temple of Heaven, examined the astronomical instruments built by the Jesuits two hundred years before, and visited the summer palace outside the city.

Then, it was back to duty—to Tientsin. Barker's admiral had arrived in the city, and now they all went down to the port of Taku, and then steamed again for Chefoo. There *Palos* was dispatched over to Nagasaki in Japan to pick up mail and supplies for the squadron.

In Japan Lieutenant Commander Barker was getting his second insight into the duties of an officer of the Asiatic Squadron: He was expected to perform anywhere. On a trip from Nagasaki to Yokohama, he was sent up to the dangerous waters of Shimonoseki Strait, between Honshu and Kyushu islands. There he learned a great deal from a Japanese pilot about the perils of that channel, for they decided to take a shortcut through the Naruto, or whirlpool passage, that connects the Inland Sea with the outside.

Lieutenant Commander Barker conferred with the Japanese pilot about the navigation problems of the passage, and the pilot did not seem to be worried about them, although Barker had heard of the danger of the rocks.

"If I can get there before ten o'clock, can do; after ten no can do," said the pilot cheerfully.

The night fell with a big bright moon, and they steamed for the dangerous passage. The approach was through a steep defile which narrowed as they neared the most perilous part of the strait; the current grew noticeably stronger, and the ten o'clock deadline came ever closer.

Barker began to worry. "I had never felt so anxious since the passage of Forts Jackson and St. Phillip in the Civil War," he confided to his diary.

The pilot stood at his elbow, serene.

The moon lay on the edge of the horizon. Soon it was ten o'clock. The pilot now stood tensely by the wheel, at the side of the quartermaster. But he looked up to smile at the American officer.

"Ten minutes we get through," he said with grave confidence.

The waves began to roar in the confined waters, and the foam boiled on the rocks so close alongside as the ship moved along.

"Rocks dead ahead!" shouted the lookout forward.

The Japanese pilot heard. He grabbed the helm and jammed it hard over to starboard, and the danger was passed.

Barker steamed into Yokohama then, after a trip of only seventy-six hours. It was something of a record—and one he was never to repeat, for he had vowed on the passage through the strait that never again would he willingly take such risks with one of the navy's vessels.

The *Palos* remained in Japan for several months, then returned to Ningpo to take an American consul to visit the newly opened port of Wenchow, farther south.

In the middle of 1877 Lieutenant Commander Barker took command of the gunboat *Alert*, and left Chinese waters on a long cruise that took him and his crew to Guam, to Bougainville in the Solomon Islands, and to the Dutch East Indies. From there they went on to Manila, then a Spanish possession.

Sailing 6,500 miles through waters where American naval vessels had not previously ventured, they added needed information to the navy's charts and finally ended their odyssey at Hong Kong. There Barker was to leave the ship and return to the United States for shore duty.

Just before he left there was one final incident which took place when the ship was anchored in Hong Kong Harbor, where currents run strong with the tides. As night fell on this day before Barker's departure —the black tropical night of the China Seas where a man could scarcely see his hand before his face without a light—a piercing cry for help was heard. A man had fallen overboard. Ensign William F. Halsey, with the reactions of the star football player he had been at the naval academy, leapt over the side of *Alert*, swam until he found the drowning man, grasped him tightly, and then tried to swim back to the ship. It was a hard go, for the current was swift and powerful. But soon a boat was in the water, lanterns were held high, and the two men were found and hauled aboard, half waterlogged. Halsey had saved the life of Cadet Engineer Worthington, a brother officer, but he had not known whether it was an admiral or a coal-shoveler or a "black gang" swab he was after until the rescue was finished.

Just another night in the life of the Asiatic Squadron.

6

"You May Fire When You Are Ready, Gridley"

In the beginning of the days of the Asiatic Squadron the American attitude toward the Chinese and other Orientals was quite correct: the ships fired salutes and the officers did everything necessary but "kowtow"—kneel and knock heads on the floor—to keep the customs of the lands they visited. But there were problems.

"I don't understand why we are keeping the Chinese out of our country, as if they were unfit to live there, while out here we are manning decks for them and giving them big salutes as though they were the greatest people on earth," said one quartermaster to another aboard the American three-masted steamship *Enterprise*. The occasion for the remark was the firing of salutes in Shanghai Harbor in honor of Viceroy Tso of the Imperial Chinese government, who was kind enough to honor the *Enterprise* with a visit that day.

But the navy men knew how to resolve an insult here if it involved other foreigners, and they showed it one day when an article appeared in the English language north China *Daily News* casting aspersions on the conduct of certain *Enterprise* officers while the ship had been standing in Foochow.

The executive officer of the ship, a big, brawny man, angrily went to the offices of the *Daily News* and demanded an apology. Instead he got a sneer. The officer picked up the editor of the paper by the scruff of the neck and shook him, whereupon the editor called the police. The police reported the affair to the captain of the *Enterprise*, who reported it to the admiral, who decided it was an affair of gentlemen, a private matter between the editor and the exec. Nothing more happened except that the officers of *Enterprise* never got another favorable line in the North China *Daily News*—only lots of brickbats.

But there was a serious side to life—as was proved in the summer of 1884, when France declared war on China in a dispute over extra-territoriality. The French ships in Chinese ports virtually destroyed the cream of the Chinese navy while the other foreigners stood by doing nothing. By this time, even the Americans were becoming as much victims of the rot of colonialism as the worst of the offenders—he who stands by when a crime is committed can surely never plead either innocence or ignorance. Violence by Japanese and Europeans against Chinese became commonplace; the Chinese retaliated as best they could with riot and occasional murder, and the Americans, like the other foreigners, began to think that force was the only way in which their "rights" in China could be protected.

Fortunately, there were few serious scrapes between the Americans and the Chinese. After all, the Asiatic Squadron was little more than a police organization created to ensure that America was represented on those occasions when the Western powers were showing the flag, and to make certain that United States traders were not abused either by the Orientals or by the Europeans.

But the pressure of events were beginning to push the United States further and further into world affairs. Between its earliest years and the beginning of the twentieth century, a tremendous transition had occurred in the United States Navy. In terms of men, the basic change was in the philosophies and tactical programs devised by Alfred Thayer Mahan (1840-1914), the father of modern naval warfare. In terms of ships, the change began with the coming of steam, but was slow in developing until late in the 1880s, when Secretary of the Navy Benjamin Franklin Tracy called for separate fleets of capital ships to police the two major oceans of the world.

It was in these years that America first became interested in an overseas empire of her own. Hawaii was first brought into the American orbit as a center for whaling and for missionary advancement, later as an area for sugar and pineapple production. It was soon traduced and in 1898 annexed. This change alone gave America a big stake in the Pacific. This era of rising national pride and interest in possessions brought William McKinley and Theodore Roosevelt to power. The President and his Assistant Secretary of the Navy shared the nation's dreams of empire. Seeing Japanese and German naval expansion in the Pacific, Roosevelt, in particular, urged the building of a more powerful

American Pacific force to strengthen an Asiatic Station that usually numbered no more than half a dozen vessels.

The American position in the Far East was still a placid one in 1897. Rear Admiral Frederick McNair refused to seek a coaling concession—in effect a territorial grab—at Chefoo, although some American officials advised such a course. But McNair was soon to be replaced by an officer who had some different ideas about the American position in Asia and what needed to be done there. The new commander of the Asiatic Squadron was Commodore George Dewey, a man whose name would soon reverberate around the world.

Immediately upon hearing of his appointment, Dewey got busy. On reaching the West Coast, he went to the San Francisco Mare Island Navy Yard and saw to it that the light cruiser *Concord* would be loaded with supplies for his new squadron. Then, on January 3, 1897, he arrived in Nagasaki, Japan, hoisting his commodore's pennant aboard the cruiser *Olympia*.

The fleet at his disposal was hardly a formidable one. It consisted of four small ships: the *Olympia*, cruiser *Boston*, gunboat *Petrel*, and the good old *Monocacy*, now regarded as a relic fit only for river service.

In contrast, the European powers had an assortment of miniature armadas. The British alone had three battleships and three armored cruisers in the Far East, plus many smaller vessels in ports and on rivers. The Russians had a battleship fleet at Port Arthur. The Germans had the East Asia Cruiser Squadron based on Tsingtao, with two heavy cruisers at the heart of it. Even the French, who had not made much pretense of naval power these days, had a stronger force than the Americans.

Besides its limited power, the American squadron still had to operate thousands of miles from its nearest navy yard. And despite McNair's attitude, there was a growing feeling in Washington in the winter of 1897-98 of a need for a port in China, especially since everyone else had one. Secretary of the Navy John D. Long so indicated in a message to Dewey, and asked him to look into the matter.

By this time, the European powers had grown very jealous of their territorial acquisitions in China, and nearly every suitable place had been taken. Japan, in fact, was looking hungrily at the Russians in Port Arthur and at the Shantung Peninsula, where the British had Weihaiwei and the Germans, Kiavichow, potentially including Taingtao. A few years before, anyone who wanted a China port had his pickings—but not at the turn of the century.

Dewey's first self-appointed task as commander of the squadron was to call on the emperor of Japan. By the time he had made the diplomatic rounds, the *Concord* had come into Yokohama to join the fleet bringing supplies from San Francisco—enough to rearm and reprovision the squadron and ready it for action.

But action was not truly contemplated at this point. The only hint to Dewey of possible trouble had come in one paragraph of his official orders, and this was a very vague mention of the Philippines. Indeed, as a Spanish possession, the Philippines were not regarded by most Americans or most other foreigners as part of the Far East—and it had been a long time since any ships of the Asiatic Squadron had called there for any reason whatsoever.

Yet, in the constantly worsening relations between the United States and Spain over Cuba, Commodore Dewey sensed crisis, and on his own initiative moved the squadron down to Hong Kong on February 11, 1898. Thus he was in position to act if anything happened in the Pacific.

It happened.

On February 18 Dewey received a message from Secretary of the Navy Long that the *Maine* had been destroyed in Havana Harbor on February 15 "by accident." That was almost assuredly a proper assessment of the cause of explosion aboard the battleship—the navy was not playing jingo that winter.

But the *New York World*, other Hearst newspapers across the land, and many members of Congress had a different view. They were itching for war and for American colonial expansion. On February 25 the Navy Department recognized the situation that was developing and prepared to do its duty: Assistant Secretary of the Navy Roosevelt sent messages to the European Squadron, the South Atlantic Squadron and the Asiatic Squadron, warning of the dangers.

Commodore Dewey was immediately cabled and told to move to Hong Kong, where he already was, and to gather all his ships there except old *Monocacy*, which probably could not have survived the trip. Dewey's orders were to shadow the Spanish Asiatic Squadron, and fight in the Philippines if war against Spain were declared.

Dewey's next move was to cable U.S. Consul General Oscar F. Williams in Manila, and, in a carefully coded message, to ask for all the available military information concerning the Philippines. He wanted to know about mines, submarines, fortifications, and other defenses. He wanted every bit of information about the Spanish squadron that could be mustered.

He then began buying colliers, laden with coal, to accompany his squadron, for the American navy had no bases closer than Hawaii. The next few weeks were trying for Dewey and the men of the squadron. Hong Kong was full of warships: British, French, German, and American vessels crowded the roadway—tension ran high. Dewey was forced to follow protocol, entertaining such distinguished foreign visitors as Prince Henry of the German Empire, brother of Kaiser Wilhelm, and Major General W. Black, the British governor of Hong Kong.

Meanwhile, off in Manila, Consul Williams was going about his espionage mission diligently. He supplied all information he could secure about the defenses of Manila, and made himself so unpopular that he was warned by the Spanish government to leave the country lest he be killed by a mob. So on April 23 Williams headed for Hong Kong.

He had done pretty well for a man who was not a naval attaché. He revealed that six new guns had been mounted at Corregidor at the entrance to Manila Bay. He reported on the changing number, type and names of Spanish men-of-war in the harbor. He told Dewey about the fortifications going up all around Manila. In all, he gave Dewey a good deal of fresh information and corrected a number of errors. For example, the Asiatic Squadron did not know that the Spanish had some twenty gunboats in the Philippines until Consul Williams informed them. Exactly the kind of intelligence lapse that could be fatal.

The cables hummed with interchanges of information. Dewey had many problems, not least of which was the shortage of coal in the Far East, for the other nations had bought up most of the colliers on the market and most of the land-based coal supply.

The crisis over the sinking of the *Maine* lasted for weeks. But the delay before hostilities with Spain began was beneficial to Dewey—it gave him time to prepare. However, it also made his officers and men edgy, and gave the potential enemy a chance to do all he could to improve the defenses of the Philippines.

March sped by. April dragged along. Dewey bought two ships, the *Nanshan* and the *Zafiro*, declared them to be American "merchant ships," topped them up to the gunwales with coal, and waited. *Monocacy* was brought down as far as Shanghai and settled on the turgid waters of the Whangpoo. Her crew was transshiped to Hong Kong to join the fighting vessels, while her captain stayed in Shanghai and conspired with various Chinese compradors to secure more coal. He also set up a secret naval base, where American ships damaged in battle might come for quick repairs. Perhaps this action was a violation of Chinese sovereignty—other nations would have held it so—but the United States was so desperate for a base in Asia that the absence of one had become the subject of a very telling joke between Prince Henry and Commodore Dewey when the two met on the flagship.

Dewey sat in Hong Kong and squirmed, while the European powers did all they could to embarrass America. The existence of the secret base remained secret—else it would have brought a storm of protest from the high-minded European nations: Britain, with Hong Kong and Weihaiwei and virtual control of the Yangtze River; France, with Indochina and parts of the neighboring Chinese province of Yunnan; Russia, with her interests in Port Arthur; Germany with her Kiaochow colony on Shantung Peninsula, and Japan, who wished a pox on all of them as she prepared to take over not part but all of China.

Dewey knew well that in time of trouble he could turn virtually nowhere, and this feeling was confirmed by cables he received from various lands. Japan in particular was insistent on maintaining her "neutrality" in case of war—which meant that American ships could secure coal in Japanese ports only for the long voyage home. So unless Commodore Dewey could arrange his own supply, he was in serious trouble if war came and lasted beyond a few brief days.

From Washington came word that the cruiser *Baltimore* was on her way to join the squadron. It was welcome news for a squadron whose might was so slight. In the Hong Kong club there were no takers for the American's bet that they would be able to get to the Philippines, fight a war, and come back to Hong Kong. The British were friendly but they were also certain. They liked the Americans too much to take their money at any odds on such a hopeless adventure.

The days of April degenerated into one long, never-ending rumor. On April 17 the revenue cutter *McCullouch* arrived, detached from customs service to be put at Dewey's disposal. Her coming only intensified the British prophecy that the poor devils in American uniforms would go to Manila to fight but would never again be seen in the bars of Hong Kong.

The movement toward war was slow and steady. On April 19 all the American ships were painted war gray, while preparations were speeded up to turn each vessel into an efficient fighting machine.

On April 21 the Navy Department sent a warning cable—war was almost imminent. Next day *Baltimore* arrived to be cheered into her anchorage by the whole American contingent.

On April 23 war came. That day Major General Black informed Commodore Dewey of the neutrality laws, and asked that the American squadron leave Hong Kong waters by the afternoon of April 25.

Dewey was not really ready. *Baltimore*'s bottom was full of barnacles and she needed to go into drydock. The gunboat *Raleigh*, which had been sent to the fleet from the Mediterranean, had a broken circulating pump, and she was reduced to crawling on one engine. But British might could not be defied, so on April 24 *Boston*, *Concord*, *Petrel*, *McCullouch*, *Nanshan*, and *Zafiro* left the protected waters of Hong Kong Harbor and headed for Mirs Bay, thirty miles away. *Raleigh*'s broken pump was stripped from the ship, taken to the Kowloon dockyard that night, worked on all night, and was back in operation on the fateful day, April 25. So *Raleigh*, *Olympia*, and *Baltimore* sailed in time to meet the British deadline of 4:00 P.M.

It was two more days before Commodore Dewey had official word from Washington that war was declared accompanied by his instructions:

> Proceed at once to Philippines Islands. Commence operations particularly against the Spanish Fleet. You must capture vessels or destroy. Use utmost endeavor.

Dewey was eager to comply, but he waited first for the arrival of Consul Williams, who had proved so valuable. When the tug *Fame* came up to their harbor on April 27 with Williams aboard, Dewey was ready to take the Asiatic Squadron to the Philippines.

The ships already had steam up. At 2:00 P.M. Consul Williams went aboard the *Baltimore*. All the captains, after a short visit aboard the *Olympia*, went to their respective ships with their instructions. The squadron began to move. Dewey formed his vessels into two columns, with the fighting ships in the front and the auxiliary vessels in the rear, and set course for Manila Bay, 192 miles away. It was a fine sunny day with a pleasant breeze and a following wind.

Just before leaving the Asiatic continent, Commodore Dewey had a message forwarded from the Singapore consulate, warning him that the Boca Grande Channel into Manila Bay had been mined by the Spanish. Further, the Spanish had fortified the approaches with three 6-inch guns on Caballo Island, three 5-inch guns on El Fraile rock in the middle of the channel, and three 6-inch muzzle-loading rifles on Corregidor. Also there were three 7-inch guns on Punta Gorda and two 6-inch guns at Punta Lasisi, which commanded the Boca Chica entrance. These two mouths to Manila Bay—Boca Grande and Boca Chica—posed a problem that must be solved.

Commodore Dewey could not believe that the Spanish had made a good job of mining Boca Grande. If it were not for the little island of El Fraile, the Boca Grande would be four miles wide, too great an expanse to be mined successfully. Dewey took the position that the re-ports from Manila, which had come from steamers there, were so much propaganda designed to delay his attack.

Dewey did not know it, but his opponent, Admiral Patricio Montojo, was laboring under the worst of difficulties. His officers were inept, and their best efforts were often nullified by Filipino rebels, who stole the Spanish mines and other weapons to secure powder and shot.

Dewey headed south from Mirs Bay, drilling the men at action sta-tions during the day and preparing the vessels for war by putting up canvas barricades around the woodwork to prevent splintering and stop shrapnel.

Consul Williams had ascertained that Admiral Montojo was prepar-ing to fight his battle in Subic Bay and to that end had moved his squadron there just before Williams sailed for Hong Kong. So Dewey prepared to fight at Subic Bay. Arriving in Philippine waters, he sent *Boston* and *Concord* into the bay to reconnoiter on April 30. They were joined later by *Baltimore*. They found nothing, and so the fleet headed for Manila Bay, thirty miles away.

Dewey had decided to run into Manila Bay under cover of darkness. Before dark he stopped and brought all his captains aboard the flagship *Olympia*, and outlined his battle plan to them. The squadron would enter Manila Bay that night—the captains would then follow the move-ments and orders of the flagship. It was as clear-cut and simple as that.

Meanwhile, Admiral Montojo had learned of the sailing of the Amer-icans from Mirs Bay from the Spanish consul at Hong Kong, who was as good an agent for his government as Consul Williams was for the United States. On April 28, in Subic Bay, the Spanish captains voted unanimously that they must return to Manila Bay to fight rather than be destroyed—as they put it—in Subic Bay. So back they went, and waited in their big harbor for the coming of the Americans.

After his council of war, which was as straightforward as Nelson's at Trafalgar, Commodore Dewey headed in to fight. The night enveloped the squadron, steaming slowly into Manila Bay, the men at action sta-tions, the lights doused or covered. In they went to Boca Grande, with a major doubt nagging at Dewey: Was the channel mined or was it not?

It began to rain. Heavy clouds came in just before midnight, obscur-ing the new moon for ten minutes at a time. Yet it was generally light enough to navigate, for the landmarks were visible and the binnacle lights were on low.

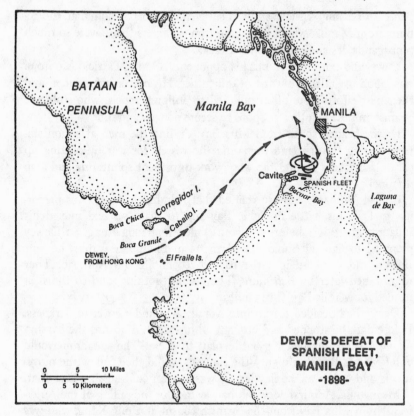

BATAAN
PENINSULA

Manila Bay

MANILA

Cavite

SPANISH FLEET

Bacoor Bay

Laguna de Bay

Boca Chica

Corregidor I.

Caballo I.

Boca Grande

DEWEY,
FROM HONG KONG

El Fraile Is.

0   5   10 Miles
0   5   10 Kilometers

**DEWEY'S DEFEAT OF
SPANISH FLEET,
MANILA BAY
-1898-**

Ten miles from Boca Grande, the men of the flagship spotted signaling ashore and apparently between ships. The Spanish had turned off the in harbor navigation lights, of course, but there was the fortress of El Fraile standing half a mile off the ship to port.

Dewey expected to be hit here by the guns of El Fraile, but the whole first column went through, and the second column—only then did the battery open up. El Fraile fired three times. *Boston, Concord, Raleigh,* and *McCullouch* returned the fire. El Fraile stopped shooting. The fort had managed to fire only three rounds.

Dewey now slowed to stall for time. He did not want to run in on the Spanish ships and the port's guns in the night—he wanted to fight by day. So the squadron slowed to four knots, headed toward Manila, and the men were allowed to catch a nap at their guns. There was no evidence of mines. At four o'clock Dewey passed the word that coffee was to be served all hands at their action stations.

As dawn broke on May 1, Commodore Dewey expected to see the Spanish fleet between himself and the city, but it was not there. The Manila batteries opened fire as the light grew stronger. Dewey ignored them; he was looking for the Spanish ships, and he found them some time after five o'clock, formed in an irregular crescent before Cavite, on the south side of the bay. Dewey did not hesitate. He ordered the *Olympia* turned toward the enemy, and signaled the other ships to close on her and prepare to fight.

The American line closed on the Spanish fleet which was protected on one flank by Cavite Peninsula and on the other by the shoal water off Las Piñas. The Spanish force, compared to the American, was a true armada. The ships were the *Reina Cristina*, the flagship; the *Castilla*; the *Don Juan de Austria*; the *Don Antonio de Ulloa*; the *Isla de Luzon*; the *Isla de Cuba*; and the *Marques del Duero*. On the other side of Cavite Point stood *Velasco* and *General Lezo*. The Spanish navy had overwhelming firepower this day.

On came the Americans, now a scant two hundred yards stood between ships, as the line of gray pressed ahead with all guns trained on the enemy vessels.

Bows sheared the sea, the low voice of a leadsman was heard above the soft engine sound; occasionally a deck officer gave an order. Periodically a shell from the shore battery was heard, only to scream overhead and burst abeam of the squadron.

At 5:15 the Spanish ships and the Cavite batteries opened fire on the Americans at long range. Still Dewey gave the order to continue standing in, keep the guns trained, but not to shoot. The speed was 8 knots. The course was converging, to keep the enemy on the starboard bow.

5:30. The men of the ships were growing anxious; the Spanish were continuing their fire, but so far they had not scored a single hit. All eyes were on the masthead of the flagship for the order to open fire.

5:40. Dewey looked sharply through his glass. He scanned the surroundings, wanting to wait until the fleet was within effective range. He now saw that they were about five thousand yards off the enemy. A range that lent his guns maximum efficiency.

He turned from the contemplation of sea and Spaniards and spoke to Captain Gridley of the *Olympia*.

"You may fire when you are ready, Gridley," he said.

7

Mopping Up in the Philippines

In the action that followed Commodore Dewey's sortie into Manila Bay, the Spanish were completely routed. Early in the action an 8-inch shell raked *Reina Cristina*, destroyed her steering gear, and knocked out 20 men. In seconds another and yet another shell hit home, and the admiral's flag was knocked down, replaced, fell again—the admiral then left the sinking ship to continue his fight aboard the *Isla de Cuba*. *Reina Cristina* sank rapidly, carrying with her to the bottom 150 men including Captain Don Luis Cadarso.

Throughout the action the American fire was fast and accurate. At 7:35 Dewey withdrew to rearm his ships; he was under the impression that they were nearly out of ammunition. He then stopped for breakfast for the men, and his officers assembled aboard the flagship for a conference. On the *Baltimore* two officers and half a dozen men had been wounded. Other ships were hit—*Olympia*, *Boston*, and *Petrel*—but not seriously enough to impede their action.

The ships then went back in to fight again, and the hail of fire resumed.

By 12:30 it was all over. Admiral Montojo had been wounded when his second flagship was shot from under him, and he had taken refuge ashore. By noon there were no Spanish fighting ships afloat to carry on the action, and the white flag of surrender flew from the forts ashore. The Americans then went aboard the scuttled Spanish ships and completed their destruction by setting them afire.

That night Dewey wrote in his diary:

Reached Manila at daylight. Immediately engaged the Spanish ships and batteries at Cavite. Destroyed eight of the former includ-

ing the *Reina Cristina* and the *Castilla*. Anchored at noon off
Manila.

The Americans had not lost a single man killed, and only a
handful wounded. The Spaniards lost 167 killed, 214 wounded,
and nearly all their ships.

So Dewey had carried out the Secretary's orders to a tee—he had destroyed the Spanish squadron. The problem of an American coaling
base in the Far East would soon be solved—Commodore Dewey had
one of the finest deep water ports in the world under his guns.

The American squadron stayed on in Manila Harbor but made no attempt to capture the port. Dewey did not have the manpower to wage
war against the local Spanish forces. That would have to await the arrival of U.S. Army contingents, the first of which reached the Philippines at the end of June.

But meanwhile the commodore got his official reward. It had been
the practice of the American government to give its squadron commanders abroad the temporary rank of rear admiral—although the government was very niggardly in bestowing flag rank. Dewey had not been
given this courtesy before because he had offended Secretary Long and
the President, both Republicans, by seeking the political sponsorship of
Senator Redfield Proctor, Democrat of Vermont. But now Dewey received his admiral's stars, and he no longer would have to sit at the bottom end of the table at conferences of naval commanders from European nations.

Dewey continued his holding operation against the Spanish, although
under difficult conditions made more so by the absence of communications. Nations of the world were in touch with the Far East by
way of the cable system, which ran around the world, but not across the
Pacific Ocean. Thus when Dewey was on the Chinese mainland or at
Hong Kong, he could send messages that were transmitted by way of
the Middle East, London, and then on to Washington. But it was six
days by sea from Manila to Hong Kong, and so the little supply ship
Zafiro became a courier, running messages to the cable head in Hong
Kong and bringing Dewey the responses. This, then, was the last of the
slow wars, where communications were still those of the days of sailing
ships.

Dewey's problems were far from over with the destruction of Spanish
sea power in the Philippines. He now had the job of keeping the other
powers from devouring the Philippines before the United States could
decide what was to be done with this strange Asian land. The Germans,
who were trying to build an international empire and thus challenge

their English cousins, were quick to learn that the Spanish Empire was falling apart. Germany rushed ships to Manila Bay and was toying with the idea of becoming truly belligerent to secure parts, at least, of the Spanish territory. But the Berlin authorities had second thoughts.

By the autumn of 1898 the navy decided to send another squadron to Dewey's assistance, this one commanded by Captain Albert S. Barker in the *Oregon*—the same Barker who, as a lieutenant more than twenty years before, had commanded the gunboat *Palos* in Chinese and Japanese waters. The war ended in December with the signing of a peace treaty while Barker and the squadron were paying duty calls in South American ports. The cruise was a leisurely one—to Valparaiso, the Galapagos Islands, Hawaii, Guam, and finally to Manila, which the squadron reached in March 1899. Dewey greeted Barker joyfully—he wanted to go home.

It was once again a spit-and-polish navy in 1899. On coming in to anchor, Captain Barker received a signal from the flagship of Dewey's squadron, which showed him where to drop his hook. He did so, and was immediately informed by the flagship: "Maneuver badly performed." This chiding note haunted Barker—it could affect his whole career—until he discovered from Dewey that night that the signal should have been "Haul fires." (Whether or not it really was "Haul fires" was a matter on which the two signalmen were ready to swear separate and different oaths.)

Dewey had hoped that once he had subdued the Spanish squadron and the U.S. Army reached the Philippines he would have little more to do there. But Emilio Aguinaldo, the Filipino insurgent leader, was not one to back down. Dewey's relationships with him were cordial until the American Army forces occupied the country. At that juncture Aguinaldo decided the Americans were just as much his enemy as the Spanish, and he fought them vigorously. So Dewey sent various ships around the islands on special missions—and soon came to realize that the Americans would have to create a special fleet of shallow-draft boats, much the same as the Spaniards' gunboat navy, if the islands were to be policed by sea.

In May 1899 Admiral Dewey received orders to return to the United States, and Captain Barker took temporary command of the Asiatic Squadron. The immediate problem remained the establishment of a fleet capable of policing the island waters, and the navy began refurbishing the old Spanish gunboats to do that job. The American warships were also frequently in action, sometimes, as Captain Barker put it, "feeling like we were using cannon to shoot partridges."

Barker was soon relieved by Rear Admiral Adolphus E. Watson, and the squadron adapted to an entirely new role for American naval officers. They were strangers in a strange land, yet they were the masters. It was the beginning of the American colonial experiment as far as the navy was concerned, embarrassing in a way because Dewey had made a number of promises and representations to Aguinaldo, while President McKinley pressed his intentions to establish a colonial regime.

This surging colonialism caused various Americans, Admiral Mahan among them, to suggest that the United States seek a naval base on the Chusan archipelago of China, at the mouth of Hangchow Bay, north of Shanghai. Tinghai on Chusan Island was the place most often mentioned.

Well, why not? It appeared that China would be cut up into pieces by the great powers in the next few years, and should not America have its share? Various advisers to President McKinley and Secretary of State John Hay urged that the United States get its share of the loot before it was all gone.

But wiser heads prevailed. And in September 1899 Secretary Hay promulgated the open door policy. This doctrine declared that the United States had no territorial interest in China, and, with strong support from Britain, maintained that all commercial ports in China, including those acquired by Russia, Germany, and France, be open to all nations of the world on equal terms. The European powers paid lipservice to the idea and America kept her ships on the Asiatic Station, some in China, some in Japan, some in the Philippines.

In 1899 and 1900 the Philippines contingent was by far the most active. After making peace with Spain, the Americans had inherited and proceeded to prosecute the war against Filipino nationalists, who did not wish to be anyone's colonials.

Life aboard the American "gunboat navy" in the Philippine tropics was varied and often hazardous. Dozens of gunboats were soon in action to support the army's four hundred garrisons all over the islands. Their duties included shelling rebel concentrations, intercepting enemy supply boats, carrying material among many others.

One of the best-known of all the American gunboats was the U.S.S. *Panay*, predecessor namesake of the famous *Panay* that was to be sunk by the Japanese on the Yangtze nearly forty years later. In the spring of 1900 Lieutenant (j.g.) Frederick L. Sawyer took command of this vessel at Cavite Navy Yard. She was a twin-engined, shallow-draft river boat of Spanish design and manufacture, with two full decks above the water line, two tall funnels, and a strange, totally enclosed navigating bridge that stood at the very prow of the vessel.

The weaponry consisted of one 6-pound 57-millimeter Hotchkiss bow pivot gun, half a dozen smaller guns and several Colt machine guns. There were rifles and Colt .38 revolvers for the officers and men, plus a rack full of cutlasses, reminiscent of earlier days. The boat was precisely designed for dealing with local outrage, when the enemy would have nothing larger than an automatic rifle or machine gun. For this purpose, as the Philippine and China gunboats were to show on hundreds of occasions, she was almost perfect.

Aboard the old *Panay* Sawyer had a force of one midshipman and thirty-three petty officers and men to uphold the United States' authority, dignity, and social position in the islands. Midshipman W.T. Clement, a youngster just out of Annapolis, was the executive officer. The men of the crew were hardly older, ranging in age from nineteen to twenty-eight.

Panay's first task was to travel around the island of Cebu, some four hundred miles south of Manila, show the flag in all ports, and generally frighten the natives into accepting American sovereignty. But Lieutenant Sawyer had scarcely begun his voyage when he received a call for help from American forces on Samar Island, over to the northwest. So it was stop in Cebu and fill up with coal and then head for Samar, which the ship reached early in July. On the way it was a question of checking insurgent vessels, which carried such important war materials as pigs and chickens. But of course these and rice were staples for the rebels and had to be captured, eaten, or destroyed.

On July 12 Sawyer stood south of Calbayog, on Samar's eastern shore, to shell a position where insurgents had been located firing into the town. Then he saw a *banca*, a native vessel, approaching the nearby Libucan Islands, and chased it into port. He found there that this *banca* and another were engaged in trade with the insurgents, and burned them both. Later that day he steamed south to Catbalogan and called on Colonel Hardin of the 29th U.S. Infantry to discuss the tactics of holding Samar with a shoestring force of American soldiers and sailors. The army was having its problems—too few men and much too much territory to cover. Basically almost all the native inhabitants were developing a fine dislike for the Americans.

Panay captured a few unarmed vessels, did a little survey work for the chart makers, and supported the troops as best she could. On July 15, the insurgents opened fire on army outposts at Calbayog, and the gunboat stood inshore so it could shell the hills where the rebels had emplaced their field guns.

Next day *Panay* responded to firing southeast of the village of Kalbayok. The gunboat *Pampanga*, under the command of Lieutenant (j.g.) Frederick Payne, had steamed here to help the army fight a heavy concentration of insurgents. Both sent in armed boats. *Panay*'s boat was commanded by Midshipman Clement and *Pampanga*'s by Midshipman Yates.

The gunboats then stood in along the shore, about a thousand yards out, and began shelling the rebel positions. The small boats moved inshore, while remaining in contact with the gunboats by semaphore signaling. As boats worked toward the shore opposite the village of Karayman they suddenly came under sharp rifle fire from a series of trenches not far from the beach. They returned fire. Then the Colt machine guns on both boats jammed—it was one of the hazards of using this particular model. They could not be cleared and the sailors continued to fight with rifles. But without their automatic weapons they were at a disadvantage and had to retreat beyond the range of the superior force of rebels in the trenches.

As soon as the boats were out of range, the *Panay* opened up with her 6-pounder and smaller guns in an attempt to take the pressure off the landing party. But the rebels had a victory of sorts that day. *Pampanga*'s boat had two casualties: Gunner's Mate First Class G. Howard was seriously wounded, and Seaman A.F. Forbeck was wounded in the left hand and arm.

With the armed boats safely back, the gunboats moved offshore. *Pampanga* had to return with the wounded to Catbalogan, the nearest place with medical facilities. *Panay* stood offshore and waited, while Lieutenant Sawyer noted the events of the past two days in his log. He had expended sixty 6-pounder shells, fifty-seven-pounder shells, and nearly a thousand rounds of machine gun ammunition; and *Pampanga* had done about the same. As far as they knew, there were no rebel casualties. The Americans had fired a lot of ammunition and taken two casualties. That's the kind of war it was—the guerrillas seemed to have all the best of it.

When the wounded men of *Pampanga* got to Catbalogan they were rushed into the tents of the surgeons, and at one o'clock in the morning Gunner's Mate Howard was operated on for a shattered vertebra. The rebel bullet from a Mauser rifle had mushroomed and made a dreadful wound. In spite of the surgeons' efforts, Howard died on the operating table.

For the next few days *Panay* and *Pampanga* worked in close support of this garrison, and then moved on. Like all the other gunboats, they knew they faced a fanatical foe. The American gunboats were constantly tangling with the rebels. They took casualties, but at least they did not have to face the enemy on his home grounds, the island jungles.

As with guerrillas everywhere, the insurgents relied on intelligence and cunning for their little victories and their constant harassment of the occupying force.

One of the favorite tricks of the *insurrectos* was to bend a small tree in the jungle into a powerful bow, using a lance as an arrow. Anyone tripping a carefully hidden line would be struck by the lance.

Another device was the *chevaux de frise*, a concealed pit lined with sharp, fire-hardened stakes, sometimes poisoned.

The rebel use of these weapons caused the American soldiers to employ equally desperate measures. To test the safety of the area, a prisoner *insurrecto* was sent ahead after being roped to a husky sergeant so that he could not suddenly escape. The prisoner carried a long pole which he used vigorously to whip the ground ahead. In many trails the coyon grass was ten feet high, so thick that a bolo man could be within an arm's length and still remain invisible.

But despite all their cunning, the insurgents could not function without their boats. And it remained the basic job of the American gunboats to capture enemy vessels. But there were literally thousands of these vessels of all sizes, many of them carrying guns, ammunition, and food. In one of the island channels the *Panay* overtook three *bancas* and burned all of them for illegal activity. That same day the gunboat stopped five more *bancas* and sent several of them off under guard because they did not have legal permits. But for every *banca* destroyed or captured it seemed another two were built.

For the most part the *bancas* were devilishly hard to catch, particularly if they had contraband aboard. They could move into shoal water where the gunboats could not, and they skirted the edges of the islands, ready to dash for the jungle and safety at the first sign of danger. Captures were made either by surprise or in deep water, where the 6-pounder gun was usually enough to make a *banca* captain heave-to.

This kind of fighting continued for months which lengthened into years. Finally an expedition under Brigadier General Frederick Funston captured Aguinaldo by a ruse, and the rebel chieftain was persuaded that the Americans would truly grant the Philippines their independence and would help them prepare for the day. Aguinaldo took an oath of allegiance to the United States and the fighting stopped in the spring of 1902. Gradually the naval forces were drawn back to the work of peacetime.

Yet the combination of events of the previous five years in China and in the Philippines had so focused American attention on the Far East that never again could that area of the world be as completely ignored by state-side authorities as it had been before 1898.

The Asiatic Squadron not only would remain there—it was soon to become the Asiatic Fleet.

8

Tangling with the Boxers

The United States victory in the Philippines and the extension of American influence in the South Pacific seemed to excite the European powers more than anything had in years. Their appetite for plunder in the Far East increased. And so pressure on the Chinese government became greater just at a time when even Chinese moderates began to realize that there was probably no salvation for their country except in a show of violence against the outrageous invaders.

For years antiforeignism had been smoldering toward flashpoint in China. Now it erupted in violence. With the tacit approval of elements close to the dowager empress, groups of fanatical nationalists began to move against the foreigners. The chief one was the Society of Righteous and Harmonious Fists, which called itself a boxing society, hence the term Boxers.

A secret society given to mystical incantations, magical rites, strange posturing, and shadow boxing, the Boxers had been taught by their leaders that they were immune from injury in battle—that bullets would turn away from their bodies. From the standpoint of the leaders, this belief was extremely valuable, because it rendered their soldiers absolutely fearless. Shouting their slogan, "Destroy the Foreigners!" the Boxers harassed and murdered Western businessmen and missionaries, burned Christian churches, and massacred Chinese Christians.

When the trouble began in the spring of 1900, Rear Admiral George C. Remey was in charge of the Asiatic Squadron. He was on the Philippine Station, his hands full with the pacification of the islands. Rear Admiral Arnold Kempff, second in command, was off in Japan with the cruiser *Newark*, having just finished several very active months in the Philippines, where many of his sailors had found themselves fighting in land actions against the *insurrectos*. Except for the wheezing old *Monocacy*, still moored in Shanghai, *Newark* was all he had under his command. And now, in May 1900, she was "taking a blow" in Japan.

One afternoon that month Captain Bowman H. McCalla of the *Newark* and several of his young officers were ashore in Nagasaki calling on the American consul and watching boat races staged by various men-of-war of the European powers. Late that afternoon Captain McCalla proceeded to the American boat landing to rejoin the *Newark*. Then he looked out at his ship—she was just disappearing up harbor, with full steam up, black smoke pouring out of her stacks. Admiral Kempff had gotten a message that day from American Minister Edwin Conger in Peking. Describing the situation in north China as desperate, Conger said an American warship was needed at Taku Bar, outside Taku, the nearest coastal port.

Admiral Kempff had ordered up steam. A quick but unsuccessful search for McCalla and his officers had been made, and their ship was leaving without them.

There they stood on the landing, watching the stream of smoke, until Captain McCalla recovered his aplomb, commandeered a steam launch from the U.S. battleship *Oregon*, which happened to be in Nagasaki, and with whistle shrieking, chased and caught the *Newark*.

In late May the *Newark* reached Taku Bar, a submerged bank in the Pei Ho estuary caused by continuous silting. Since she drew too much water to cross over, she anchored outside. Admiral Kempff had asked Washington to dispatch another vessel or two to these waters, but he had been rebuffed—the U.S. government was spending quite enough money on the Philippine operation. So here sat Kempff with a single American ship, riding the rough waters off Taku.

Aboard the *Newark* Naval Cadet Joseph Taussig described the scene:

A more desolate anchorage than that off Taku cannot be imagined. From the deck of the ship not a vestige of land is in sight. The wide expanse of muddy greenish water is depressing. The Taku Bar . . . is the barrier.

Outside the harbor with the *Newark* were several other warships, including the French cruiser *D'Entrecasteaux* and gunboat *Surprise*, and three Chinese cruisers.

At about that time things began to happen near Peking. The Boxers attacked the railroad station at Fengtai, a short way down the Peking-Tientsin line. This action threatened the escape route of the foreign diplomats and their families stationed in Peking, now threatened by antiforeign violence. So Minister Conger asked Kempff to put a force ashore.

At four o'clock the next morning the *Newark* bustled with preparations for the landings. Two groups were to go ashore—marines under Captain John T. Meyers and sailors under Ensign Daniel Wurtsbaugh. The men put on their marching clothes and strapped on haversacks. Besides their rifles and ammunition, the sailors took along a 3-inch fieldpiece.

The sailors' landing operation was miserable—no spit and polish this time. First the *Newark*'s steam launch, towing two smaller boats, got stuck in the mud and some of her men had to be transferred to the other boats to lighten her. Then the two smaller boats, put under sail, were stopped dead by the unfavorable winds and tide. Finally, as the tide turned, the steam launch got under way and, taking the other boats and two commandeered sampans in two, led them over the bar. Five and a half hours after leaving the ship, the troops landed at Taku and piled into their field rations of bully beef and hardtack.

At Taku the naval contingent joined the marines, who had landed ahead of them. Together, in a chartered tug and lighter, they started for Tientsin, some thirty miles upriver, remaining under cover near the river bank so as not to be seen by the Taku forts. Up they went along the low, muddy river bank, passing rice fields and fishing villages, until 11:00 P.M., when they finally reached Tientsin.

There they were greeted by the whole foreign colony, led by a brass band.

"Three cheers for Uncle Sam!" was the cry—and the Germans, Frenchmen, and Britishers responded with a will, for there was very grave fear of the Boxers these days. The American sailors and marines were then led off to Temperance Hall, on the Taku Road, where they would be quartered, the crowd following along all the way, cheering long into the night.

The American force sat there for several days. In the interim several other countries managed to get their ships and troops to Taku in response to frantic calls from the legations at Peking. But the Chinese had stalled for days to prevent the Americans and others from using the rail line to Peking. Finally, on May 31, permission for a special train was given. The men entrained. And by June 2, some four hundred men, including Russian, British, French, American, Italian, and Japanese, reached the capital and took up positions in the legation quarter. The American contingent consisted of fifty marines.

The rest of the Americans remaining in Tientsin, including fifty-four sailors under Ensign Wurtsbaugh and Cadet Taussig, moved to the compound of the American Board Mission, a group of buildings sheltered behind a high wall.

Nothing happened in Tientsin in the next few days, but the Boxers roamed the countryside along the roads and railroad. As they went they burned missions and railroad stations, murdered some missionaries and Chinese Christians, and tore up sections of the railroad.

When word came that the Peking Tientsin rail line was severed, Admiral Kempff and Captain McCalla ordered another fifty sailors ashore to strengthen the defenses of Tientsin. Two days later, on June 8, the telegraph line between the two cities was cut. Peking was isolated, and no one knew what horrors might be in store for the Westerners there.

As the air of crisis thickened, more warships arrived at Taku, including British, French, Japanese, and Austrian vessels. The British had brought up *Centurion, Endymion,* and *Aurora.* The international force ashore grew to a formidable size. With the largest force, the British under Vice-Admiral Sir Edward Seymour took charge of the situation. And much to the Americans' annoyance, they grabbed control of the rolling stock in the Tientsin yards.

There was no really unified command, as accounts by the Americans showed. Cadet Taussig later recalled that at a general meeting of representatives of the various powers Captain McCalla declared that the Americans were going to the aid of their Peking mission. The other nations fell into line—a natural reaction, perhaps. But when McCalla got to Tientsin station and found the British in charge of all the trains, he lost his temper and demanded space on the first one out. He was refused. He then created a storm, railing at Captain E.H. Bailey of the *Aurora,* who had been put in charge by his admiral. By what right did Bailey take control? demanded McCalla. By Admiral Seymour's orders, said the captain.

To which McCalla retorted that he wanted it clearly understood that Captain Bailey could not issue orders to him.

Finally the troublesome Americans were accommodated in that first train, with the officers riding in the baggage car, along with Admiral Seymour's baggage. An admiral traveled in style those days, no matter where he was going. The American enlisted men were put on a flat car.

On June 11, some 1,950 men strong, the expedition for the relief of Peking set off. This time it consisted of troops from eight nations—Britain, Russia, France, Germany, Japan, United States, Italy, and Austria. They expected to arrive in the city in a day or so. Under normal conditions the journey was only a few hours' run by train. Thirty-five miles out they passed Yangtsun station. On the way they noticed the Imperial Chinese army of General Nieh Shih-ch'eng encamped along the Pei Ho, apparently to guard the rail line against the Boxers.

But seven miles farther on, the train had to stop because of torn-up rails, and from then on the harrying effect of the Boxer rail busters was almost continuous. It was move a little, stop, repair the line, and move on.

At dusk the force arrived at a long trestle over a dry wash and found some ties burned at the farther end. Admiral Seymour decided to wait there for the night and repair the trestle, so that no damage might occur to this or following trains. But only one man in the whole force knew anything about rail-line work—a six-foot-tall member of the American contingent who served in the *Newark*'s black gang, and who had been at one time a section hand on a railroad. So he taught the others how to drive a spike.

Spike driving, however, was not the fashion for navy men, and it was not long before Admiral Seymour had recruited a gang of Chinese coolies to do the work. This was the Orient, and this was how it was done—the lives of the expeditionaries were entrusted to the mercies of Chinese who had little interest in the proceedings. Finally, at dark, the Americans lay on the ground and slept.

Next day, the line repaired, the force moved on to Lofa station, twenty-five miles outside Tientsin. Here they encountered a band of about a dozen Boxers, recognizable because they wore red caps, red belts, and red anklets, and carried white and red flags. They also carried knives or long spears.

It was three o'clock in the afternoon when this small group of Boxers attacked a train carrying more than 1,500 heavily armed soldiers of various lands in a frontal assault.

The Boxers advanced slowly and steadily, making many salaams and gestures—a most picturesque group. As Taussig put it:

> We had heard that these poor superstitious creatures thought they were bullet-proof and that their peculiar movements turned the missiles aside, giving them nothing to fear. When fire was opened they had no time to appreciate the fallacy of their belief. In a few moments they were riddled with bullets, all of course being killed. Our skirmish line then advanced through a nearby village but saw no more Boxers.

The villages had been temporarily abandoned.

The Lofa action brought Admiral Seymour's disciplinary problems to a head. For here the allies had behaved with little sense of mutual responsibility, and the admiral had difficulty keeping the troops from rushing off in all directions at the behest of their own officers. Now Seymour called a meeting of national commanders and laid down the law.

Discipline then improved, but other problems arose that were as serious. The troops had brought food for not more than six days, and they were already beginning to realize they were facing a long trip. Water was a problem; first the Westerners had to test it—so they let the coolies drink it. Even if the wells had not been poisoned, as they feared, the water still had to be boiled to prevent cholera and typhoid. Then, too, they had to water the train, where the Boxers had destroyed the pumping apparatus, it took a thirty-yard-long line of men with buckets six hours to fill the 4,500-gallon water tender of the engine.

Most of the Westerners were having their first experience with the Peking plain in midsummer, when the hot, dry ground absorbs all the water about, and the winds from the northwest hurl red dust along the land, drying out whatever was not cracked or seared by the sun. And the hot days were often replaced by freezing nights, forcing the men on watch to move about and stamp their feet. The rest of the troops slept curled up in woolen blankets that had been repulsive to the touch a few hours earlier.

The expedition laid over at Lofa until supplies could be brought up by other trains. Then, leaving a hundred British sailors and marines from *Endymion* and taking a hundred coolies to work on the railroad, the relief force moved ahead for Langfang, just five miles away.

Reaching Langfang, they realized how serious the problem of the Boxers could be. Another handful of badly armed men had torn up the rail line so that it would take several days for coolies and sailors to repair it.

Here at Langfang, the Boxers made another attack. Several hundred of them suddenly appeared out of a peach orchard behind the Chinese village, chasing five Italian sailors who had gone wandering off beyond the picket line. The foreign troops watched as the Boxers first caught and then cut down all five Italians. Maddened by the blood and the slogans they were shouting—"Death to all Foreigners; the Government has ordered it"—the Boxers came on, sure of their mystical strength and invulnerability.

A British officer rammed his sword down a Boxer's throat. Captain McCalla seized his orderly's rifle and shot down several Boxers as they

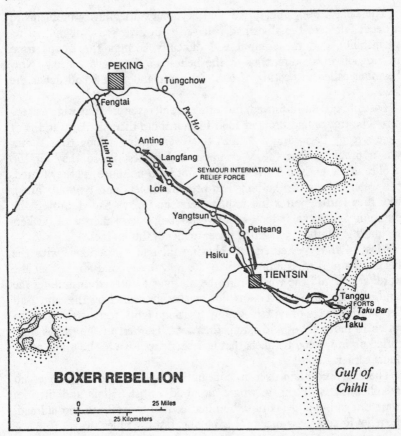

PEKING

Tungchow

Fengtai

Peo Ho

Hun Ho

Anting

Langfang

SEYMOUR INTERNATIONAL
RELIEF FORCE

Lofa

Yangtsun

Peitsang

Hsiku

TIENTSIN

Tanggu
FORTS
Taku Bar
Taku

*Gulf of
Chihli*

BOXER REBELLION

0   25 Miles
0   25 Kilometers

ran toward him. Then the machine guns opened up with deadly fire,
and the Boxers still rushing forward, began to fall. A dozen died and
another dozen, and then the ranks wavered as those behind saw that
the charms of the mystical rites did not really protect them from the
foreign bullets. The assault crumbled and broke, and the Boxers turned
and ran, dropping their swords and slogans.

The Westerners went out cautiously, guns in hand, bayonets at the
ready, and turned over the bodies. There were 102 Boxers on the field—
all dead. The five Italians were the only casualties among the Westerners.

That day the expedition finally received a message from the American legation in Peking, carried by an old Chinese servant who had dis-
guised himself as a ragpicker and worked his way from village to village

along the road to Tientsin. The messenger reported that foreigners in Peking were hard-pressed by the Chinese, and that the column must arrive soon if it was to save the lives of the diplomats and their families.

Having been twice attacked, suspecting that the Imperial Chinese government was behind the Boxers, and seeing the difficulty of using the rail line, Admiral Seymour now decided to move up to Anting, fifteen miles from Langfang, and abandon the railroad. From that point they would try to march overland to Peking. He also decided to burn the villages along the way, since they seemed to harbor Boxers.

Now came another blow. Captain McCalla had taken the construction train along the road toward Anting to supervise the relaying of track to that town. He then received a message from Admiral Seymour: Bring back the train. For General Nieh's Chinese army that had been camped along the river had deserted the area, and the Boxers had rushed into the vacuum and torn up many miles of track between Yangtsun and Tientsin. The relieving force had been cut off from its supply base. So on that day, June 17, the expedition found itself in a perilous situation.

Back in Tientsin Admiral Kempff had begun to realize that the Chinese government had more than a passing acquaintance with the Boxers, and he asked for reinforcements. In Washington navy officials were coming to realize the seriousness of the situation. Already other nations had sent almost thirty warships to the scene. Perhaps the United States was lagging. They queried Admiral Remey in the Philippines. Could he help? But Remey, who considered his problems in the Philippines to be much more important than anything that could possibly be happening in China, said he had no ships to spare.

Finally, with faint hope, old *Monocacy* was dispatched from Shanghai—many in Washington doubted she could survive the voyage north. But survive she did. *Monocacy* arrived at Taku Bar on June 15, and, wonder of wonders!, managed to cross the bar and anchor at Tangku, a few miles upriver from Taku. And out from the Philippines, by dint of flat departmental order, steamed the light cruiser *Nashville* with a contingent of marines.

So the international fleet lay off the bar while the Chinese coastal forces held a trump card—the Taku forts on either side of the Pei Ho estuary. The forts could block the flow of reinforcements up the river, sealing the fate of Seymour's forces, and they were already active and menacing. The Westerners got word that the Chinese were sending troops to strengthen the garrisons, and they also learned that Chinese were laying mines in the river. Then other informants claimed the "mines" were nothing but buoys.

This was the way "intelligence" was served up during the entire Boxer Rebellion. Foreigners, most of them not speaking the language or knowing the customs of China, were largely at the mercy of native interpreters, who might or might not have axes of their own to grind.

The Western naval commanders now held a council to decide what to do about the forts. The result was an ultimatum to the Chinese, delivered on June 16, demanding surrender of the forts by 2:00 A.M. the next day. And gunboats of the powers began to deploy in the shallow waters of the Pei Ho, within easy range of the forts.

Admiral Kempff refused to participate in the ultimatum, feeling he could not take such overt action against China without authorization. But to make sure he was doing the right thing he did send a telegram to Washington for information. The telegram went southward to Shanghai and thence to Hong Kong, and then over the long British cable system to reach London and finally Washington. It took ten days to arrive. Kempff must have suspected how slowly it would travel. The world was still in that period of communications when the telegraph was useful but limited, and sometimes created more ill than good.

The Chinese fort commanders ignored the allied ultimatum and shortly before its expiration, at about 1:00 A.M. on June 17, they opened fire on the foreign ships. Immediately Russia, German, French, and British gunboats attacked the forts.

Soon afterward poor old *Monocacy* took a shell in one of her cutters. Commander Frederick Wise, her captain, wanted to fight back, but he had orders from Kempff not to do so, and he was carrying thirty-seven American women and children from Tientsin who had taken refuge on his boat. So he moved back to the mooring just after dawn.

But Admiral Kempff was now relieved of the responsibility of starting trouble with the Chinese, and he ordered Commander Wise to cooperate with the other gunboat captains for defense and combat. By this time the allied commanders had sent landing parties ashore and captured the Taku forts. "A state of war [with China] practically exists," said Kempff in his next message to Washington.

Events, more than policies, decided American actions in the next few days and the biggest was an attack by regular Chinese troops on the foreign colony at Tientsin on June 17. Now China was truly at war. Kempff decided to send men to protect the foreigners at Tientsin. Some from *Monocacy* moved to take control of the Tangku station and yards. Commander Wise took over as trainmaster and began sending trains full of troops to Tientsin. Major Littleton Waller arrived from Manila with his contingent of marines. Wise found a train and dispatched him to Tientsin. Off he went, leading a group that included British and Russians. But they had to fight their way up the line to the city.

And what of Admiral Seymour and his expeditionaries on the Peking-Tientsin line while all this was going on? On June 18 a force of Boxers and regular Chinese army soldiers attacked the relief column at Langfang, and for the first time the Westerners found themselves under fire from artillery and machine guns. In the fighting, the well-trained international soldiers killed some five hundred Chinese, while losing only a handful killed and about forty wounded. But now they knew they had a real war on their hands.

This grave turn in affairs caused Admiral Seymour to change his plans. Surmising that the Chinese commanders had an army of thirty thousand in or around Peking and an additional ten thousand in the vicinity of Tientsin, he decided he must try to get back to Tientsin and secure reinforcements rather than head into a suicidal attack against a force fifteen times as large as his own.

The Westerners thereupon brought their trains back to Yangtsun, where the railroad crosses the Pei Ho, set the trains on fire, and prepared to retreat to Tientsin overland. First they moved to the left bank of the river, the soldiers crossing over the railroad bridge, while the American fieldpiece was ferried over in a junk. At noon on June 19 the retreat began.

Admiral Seymour rode a horse. Captain McCalla was astride a small white mule. Nearly everyone else walked. Some of the stores were packed on other mules the party had commandeered. The remaining stores and the wounded were moved in junks and sampans picked up along the river and manned by Germans and the Americans.

The entire column had three field weapons: the American 3-inch gun and two British muzzle-loading 9-pounders. The Americans led the way as advance guards. First came a marine sergeant and three marine sharpshooters; then, at successive intervals of a hundred yards, marched ten marines under Paymaster Jewett, twenty men under Cadet Taussig, and the main body of Americans with the field gun.

Night found the column only a few miles beyond the abandoned trains—they knew because all the way along they could see the smoke and flames of the burning cars.

At six o'clock the next morning the retreat began again. Now the Boxers and the Chinese troops knew that the Westerners were on the move, and they attacked at about ten o'clock that morning. The Americans set up their fieldpiece behind a mud wall. The Boxers came on, and this time they had rifles—another sure indication of the change in Chinese government policy.

Some two hundred Boxers bore down on the American advance party. The Americans held their fire until the Boxers came up to within five hundred yards, and then the fieldpiece began firing. Two shots and the Boxers turned. One more and they fled, and disappeared into a village.

The Boxers fought through the villages, hiding in the houses and shooting through the windows and doors, then ducking and escaping to stop at the next bit of cover. The expeditionaries moved on down the crooked river line, fighting their way toward Tientsin. At one point the Chinese put up a tremendously noisy fire from a village, and the Westerners stopped—until a Japanese captain discovered that the noise came from firecrackers.

That night the troops camped between two villages, and burned them both for protection. Next morning they set out across the plain to the city of Pietsang, which lies on both banks of the Pei Ho less than ten miles from Tientsin. There they came under fire again from the rifles and field guns of the regular Chinese army.

But with the Americans leading the attack, the force moved on through Pietsang, taking every street until the Chinese were forced out of the city.

In this struggle Captain McCalla on his white mule was everywhere along the line. Cadet Taussig tried to persuade him to move back.

"Captain, they are using you as a target."

"Now, don't mind me, don't mind me," came the answer—and Captain McCalla moved on. A bullet passed through his hat, one hit his sword scabbard, and one grazed his back. He kept right on going on the small white mule.

On the levee on the other side of the city, the Chinese decided to make a stand. The men dragging the fieldpiece were exhausted from the heavy work, and Captain McCalla ordered Cadet Taussig to take over the task for a time. It was here that Taussig was wounded in the leg. He was picked up by British soldiers and put under the care of the surgeon of *Endymion*, and the force moved on.

That evening of June 21, while Taussig was lying in a junk on the river, the Westerners closed up and concentrated on the riverbank. Ensign Charles Gilpin was with the American force, which was just behind the British marines at this point. Gilpin recalled it:

> In fact we were so close to the British Marines when they halted a short distance from a village, or rather a cluster of mud brick houses, that I could distinctly hear the Chinese in the village shouting, "Sha! Sha!" ("Kill! Kill!")

The British and the Americans advanced and took the village. As usual, the Boxers melted away into the underbrush—not even a chicken or a Chinese village dog was to be seen.

As they approached a bend in the stream near dawn next day, the forward allied patrols spotted a pair of 90-mm. Krupp guns, surrounded by gun crews, and pointed directly at the column. A Chinese officer paced up and down the earthworks with sword drawn. As the sun came up over the Pei Ho, Admiral Seymour's interpreter stepped up and hailed the Chinese officer:

CHINESE OFFICER: Who are you and what do you want?
INTERPRETER: We are Europeans who wish to go down stream without any more fighting, if possible, but we will fight if necessary.
CHINESE OFFICER: Fire!
KRUPP GUNS: *Bang! Bang!*

Bugles began to blow. The guns fired again, and then machine guns and rifles opened up on the expeditionaries from the earthworks on the other side of the Pei Ho.

In the fighting, Cadet Taussig, in his sickbed in the junk, was nearly killed when the boat ran into the line of fire. A Britisher, Midshipman B.J.D. Guy, rescued the junk and its cargo of wounded, and was later awarded the Victoria Cross for his gallantry.

By this time the soldiers of all the allied nations were nearly exhausted. On June 22 the Chinese suddenly stopped their fire and the column moved along until the troops came to a fortress surrounded by a high wall and a moat. Again came the challenge:

Who comes?

And the answer: Peaceful foreigners going to Tientsin.

Again, gunfire.

Admiral Seymour concentrated his fire against the fortress, and slipped a flanking party of Royal Marines to the rear, where they came up behind the fortress. When the marines added their fire to that of the frontal party, the Chinese suddenly abandoned the position and fled.

The allied force marched into the next river town, Hsiku, and captured the local arsenal. There they discovered stacks of modern Winchester, Mauser, and Mannlicher rifles, and hundreds of thousands of rounds of ammunition. It was a lucky break, for the Americans were down to twenty-five rounds per man by this time and most of the other foreigners were in the same state.

The Seymour force occupied the arsenal, and the wounded were brought in and put in a big comfortable room. Lieutenant Bates of the Royal Marines volunteered to lead a party to Tientsin, now only a few miles distant, to seek aid. He went out with a detachment, but they did not make it. The Chinese captured them and beheaded every man.

The Chinese now laid siege to the position they had abandoned. At night the Seymour force fired rockets in the hope of attracting the attention of the international forces in Tientsin. By day they fought the dust and the Chinese—and waited.

On the second day they saw a dust cloud on the road.

It turned out to be a Russian-led international relief force. After driving off the Chinese, moving the wounded, and burning the arsenal, the Seymour force and their rescuers headed back to Tientsin, by now a burned and silent city protected by the foreign troops.

The Americans counted heads: They had set out with 112 men; 5 had been killed and 26 wounded. The wounded were cared for in Tientsin by doctors and others of the foreign community. The remaining troops were sent back to their ships, to await the gathering of the much larger international expedition that would soon march on Peking, carrying its own baggage and supplies for the siege-breaking operation.

Captain McCalla went back to the *Newark* with the praises of Admiral Seymour ringing in his ears.

"Why, if he had been thoroughly British," said the admiral in some surprise, "he could not have rendered more loyal service."

That was quite an accolade for a sailor of the Asiatic Squadron.

The situation in China kept the world on tenterhooks. Admiral Kempff gladly turned over the delicate American role to Admiral Remey when that commander steamed up to the Taku Bar in the cruiser *Brooklyn* on July 8. But the show shifted in July to military operations bossed by the generals in Tientsin, and the navy's land participation ended.

In August that year an international force of about 18,000 troops—Japanese, Russian, British, French, and American—marched on Peking and broke the Chinese siege of the legation quarter. The expedition included 2,500 Americans. The Chinese court fled into the interior.

Later the allies imposed a $330 million indemnity on China for damages and expenses incurred. But the United States returned the bulk of its share of the indemnity to China, to be used as a fund for educating Chinese students in America.

9

The Fleet Gets Around

The most important outcome of the Boxer affair for America was the realization that something had to be done if American trade interests in the Far East were to be protected and the navy was to have the influence it needed there. The question could not be easily answered: the United States' ambivalence toward overseas expansion was indicated by the size of its standing army—97,000 officers and men, of whom 61,000 were stationed in the Philippines.

But the Navy Department sent the battleship *Oregon* to Taku Bar to join Admiral Remey in the *Brooklyn*, and also dispatched two other warships to central China to await developments.

An incident involving the *Oregon* during the Boxer troubles had further demonstrated the kind of maintenance difficulties faced by American warships operating in China waters. One day the battleship struck a rock off the Shantung Peninsula and went aground. She was assisted in getting afloat by the Chinese cruiser *Hai Chi*, and in turn let *Hai Chi* fly the American flag at a critical moment when the Chinese ship was about to be captured by the Russians.

When it came to repairing the *Oregon*, there was a problem: The Russians were annoyed by the *Hai Chi* incident and made excuses about their drydock at Port Arthur. Finally the Japanese let the Americans bring *Oregon* to Kure for repair. Once again Washington had learned a hard lesson in the need for naval facilities in Asia if America was to maintain ships in the area.

In the autumn of 1902 Rear Admiral Robley D. Evans, known in the navy as "Fighting Bob," succeeded Admiral Frederick Rogers as commander of the Asiatic Squadron. The Navy Department was at last toying with the idea of promoting the Asiatic Squadron into an Asiatic

Fleet, as most aggressive naval advisors were suggesting. When the decision to do so came that year, Bob Evans found himself in a tough spot: As first commander of the Asiatic Fleet, he was given fleet obligations with only twenty ships to handle them. But that of course was not the navy's fault. It was just the way of the American Congress in those times.

Now came the period in which the niceties of life and discipline overtook the American navy in the Far East. One of the big issues in the service in the fall of 1902 was the question of dressing officers for dinner.

The other foreign navies dressed their officers in "mess dress" which consisted of formal trousers, a formal shirt and tie, and a short jacket cut off at the waist and fitting snugly about the body. The Americans had to have mess jackets if they were not to look foolish when they went to dinner with the British or the French.

"Fighting Bob" considered this weighty problem for days and then issued his edict, Fleet General Order No. 4. It specified the dinner uniform: either mess jacket or evening dress. And that was to apply to all ships except the small gunboats.

Some officers bridled.

Who the hell was the admiral to tell them what to wear to dinner?

The order stood, and so one grizzled veteran ate in his cabin for a week while he sulked and thought it over. Finally he emerged in the splendor of a new mess jacket, and the war was won.

The ways of the Orient, with their little additions to the body military, also began to seep into the American Asiatic Fleet.

The maneuvers in Amoy in November 1902 were typical. The Americans assembled and had their drills and war games and gunnery competitions. They were landed ashore in the afternoons to play baseball and football and to participate in track and field events. This athletic program was a definite part of the fleet's attempts to preserve camaraderie and well-being.

"It was necessary," said Admiral Evans, "that the officers and men should work hard at their drills aboard ship: it was also of great importance that they should be kept in proper condition by playing hard on shore."

As the time neared to leave Amoy, the command arranged sailing races and rowing races for all classes of boats. The British battleship *Goliath* was invited to join in, and when the British could not compete because of the difference in the style and weight of their rowing boats, the Americans lent them American boats to practice in for a week—and then went on to beat them. The men of *Goliath* had their revenge in the sailing races, which they won with ease.

Admiral Evans then discovered that his flagship, *Kentucky*, was badly in need of defouling. Vice-Admiral Sir Cyprian A.C. Bridge of the British navy offered the Americans the use of the docks and facilities at Hong Kong, and so Evans took his flagship there, dependent on British charity, as he was to be again and again.

Evans moved over to the cruiser *Helena* during the refitting work, and sailed to Canton to show the flag, and particularly to check on rumors of a revolution brewing against the Manchu rulers there.

He visited the viceroy of the region, a necessary bit of protocol, and found that Chinese gentlemen very much worried about the future and his own fate. The admiral left orders with the American gunboats in the region to check all shipping coming from Hong Kong to Canton, and a few weeks after Evans left, the Americans found a steamer load of "barrels of cement" was really a load of Mauser rifles. They were confiscated, putting an end to revolution for that season.

Then the Asiatic Fleet was off to Cavite, its anchorage near Manila, to help in the basic American commitment in the Far East, the subjugation of the Philippine *insurrectos*.

Manila was then a dreary and in many ways a dreadful place. There was only one decent hotel in the city, and that was reasonable only by comparison with the others. Transportation was impossible; the officers and men had to use carriages that were about to fall apart, and pay exorbitant rates for the privilege. There was no public transportation system, and only the main streets were paved, these so badly that the iron tires of the carts banged and bumped across the rocks.

Americans, who had been the conquering heroes for a brief time in 1898, were now far more despised than the Spanish had ever been—because Filipino patriots knew in their hearts that they had been betrayed by the one land they had expected to free them from the yoke of colonialism. The Americans came, and where they camped they brought sanitation and employment, but the Filipinos hated them so that Admiral Evans said he did not like having his men go out of Manila lest they be murdered.

The "snug harbor" of Manila for sailors was the Army and Navy Club, a luxurious establishment, but one the navy men could reach only occasionally, since they were usually expected to stay aboard ship. Admiral Evans set the style. He very rarely visited the city, he was far too busy keeping his fleet in shape, so he lived aboard the *Kentucky*.

Washington provided little or no support during this time. Throughout the period of Admiral Evans' command of the Asiatic Fleet he made constant efforts to secure the base the navy wanted in Asia. The governor of Amoy once told Evans that if he were to raise the American flag over that port, no Chinese would object. But Washington refused to act. In the Philippines navy planners wanted to build a big base in Subic Bay, but they fell to squabbling with the army engineers over the facilities, and Congress did nothing. So time went by and the American base in Asia did not materialize.

But Evans did his best with the Asiatic Fleet. And on the day after Christmas, 1902, he took his twenty vessels (scarcely more than a squadron in real size) out of Manila Bay for fleet drills.

What a fleet! The 12,000-ton battleship *Kentucky* led the procession. After the flagship came the cruiser *New Orleans,* a pair of gunboats, then cruisers *Helena* and *Wilmington,* four more gunboats, and what might be called the pirate squadron—a dozen vessels captured from the Spanish which would not fit into any American naval categories.

To "Fighting Bob" Evans' sharp nautical eye, his fleet was a monstrosity, incapable of any kind of fleet performance. As he put it:

> Their appearance was grotesque. Before we had been steaming one hour the speed had to be reduced to allow some of the smaller ones to keep in position, and before the second hour was completed four or five of them were being towed by the larger gunboats.

Yet they were not joking in their drills. When they ran into Subic Bay the *Kentucky* maneuvered outside while a minelayer planted a double row of mines across the entrance to the bay. This protection would keep out snoopers, Filipino or otherwise. The guard vessels were ordered to fire on any boats approaching the field or the entrance to the bay.

Then half the fleet became the "enemy" and tried to break the blockade. One young midshipman, with two companions, even swam out towing a small raft containing a buoy and "blew up" part of the minefield by planting the buoy. To do so he spent half an hour in the company of the bay's sharks, which were known to eat men as well as fish. When Evans heard that tale, since he knew the midshipman's mother, he hastily put an end to swimming "attacks."

After maneuvers in Subic Bay the fleet returned to Manila Bay. A few more attempts at fleet maneuvers, and Evans gave up the idea. Only half a dozen of his ships could even make a show of working together.

Next summer, in 1903, Admiral Evans was in on the Shantung Peninsula, one of the most pleasant ports in China and a center of American activity. By this time the Asiatic Fleet had been split, and Rear Admiral P.H. Cooper had arrived with his flagship, the battleship *Wisconsin*, to take command of the northern division, which operated in Chinese and Japanese waters. The battleship *Oregon* was also in port. Altogether there were some twenty American warships in Chefoo, and the Russians, already edgy about the prospect of war with Japan, wondered why so many American ships were present.

To look into the matter, the Russians sent an agent to Chefoo— General Desino, who brought his wife and children and set up headquarters at a big resort hotel. He had one question for Admiral Evans: Why are you here? Evans answered: "For our health." He could not help it if the Russian general did not believe him.

But the Americans had chosen Chefoo as the summer port for precisely that reason. Why be in Hong Kong or Manila or even Amoy in the worst of the fly season, when the streets were lined with the bodies of victims of the cruel Oriental diseases? Not when they could be on the cool, sunswept coast of the Shantung Peninsula with the ocean breezes caressing them.

The wives of the officers of the fleet usually came to Chefoo for the summer and lived in the hotels or took houses. One Secretary of the Navy had gone so far as to prohibit wives from doing such things—but wives, being citizens and not subject to naval discipline, paid the Secretary no attention, and the admirals on the Asiatic Station were as eager to see their families as anyone. So Chefoo had a summer civilian colony that quite belied its military status.

In September the idyll was ended by a typhoon. The tail of the storm struck Chefoo. The wind hurled boats ashore, small streams became raging torrents, and the surf pounded the beach. Some of the smaller American ships lost their anchors, but all rode out the gale in the harbor, and not an American life was lost.

Not so with the Chinese. Following a cloudburst on the mountains behind the city, houses, trees, animals, and even people were washed down from the mountains to the beach and into the surf. From the windows of a hotel overlooking the beach, Admiral Evans stood and watched for some time, unable to do a thing to stop the destruction or to help these people who were so close at hand, yet whose lives were lived on a plane that barely intersected the lives of the foreigners.

When the storm ended, Evans and his family looked out on a scene of destruction. On the beach in front were several timber-laden junks, which had grounded and were going to pieces while the crews struggled to save what they could. The whole of the surface was dotted with bodies of animals and people—some washed out of vessels, most washed down from the mountains into the sea.

In all, some 2,500 Chinese lives were lost in the dreadful storm, and there was absolutely nothing the foreigners could do to help.

One reason for the gulf between the foreigners and the Chinese was the failure of the Westerners to learn about the real China in which they lived. Certainly the fleet and the fine hotels and the foreign quarter were a reality, but they were a reality far removed from China and Chinese ways. How far apart the two groups were was demonstrated when, one day not long after the storm, a large packing case was delivered to the *Kentucky* for the admiral. It was a gift from the dowager empress, whom he had visited at the Summer Palace outside Peking not long before. The box contained a large number of jars of Chinese delicacies. There was chicken in wine, preserved pork, and "thousand-year-old" eggs—the best that China had to offer. But nearly all these rarities went to waste because the Americans did not know how to prepare them for the admiral's table.

If Evans and his men were fearless and forthright in carrying out their duties, they were hardly any more responsive to the Chinese than most nineteenth-century Europeans. The Westerners knew that China was weak, backward in the modern scientific sense, and feudalistic. They insisted that their nationals who had invaded China be treated with the same respect they would receive in their own lands.

Thus when in August 1903 Admiral Evans learned of troubles threatening American merchants and missionaries in the Poyang Lake district, on the Kan River, he sent the gunboat *Villalobos* up the Yangtze to investigate. This action outraged Chinese officials because it caused a loss of face by the *tao-tai*, or governor, of the province. But Evans took the position that the gunboat had been sent properly and had shown the flag and frightened the warlords and their bandit friends, and that he would do it again. In Peking American Minister Edwin Conger tended to side with the Chinese in their contention that there had been an invasion of Chinese sovereignty. But Minister Conger had his wrist slapped when Secretary of State Hay agreed with Admiral Evans that the presence of Americans in the district was reason enough for sending a gunboat.

10

Yangtze Patrol

Once the Boxer Rebellion was over and the Filipino insurrection was more or less under control, the major task of the Asiatic Fleet was to emphasize the reality and seriousness of America's open door policy, which advocated equal trading opportunity in China for all nations and supported the principle of Chinese territorial integrity.

One opponent of that policy was tsarist Russia, which had not only built a naval base at Port Arthur on the Liaotung Peninsula but had also occupied Manchuria.

In that Chinese province there was only one international treaty port —Newchwang (Yingkow), on Liaotung Bay about 150 miles north of Port Arthur. There the United States maintained a consulate, along with other nations. And the Asiatic Fleet sent ships to show the flag and remind the Russians that they could not do as they wished in this northern country.

Commander E.B. Barry in the gunboat *Vicksburg* was sent to Newchwang in 1901, arriving just in time to be frozen in for the winter, in company with the British boat *Algerine*. It was a rough Manchurian winter in more ways than one. The Russians believed that the Americans and British were conspiring against them. They harried the Westerners. They invaded the American servicemen's club and charged the Americans with twice attacking Russian sentries in the street, although there was no proof to support the charges.

The Russians and the Americans argued at Newchwang while the State Department remained aloof and warned the navy to use extreme caution in pressing its case. Next summer at Chefoo Admiral Evans was faced with a big Russian fleet at Port Arthur across the Gulf of Chihli, but the American and British presence, plus the sharp diplomatic pressure employed by President Theodore Roosevelt, kept the Far Eastern situation from deteriorating completely.

Then, in the autumn of 1903, American attention was diverted from the Far East when Admiral Evans was suddenly ordered to take the Asiatic Fleet to Honolulu. The reason, which Evans learned much later, was the revolution in Panama. President Roosevelt foresaw that he might have to use this fleet in Latin America, and he was prepared to do so, although the need did not actually arise.

The result of the withdrawal of all the American ships from China, except for a handful of gunboats, was a survey by the Naval War College of the prospects of the Asiatic Fleet in time of war. The college found them dismal, and this finding would affect the course of American Far Eastern policy for the next four decades. In December 1903, the War College recommended that since the Asiatic Fleet was not defensible, its battleships should be withdrawn and added to the Atlantic Fleet. Oddly enough, the decision to withdraw these ships was made over the protestations of the Japanese, who favored the retention of American battleships in Asia as a great force for peace!

But while the power of the Asiatic Fleet was reduced in the first years of the twentieth century, the American responsibility in the Far East was not. In 1903 the Yangtze Patrol had begun, under the control of the station ship *Monadnock* in Shanghai. *Monadnock* had originally been a floating fortress in the Civil War years. She had been rebuilt in 1883 into a sturdy, if odd, steam fighting ship, with 10-inch guns, and she served for a long time on the Whangpoo. Under her wing in 1903 came the river gunboats *Elcano*, *Villalobos*, and *Pompey*. In the summer they alternated on the Chefoo Station.

Other ships of the fleet plied more distant waters. And in the winter of 1904 the Americans came uncomfortably close to being involved in the Russo-Japanese War that had erupted over Japanese designs on Manchuria. The gunboat *Vicksburg* was in Chemulpo, Korea, when a Japanese squadron attacked Russian ships just outside the harbor. "Fighting Bob" Evans wanted to do something about the Russian incursions into Chinese territory. But the Navy Department told him to go slow, stopped him from moving his troops about, and canceled the fleet summer exercise scheduled to be held at Chefoo.

Soon afterward Bob Evans was recalled. He was too much the fighting admiral for Washington in these days of delicate diplomacy. Evans was replaced by Admiral P.H. Cooper, and he very quickly was supplanted by Rear Admiral Yates Stirling, who was as vigorously aggressive as "Fighting Bob" Evans had ever been.

It was small wonder that under Stirling the American Yangtze Patrol came into its own. The captains of the river boats were nearly godlike in their powers on the stream, and sometimes off it. Stirling took the position that the absence of vital communications, as shown many times before, made it necessary to trust responsible officers to do their duty, and that the least an admiral or a Navy Department could do was to stand behind them.

During the Russo-Japanese War the American naval men were forced to watch some strange demonstrations. One day the Russian destroyer *Ryeshitelni* steamed into Chefoo Harbor and requested a mooring at this international port. American ships were there, as well as ships of several other countries. But no one did anything when two Japanese destroyers, over Russian and Chinese protests, towed the *Ryeshitelni* off as a prize of war.

But on one occasion Admiral Stirling was able to thwart the Japanese. After their great naval victory at the Battle of Tsushima Straits in 1904, the Japanese were anxious to mop up all the remnants of the Russian navy—either to take the ships for their own use or simply to deny access to the Oriental seas to the Russians. Among the Russian ships in the Tsushima debacle was the cruiser *Askold*. She had been hurt badly but had managed to limp into Shanghai, where she sought the protection of the international community and the neutrality of China.

Under international law, *Askold* was entitled to such repairs as she needed to be ready for sea, plus enough fuel to take her to the next closest neutral port. But the Japanese had no intention of letting her go, or giving her even another day of life and had come after her with three cruisers and several destroyers. They intended to capture their prey.

On the night that *Askold* arrived in port, the governor of Shanghai gave a banquet, and seated next to the aide of Admiral Stirling was the Japanese consul general of Shanghai. The consul, in his most pleasant, languid fashion, made it quite clear to the young aide that the Japanese were going to take *Askold*, and that it would be ever so wise if the Americans did not interfere. There were a number of American ships in the harbor and just outside, including battleships *Wisconsin*, now the fleet flagship, and *Oregon*. *Monadnock* was also there with her 10-inch guns, and five American destroyers were in the port, along with a collier and several other ships. So the American presence was about as strong at Shanghai that day as it was ever likely to be.

Now, the young aide of Admiral Stirling happened to be Lieutenant Yates Stirling, Jr., the son of the admiral, and he listened very carefully as the Japanese consul smiled and warned the Americans to stay away from any action. Immediately after the last cup of tea, young Stirling was off to the flagship to inform his father of the disturbing news. The admiral listened carefully.

He knew that because of Russo-British animosity the British would not be at all upset if every Russian ship in the world were sunk by the Japanese. He also knew that the *Askold* was lying next to the Standard Oil compound. Since Standard Oil was one of the big American interests in China, it was important that it be protected from any untoward events, so that night Admiral Stirling issued orders that sent sturdy old *Monadnock*, with her big guns, to stand off the Standard Oil docks and prevent any damage to the company's tanks or holdings. Just incidentally the *Monadnock* next morning was positioned off *Askold*'s drydock so that it was virtually impossible for anyone to take a potshot at *Askold* without endangering *Monadnock*. Or if they missed *Monadnock*, they would scarcely miss the collier and the three destroyers that had dropped their hooks right out in front of the drydock where the *Askold* was enjoying Chinese neutrality.

Outside, off Woosung, down the Whangpoo from Shanghai, the *Oregon* and the *Wisconsin* were on the alert. Who knew what kind of maneuvers might be needed before the day was out? The sea was full of surprises. The battleships were surrounded by American destroyers and other ships.

On the next day, around noon, a Japanese destroyer passed by, at flank speed, headed for the entrance to the Whangpoo.

After her! commanded Admiral Stirling, who was very much interested in the activity of this ship of the Rising Sun.

The order went to Lieutenant George Williams, commander of the American destroyer *Bainbridge*. Williams knew the game, and he went his commander one better. *Bainbridge* worked up speed in a few moments (her boilers were anything but cold) and just as the Japanese destroyer slowed to glide over the shallows of the Woosung Bar, *Bainbridge* came charging up, and passed her, sending an afterwake that very nearly turned the smaller Japanese ship onto her beam ends. Then *Bainbridge* hustled up the Whangpoo toward Shanghai.

The near accident had caused such consternation and chaos aboard the unsuspecting Japanese vessel that her captain was forced to anchor while he inspected for damage. He sent a boat to the *Wisconsin* to make a formal protest about the bad manners of Skipper Williams in the *Bainbridge*.

Yes, said Lieutenant Stirling, the diplomatic aide to the admiral, Mr.

Williams would be spoken to. It was most regrettable, but the lieutenant was in a hurry to see that the Standard Oil property was well protected.

The Japanese listened and went away. And *Askold* lived to fight another day. But the incident was not forgotten—not that Yates Stirling would have given a damn one way or the other.

The battleships *Wisconsin* and *Oregon* remained in Woosung during that summer of 1904, but they carefully avoided any action, in spite of various provocations. The battleships, like the whole American navy, were carrying out their function as instruments of American foreign policy. And although there were limits to the provocation they would endure, they were following Washington's orders: stay out of trouble.

For the next few years American policy was marked by indecision. The basic problem was that most American military men were Europe-minded. In addition there was still sharp controversy over where an American naval base in the Far East might be located—that problem had not been solved in half a dozen years. Generals and admirals were still debating Subic Bay as the proper place for the major American base.

New problems came quickly. The Russo-Japanese war, ending in a complete Russian defeat, brought about a revolution in ship design, and the American "battleships" were suddenly reduced to the relative size of cruisers. The dreadnought-type battleships, patterned on the new British *Dreadnought* and equipped with floating gun platforms, were the order of the day. They were almost twice as large as the old-type battleships and carried twice the fire power, the British *Dreadnought* boasted of ten 12-inch guns.

These considerations did not concern the United States at this time, however. Congress was interested in economy, not defense, and the American navy had in commission only ten battleships. But the situation improved in 1906, when the General Board of the Navy recommended the building of two battleships each year until the United States had a total of thirty battleships. A building program was then launched.

Meanwhile diplomatic friction developed between the United States and both China and Japan over U.S. immigration laws, which discriminated against Orientals, and over the treatment of Asians already in America. In 1905 the Chinese government took violent exception to the mistreatment of Chinese nationals who had settled in America during the gold rush days, and who were now being murdered, beaten, or, if they were lucky, just run out of town. In 1906 and 1907 there were sharp protests from Japan against limits placed on Japanese immigration into America and treatment of Japanese there. It all meant that American prestige was falling to a new low in the Far East from which it would not recover for many years.

In 1908 and 1909 American planners had two new factors to consider in the world naval situation: the Panama Canal was abuilding, and Germany displaced the United States as second to Britain among the naval powers. It was in those years, too, that certain naval thinkers began to draw up theoretical war games with Japan as the potential enemy in the Pacific.

Meanwhile, the Asiatic Fleet—the Cinderella of the navy—was subjected to new indignities. In April 1907 the fleet was disbanded and made a squadron of the U.S. Pacific Fleet. The Yangtze River gunboats were demoted to nothing more than a division of the Third Squadron.

But the Americans who lived along the Yangtze had come to depend on the boats for refuge, and this was never better shown than in 1908 when a political disruption of the Anking area, between Nanking and Hankow, sent missionaries and businessmen scurrying for the river and the protection of the foreign naval vessels that roamed it. The Americans had to seek the safety of the British cruiser *Flora*, for no American vessels were in the area.

Incidents like this finally impressed the brass in Washington. The river boats, which had mysteriously disappeared, were restored to the Yangtze. Better still, in 1910 the Asiatic Fleet was re-established as a force in its own right. And it was not long before the cruiser *New Orleans*, with her ten 5-inch guns, was anchored along the shore at Hankow, with gunboats *Villalobos*, *Samar*, and *Elcano*.

Life was pleasant for a sailor on the Yangtze except in the heat of summer when it was far, far better to be at Chefoo than anywhere on the steaming river. But there were always compensations. A case of Haig Scotch whiskey cost only ten dollars, and Gordon's finest gin was three dollars a case. Through the French commission agents at Shanghai one could secure the finest wines and champagnes for equally low prices. Of course, in July and August the temperature at Hankow hovered around 100°, but if you had to live in the heat, there was nothing like a punkah fan whirling overhead and a few gin slings to make it bearable.

Most of the men and officers of the patrols—including British, French and American—were a hard-drinking lot. The Hankow town club welcomed them all to its three billiard rooms and bowling alley, its restaurant, and its bar. One who hankered for knowledge could spend a few hours in a good solid library, surrounded by black leather chairs and tables spread with the most erudite, if not the most up-to-date issues, of the magazines of the Western world. But the bar was the place, and this was where Hankow's river men congregated night after night to spin their tales of the river.

From 6:45 in the evening one could find them drinking pink gins in the winter to keep warm and gin and lime in the summer to keep cool. Those who did not hold their liquor well or who were not adept at the skills of bridge and poker—and particularly bridge—did well to stay away from these high stake games.

The American sailors seemed to give more trouble along the river than any of the others. For one thing, they had more money than their British counterparts. For another, they were mostly "country boys," and they did not hold their liquor well because they were deprived of it on shipboard, particularly by various acts of their own government (that situation would end in 1914 with Secretary of the Navy Josephus Daniels ordering all liquor removed from American ships forever—except for medicinal purposes).

The Americans, not having a tot aboard ship each day to give them solace, developed a reputation from Shanghai to Chungking as hard-drinking hell-raisers when ashore. And the British shore patrols could count on a little extra work when American ships were in town. The Americans threw their money around, stealing the best girls with it, and the British tars took offense. There were fights and bloody heads, and many nights in the brig for both sides.

The year 1911 was tense in all of China. Revolution against the Manchus was afoot, and, as if knowing it, the Americans and others congregated in the big ports with their cruisers and destroyers and gunboats—and waited. In September that year, Rear Admiral J.B. Murdock, commander of the Asiatic Station, came to Shanghai to see how things were going. Aboard his flagship, the heavy cruiser *Saratoga* (no more battleships for the Americans in Asia), he came upriver to Nanking with *New Orleans* and *Helena*. At Nanking the admiral switched over to the shallower draft *New Orleans* and moved on to Hankow. The admiral went to the races, visited the governor, as was customary, and then went downriver. Two weeks after he left China, the revolution began, and neither the Yangtze nor the Asiatic Squadron was ever to be quite the same again.

II

The New China

Early in the autumn of 1911 the German armored cruiser *Gneisenau* was cruising on the Yangtze, showing His Imperial Majesty's eagle war flag and keeping order. This was never a very easy job. The Germans upriver were having some difficulty, and S.M.S. *Emden* under Fregattenkapitan Karl von Mueller had to put a half dozen shells into one of the Yangtze River fortresses to teach a certain warlord that he had best not bother German ships in the channel.

The Americans were around—*New Orleans* was on the river that season, patrolling and keeping in touch with the radio station at Shanghai. In October, as the clouds of revolution hovered over south China, the navies of the Western powers clustered together at Hankow. On October 9 the rebellion began there with a loud bang. Some conspirators of the Kuomintang, the revolutionary party, made a mistake and exploded a handful of homemade bombs in the Russian concession by accident. Nervous police descended on the area and called for army reinforcements—the revolution was on.

The foreign ships began the process of protecting their nationals. The American cruiser *Helena* sent out boats to pick up the missionaries and businessmen who lived at Wuchang, opposite Hankow on the south side of the Yangtze, and bring them to the concentration of Hankow, where the combined foreign military units could offer more protection.

The foreigners acted as a unit in this time of stress. The senior officer in the region was Vice-Admiral Kawashima of the Imperial Japanese Navy, and he took charge. Under his direction, *Helena* that same evening put ashore a landing force of three officers and fifty marines and sailors with two Colt machine guns. They joined a German contingent, and moved to the German concession near the race course, where they began the suppression of brigandage and looting. As the Chinese Imperial armies lost control of Hankow and the rebels won adherents, the poor rose up to take their revenge and better themselves in any way they might. They broke into shops and stole anything they could grab—somehow, somewhere, it would bring them a little more rice and fish. The foreign troops stood by to prevent the looting of the foreign concessions and shops—machine guns rattled all night long.

On October 13, the men of *Helena* patrolled the French concession. Marine Second Lieutenant A.B. Miller spent the next day guarding the American consulate, while Ensign A.D. Denny took some twenty sailors to protect the Russian municipal building. Later in the day the Americans guarding the Russian site were relieved by Italian marines. American marines and sailors also went out from *Villalobos* and *Elcano* to guard the Japanese concession.

All these foreigners were doing just as they said—guarding foreign property in the cities. The revolution was being fought all around them. The Chinese part of the city, along the Yangtze and the Han and at the confluence of the two rivers, was almost entirely destroyed by fires set by the rebels to distract the Imperial troops. Out in the countryside the Imperial troops lost heart as they learned that the people were going over to the rebels. They retreated, then began to melt away and doff their uniforms to join the insurgents. By the third week in October the Yangtze cities were falling like ninepins and so were other important places in China. Ichang, Kiukiang, and Changsha all succumbed. Two weeks later the Kuomintang force held that greatest of prizes, Shanghai.

The war continued for two more months, until the Imperial forces saw they could not win, and then the Imperial advisors brought about the abdication of the child emperor, Hsuan T'ung—China was a republic.

By this time the Hankow international force had been strengthened with the troops of many nations, and the Chinese were at work with foreign help in rebuilding their city around the foreign concessions. By spring 1912 it was business as usual along the Yangtze. Shanghai hardly noticed the difference—that is, the International Settlement and other foreign concessions of Shanghai. For then, as later, the Westerners had virtually no understanding of, or interest in, Chinese affairs.

The race course in Shanghai hardly ceased a beat during the whole rebellion. Snipe hunters were out constantly. There existed in Shanghai a typically English organization, the Shanghai Otterhounds, consisting of a group of businessmen and officers whose great interest was the chase of otters and lesser beasts. They made thirty-six hunting excursions with horses and hounds during this revolutionary year, chasing otter, gray fox, badger, ring-tailed civet and even rabbits if nothing else showed. The Chinese thought the foreign devils were crazy, and on one occasion, when the excited hunters in their red coats had the scent of an otter and were after him hot and heavy, the villagers took the side of the beast, crowded around the hunters at every turn, and managed to help the otter escape his pursuers. That was the kind of frustration an otter hunter had to put up with in the Shanghai area. The Chinese just had no sense of the game.

Hardly had the revolution ended when the Navy Department in Washington discovered there was a revolution in China, and in November sent orders that five heavy cruisers were to prepare to go to the Far East. But then the end of the carnage was discovered, and the plans shelved.

By the summer of 1914 China was beginning to quiet down amid the rebuilding of the Yangtze cities, even as Europe heated up after the murder of the Archduke Franz Ferdinand of the Austro-Hungarian Empire. The armored cruiser *Saratoga* came to Hankow that summer because Rear Admiral Walter Cowles, commander of the Asiatic Fleet, had never been there before. The gunboats were spread around and went to work to protect the American interests along the river from the new breed of revolutionary functionaries, whose intentions were not yet known.

That summer, the gunboat *Elcano* went downriver from Hankow. *Samar* was also downstream in Kiukiang, while the remaining boats visited other ports on the lower river. But most of the Yangtze Patrol craft drew too much water to go upstream, until the American navy assigned two shallow-draft gunboats to the Far East—*Palos* and *Monocacy* (successor to the old *Monocacy*, which had finally withered away). These boats were brought to China in pieces, assembled and launched at Shanghai, and sent upriver in the summer of 1914.

In that fateful summer of 1914 the foreigners in China were living almost as usual, while war clouds gathered in Europe. True, the Germans were edging their way downstream to Shanghai, and German businessmen and sailors alike made plans to go to Tsingtao, in the Kiaochow colony on the Shantung Peninsula. But for the English, Americans, French, and Italians it was tennis as usual at the club in the steaming Yangtze summer heat, or a round of golf just after dawn, when the river's mist still hung low over the valley.

The foreigners lived no more with the Chinese than before, when the ancients of the Manchu empire discouraged mingling of the chosen people with the red-necked Caucasians. Whereas half a century earlier the contempt had been on the side of the mandarins for the foreigners, now it was the foreigners' contempt for Chinese ways that kept them apart. At the clubs and in the foreign concessions Europeans were warned not to use the Chinese waiting rooms, unless they liked bugs, and not to mingle on the trains with the people who ate water chestnuts and peanuts and buns and spat their residue on the floor or out the open windows. The Western preoccupation with sanitation was driving the races as far apart as the emperors' edicts had ever done.

One day in July Lieutenant R.A. Dawes decided he would take *El-cano* over to Poyang Lake, south of the lower Yangtze, where Americans had encountered dislike and trouble a few years earlier when "Fighting Bob" Evans commanded the fleet in Asia. He ran into Nanking, and found a typical Chinese city, almost untouched by foreign hands. There was no club. Those missionaries who graced the place had long since moved up to higher ground at Kuling for the summer months to convert sensible Chinese who lived in the mountains, rather than foolish idol-worshipers who stayed in the cities during the summer.

No club, no foreign concession, no missionaries; nothing to do. The Chinese functionaries were not aroused by the visit of the gunboat—they were not even interested. A bored police sergeant made a duty call and that was all. The Americans were left to their own devices.

The captain went for a long walk in town, making sure, by the standards he had been taught, that he did not drink any water, or eat anything, or touch very much. The ship's doctor went fishing. There was absolutely no recreation for the crew which the officers would approve, and so sails and spars were broken out for the ship's boats, so they could go "yachting" on the lake.

Elcano stayed only a short time and then headed back for the excitement of Hankow, arriving just about the time war was declared in Europe. The Germans were hustling off downriver as best they could, after being refused transportation by the British river boats and the British-controlled railroads. British reservists were heading for Hong Kong, where the battleship *Triumph* was laid up out of commission and trying to raise a crew.

The homogeneity of the foreign contingent in China was sharply broken, and would never again be the same. Only a few days passed before American warships were the only ones patrolling the Yangtze, as the

Europeans headed home and the Japanese returned to Shanghai to assess their role in the coming hostilities.

This change caused problems for the Americans, who were relatively new on the river. Most of the American gunboat captains did not know the Yangtze very well. Because of Washington's parsimoniousness, they did not use Chinese pilots, and this penny-pinching got *Elcano* into difficulty one summer day. She ran hard aground in eleven feet of water. In the past it would have been simple enough to call upon a British boat or a German boat or a Frenchman or even a Japanese for a hand—but they were all gone. The S.S. *Kutwo*, a Chinese steamer, passed her by, for the Chinese tradition of the rivers and the sea did not include becoming involved in foreign seamen's difficulties. *Elcano* sat on the river in the mud.

Next day the Chinese steamer S.S. *Kiang Foo* came by. Her captain had been sufficiently exposed to Western ways to know that in America sailors helped one another. He offered a tow, and *Elcano* broke out a hawser. But when *Kiang Foo* moved ahead with a jerk the hawser broke —and all the old training came back to her captain: He had absolutely no business messing about with the foreign devils. He steamed off majestically in a cloud of black smoke, leaving *Elcano* sitting on her mudbank.

More time passed. Finally S.S. *Tuck Wo* approached, took pity on the American gunboat, and worked her off the bank.

Captain Dawes hurried straight downriver in the middle of the stream, where the water was deep, until he reached Shanghai and safety.

World War I changed China for the foreigners so that it would never again be the same in another respect—the atmosphere of many of the cities was drastically changed. Before the war the enlisted men had virtually nothing to do ashore, unless they wished to eat a Chinese meal, visit a Chinese bathhouse, go to a Chinese brothel, or smoke opium. Otherwise they could walk the streets, take a rickshaw ride, or stay aboard ship. There were no facilities except for "gentlemen"— which meant officers.

Shanghai, of course, was a different matter. It was big enough, and the International Settlement was profitable enough, to cater to all types. It was better there, although most of the places that appealed to the men were "dives." As for the officers, there was the Carleton, a restaurant that also appealed to the ladies (and to ladies of the evening); there was the Astor Hotel and the Palace Hotel, which was even then famous for its afternoon tea service. The Shanghai Club existed for the wealthy businessmen and the officers of upper rank. But even Shanghai was staid in 1914 compared to what it became later.

The big change, for all China, resulted with the arrival of the European refugees. At the end of World War I, millions of people were displaced by changes in national borders. A Czechoslovak legion had fought its way across all Russia, to leave the Far East at Vladivostok. Down from Siberia swept hundreds and thousands of stateless Russians, "Whites" who had defied the Soviets in their drive for power and could not expect to survive in communist-dominated Russia. Along came thousands of nonpolitical people, army and navy officers and their wives and children, Poles and Lithuanians and other nationalities, people with intriguing, confused backgrounds. China welcomed them. China, the great mother, had few of the niceties to which they were accustomed, but still she embraced these people when other lands were turning them away, and they came gratefully eager to establish themselves and eager to survive.

Immediately the cities of Harbin, Mukden, Port Arthur, and particularly Shanghai began to change. Shanghai became the Broadway of the East. Bright lights, soon enough to become neon, began to emerge along the streets of the city. Peking Road, Nanking Road, and Kiangsi Road all sprouted clubs and tearooms, bars, and restaurants. Hundreds of White Russian girls became available to servicemen as dancing partners—and there were dance halls and clubs to appeal to every rank. South of Soochow Creek the city burgeoned, and even seamy North Szechwan Road was tamed. In 1916 the American high command in China complained about the "low character" of the dives on that street, but ten years later their character was considerably higher.

As far as China proper was concerned, the years of war were relatively quiet. The Germans were gone for the most part. But other foreigners were more welcome than they had been for many years, particularly after China joined the Allied cause to strengthen her position at the peace table. What trouble there was occurred upcountry, when war lords clashed among themselves. A typical incident occurred in the fall of 1917 when the gunboat *Palos* was briefly involved in a struggle between troops of the governors of Kweichow and Szechwan provinces. She soon found her men under fire as they protected the American consulate in Chungking.

But it was a more serious matter for the *Monocacy* when she ran into a hail of fire on the upper Yangtze in the beginning of 1918. At the time she was proceeding upstream and was fifty miles above Chenglim

—at a point where the Yangtze gorge brings the steep sides of the river to within thirty yards of the channel in low water.

The war lords were fighting again for control of some bit of territory, or of a whole province—it was all the same. By this time the Navy Department was willing to pay for river pilots, so *Monocacy* was not in terrible danger of running aground inadvertently, but there was the danger of enemy action. The enemy, as far as the men of the patrol were concerned, was anybody who shot at them.

Monocacy was dressed in war gray rather than gunboat white, for orders had gone out to the American fleet as soon as the United States entered the war that all ships were to go gray for the duration. Her captain had learned of the presence of warring war lords on the river, and had taken precautions. Bags of coal had been heaped on the rails to provide bulwarks. But this was scant protection here, because the banks of the river rose up thirty feet above the deck of the gunboat. She was in grave danger while in this gorge and everyone aboard knew it.

To anyone who cared to observe, the gunboat was very obviously an American ship. At her stern flew the largest American flag she owned. And she was minding her business, going upriver with her men as far under cover as they could get.

Then a shot rang out, and then another. They were followed by a volley of hundreds of rounds from Chinese soldiers on the riverbank. A stream of bullets hit the ship and glanced off the bridge. A minute later *Monocacy* began returning fire as her men opened up with rifles from behind their barricades.

Five minutes later, there were only a few sporadic shots, but one of these hit Chief Yeoman Harold L. O'Brien, who was standing next to the captain on the gunboat's bridge, and knocked him off his feet.

Monocacy then opened up with her 6-pounders, and the Chinese quieted down. Soon she came upon the Japanese steamer *Tayuen*, which was heading downriver, also under fire. *Monocacy* moved to a point where the river gorge widened, turned around, and came back to follow *Tayuen* and protect her. That was the end of the incident, but Yeoman O'Brien died of his wounds. The Chinese apologized and paid an indemnity of $25,000 to O'Brien's widow. But it was the Americans' own fault, they said. The gunboat should have been painted the old buff and white.

By 1919 a semblance of the old had returned to China, along with the exciting movement of the White Russians who turned Shanghai into the most beckoning, sinful city in the world. The Asiatic Station was strong for a change, with four-star Admiral Albert Gleaves in charge. He had the battleship *South Dakota* and cruisers *Brooklyn*, *Albany*, and *New Orleans*, plus cruiser *Wilmington*, which was in charge of the gunboats. There were now six U.S. gunboats in central China, and two more down in Hong Kong and Canton, keeping an eye on the celebrated pirates of the south.

Washington was always a thorn in the side of the Yangtze Patrol. The denizens of the Potomac did not seem to understand the Oriental requirement of keeping "face" and of maintaining national prestige by a little show. But Admiral Gleaves knew. He asked the Navy Department to put a flag officer, with rank above captain, in charge of the Yangtze Patrol, as the British had done. Too expensive, said Washington. And that was that. So the Americans continued to sit at the bottom of the table.

But on the rivers, the American gunboats were always welcome when the war lords acted up.

In the summer of 1920 another adventure on the river indicated the kind of warfare in which the gunboats were likely to be involved in these ticklish days when the Chinese politicians settled their differences with peasant power. Once again the *Monocacy* was involved. She was lying off Wanhsien, downriver from Chungking, on July 8, when she received an appeal from the postmaster of the city. He was a foreigner. This was not as unusual as it sounds. In China foreigners were often chosen to fill administrative posts because foreigners could read many languages, and only now were the Chinese gradually accepting the accomplishments of the Western world that had been so greatly despised during Imperial rule.

The postmaster of Wanhsien was upset because he had a safe full of money and the local war lord's troops were eager to steal it. Captain C.D. Gilroy agreed to take charge of the money while the "crisis" continued, and so at noon that day an armed party from the ship picked up $5,600 in Chinese dollars for safekeeping.

How right the postmaster was.

Before nightfall the city was filled with sounds of gunfire as the Chinese bandits moved the center of their activity toward the post office, and before the night was out the *Monocacy*'s men were standing at action stations and wondering if they were going to have to repel boarders.

But that did not happen. The night quieted and the firing did not begin again until 7:30 in the morning. In fact, whenever firing began around Wanhsien it seemed to start at 7:30 in the morning. That, said the men of *Monocacy*, was when the Chinese generals got up.

It was three days, this time, before the area quieted down enough so that Captain Gilroy could deliver the cash back to the postmaster of Wanhsien. It was done. Then, five days later, the fighting started again. Shells and bullets began whizzing around the Standard Oil tanks on the bank of the river, and Captain Gilroy was upset. He did not want anyone wrecking those tanks.

He called for Ensign Stanley Haight, the executive officer of the gunboat, and gave him some instructions. Those Chinese bastards, he said, were to be told in no uncertain terms to stop shooting around the oil tanks.

Haight buckled on his web belt with the big, .45-caliber Colt automatic, filled a canteen with hot coffee, buckled it on the belt, and headed ashore in the ship's boat. Alongside padded a Chinese messboy, who would serve as an interpreter.

The American and his messboy marched up the hill, and there searched out the commander of the government artillery that was shooting at rebels so close to the Standard Oil tanks. The commander was a thirty-year-old officer named Li Tan Hsai.

Ensign Haight turned to his messboy interpreter.

"You tell him I am here to warn that if they destroy the oil tanks, *Monocacy* will have to shoot back."

The mess boy began . . .

"We are interested in stopping the bandit forces across the river. They are out to raid and sack Wanhsien," said the officer in perfect English.

They stood there. Ensign Haight looked through his binoculars and explained his complaint: The shells were dropping less than a quarter of a mile from the tanks.

Li had no glasses, so he borrowed Haight's. He looked. Then he suggested that Haight lay out a limiting arc for the fire of the guns, and Haight walked about fifty yards ahead of them and built a little cairn of stones, which was to be the left perimeter of the gun-training arc.

They then settled down, and Li gave them tea, while Haight offered the contents of his canteen.

At about this time along came a messenger puffing up the hill to report that the rebels had just crossed the river and were heading for the government artillery. Haight and his messboy hurried back down the hill. Just as they left, Li spoke:

"I would like to buy one of your 6-pounders and a thousand rounds of ammunition."

Haight waved and smiled and left. All the way down to the riverbank

he considered the offer, and how Uncle Sam would feel about an ensign
selling a Chinese officer one of *Monocacy*'s 6-pounders.

It was an interesting offer, of a kind the men of the Asiatic Fleet
were to have from time to time in the next few years. This was the new
China, but it was suspiciously like the old.

12

The Siege of Socony Hill

In the 1920s and 1930s the people of China warred endlessly among themselves. The chief conflict was between the Nationalist forces of General Chiang Kai-shek, the successor to Dr. Sun Yat-sen, and the Chinese Communists led by young Mao Tse-tung. That war subsided temporarily with the defeat of the Communists in the campaign that began in the summer of 1926 at Canton and moved up to Hankow. In 1934 the Communists began the long march through Kweichow and Szechwan provinces to the hills of Yenan in Shensi, and there they reorganized and regrouped.

Chiang's main problem then became the unification of the rest of the nation, which entailed wresting control of various provinces and regions away from the war lords. So the guns sounded constantly throughout China, and the foreign gunboats, cruisers, and destroyers were still deemed necessary to protect the privileges of the colonialists, the persons of the missionaries, and the business of Standard Oil and other traders.

The war lords of the river provinces were forever needing money. One way to secure ready cash was to collect "taxes" from ships and boats moving along the waterways. The foreigners called this taxation extortion and piracy, and so the guns sounded more often.

One day in the summer of 1920 a junior war lord set up shop at Tang Chia To, upriver on the Yangtze, some eight miles below Chungking. He tried to stop the U.S.S. *Alice Dollar* to collect a toll, and when the vessel refused to pay, the general's troops opened fire on the ship from the banks. No particular damage resulted, but passengers, and particularly foreign passengers, did not relish a peppering from the banks of the river as part of the tour up the Yangtze, so the next day *Monocacy* tagged along behind *Alice Dollar* as she steamed back downstream.

Four miles above Tang Chia To, the shooting started. The men of *Monocacy* threw half a dozen shells from the 6-pounders into the hills, and the noise subsided. But not for long. The general had apparently stationed his men in detachments, figuring that by the time the first group had finished with a ship and the second started, the captain would be willing to pay to stop the buzz of bullets. A few hundred yards downstream the shooting started up once more and continued until the vessels passed Tang Chia To. Then it stopped.

Monocacy escorted the steamer on her way downriver and made sure that the bandits did not pull out in launches from behind some promontory and try to capture her, and then headed back upstream. The captain pulled in on the edge of Tang Chia To and anchored, while the guns were ostentatiously manned, the .30-caliber machine guns were moved back and forth, sighting along the shore. Nothing happened. *Monocacy* then headed back upstream to her anchorage at Lung Men Hao lagoon in Chungking. She was unopposed. The men of *Monocacy* treated their two slightly wounded fellows and plugged up the bullet holes in the hull of the ship. It was all in a day's work.

At anchorage, the captain sent an emissary ashore to visit the American consul and make a protest to be transmitted to the local governor. It was. In time an apology would be received that would be meaningless, as everyone knew, because the central government forces were not really responsible—they simply did not have control of the river.

But as the Chinese fought among themselves along political lines, nationalism brought them a distinct distaste for the foreigners who had invaded their country and had more privileges than nearly any Chinese. The year 1925 was notable for violence along the rivers and waterways. There were riots in the mills at Tsingtao, which the Japanese had seized from the Germans in World War I and where Japanese influence remained strong, although the port was returned to China in 1922. There were also antiforeign riots in Shanghai. The Chinese began a boycott of British and Japanese goods, and this led to more violence.

At Wanhsien, on the upper Yangtze, where the U.S.S. *Monocacy* had been attacked in 1920, the British engaged in a bloody gunboat battle six years later with the local war lord's troops. It ended in heavy casualties on both sides, including the death of Commander F.C. Darley, the gallant chief of the British forces. Two British gunboats, the *Wanhsien* and the *Wantung*, were virtually destroyed in this first serious free-for-all between the Chinese and the foreigners.

The Wanhsien incident between the British and the Chinese was an indication of the national disorder of China in the 1920s. Nanking, for example, was held by the Marshal Sun Ch'uan-fang. He was being challenged in the late 1920s by Marshal Chang Chung-h'ang, who had come over from Shantung province to increase his holdings and stood at the gates of Nanking.

These two were more or less reluctant allies against Chiang Kai-shek, who was trying hard to unify China under the revolutionary banner of the Kuomintang, or People's Party. By March 1927, after much maneuvering, Chiang Kai-shek was marching on Nanking, and foreign consuls were calling for the warships of their nations to come and protect their nationals and their business interests. So up the Yangtze to Nanking came the American destroyer *Noa*, commanded by Lieutenant Commander Roy C. Smith, Jr.

On the afternoon of Monday, March 21, Ensign Woodward Phelps landed from the *Noa* and took a party of ten men to the American consulate in answer to appeals for personal protection. They carried no arms except a half dozen .45s smuggled under their coats—because the Chinese troops swarming through the city took exception to foreigners bearing arms, and besides that there was a small arsenal of Springfield rifles in the consulate which the navy men could use if need be.

The sailors began evacuating Americans, sure that the city of Nanking was going to be the site of a major confrontation between the war lords and Chiang. The U.S. destroyer *Preston* arrived in Nanking next day, and the evacuation began. By noon on March 22, 102 Americans had boarded *Noa* and 73 were on *Preston*. Late that day the sounds of battle could be heard from the south, where the troops of the war lords were meeting Chiang's advancing Nationalists.

March 23 was the day of real action. The morning was quiet enough, and the destroyers sat in the river, waiting. Officers and small detachments went ashore to be sure no Americans had come in from up-country to seek sanctuary—they found none. But by midafternoon thousands of the war lords' troops, recognizable by the yellow arrow brassards they wore on their arms, began pouring through the city in a rout. Some seventy thousand retreating northern troops were ferried across the Yangtze that day to escape Chiang's men from the south, who were moving up to the river.

Then Chiang's men were upon the city. At the American consulate troops guarded the walls to keep invaders out. The first to arrive were the soldiers of the war lords, who wanted sanctuary and knew that if they could gain the sympathy of the Americans they might be saved.

But these were harsh days: A wounded officer who cried out for help at the gates was brought in, his wounds were dressed, and he was then thrust back outside, where he cried for readmission until he died. Others banged on the gates of the compound, but the sailors kept them out, afraid that if the advancing Chiang Kai-shek found any war lord troops inside, he would massacre the Americans too.

All night long the shooting continued, and from the consulate compound the Americans could see the lights of fires as the city was looted and partly burned.

Although the town was deserted—the foreigners and the Chinese businessmen had either left or were locked up in their walled compounds—the telephone services still worked (possibly more efficiently than in ordinary times) and the American consul was in touch with the outside world. Early in the morning came the word that the Japanese consulate had been overrun, the consul killed, and the consulate looted. Two hours later came news that the British consulate had been looted and several Britons killed or wounded.

Then a detachment of Chiang's soldiers arrived; they told Consul John K. Davis that his big American flag would not be necessary and that all those sailors with guns simply showed how little the Americans trusted the Chinese liberators.

The fact was that Chiang Kai-shek hated foreigners and had decided to make an example of them. The Japanese consul, it turned out, was shot at—not killed. But the president of Nanking University was threatened and its vice-president, J.E. Williams, murdered. A Chinese government soldier shot Anna Moffat, a Presbyterian missionary, in the stomach but she was rescued and recovered.

Learning of the violence, Consul Davis issued arms, and set out with his wife and his troops for a compound up in the hills where he felt they might better defend themselves. Several missionaries decided to join them on the dangerous trip across two and a half miles of hilly country. The Americans carried arms, and the missionaries, much to their disgust, were forced to lug along the parts of the party's machine gun, protesting all the way that this was not the way of God and guns would not save them. One missionary was given the task of carrying the American flag on a staff, for what good that might do. Although normally a protection, a foreign flag might now be an invitation to murder.

Almost immediately after leaving the consulate the Americans met a soldier who asked them where they were going, waved them on, and then began shooting at them. Like most Chinese soldiers he had never learned how to shoot. The party speeded up, still safe.

The missionaries, grumbling at every step, began abandoning the parts of the machine gun. A Chinese coolie employee of the consulate was carrying some baggage that belonged to the Davis family. He was shot and the baggage was lost.

They had gone over a mile and a half when a bullet hit Fireman Third Class Ray D. Plumley. At this the navy men stopped running and stood and fired at the Chinese, killing two of them and routing the rest. They reached the compound, where they found some thirty men and the owners, Mr. and Mrs. E.T. Hobart. (He was a Standard Oil man; she was Alice Tisdale Hobart, who later wrote *Oil for the Lamps of China*.)

Soon the compound was approached by Chinese Nationalist soldiers. At first the Americans tried to parley with them, but it became apparent that they were bent on murder and loot, and that they would not be stopped by their generals. So the arms were readied, the loss of the machine-gun parts was lamented, and the missionaries were subjected to many black looks.

The Chinese kept knocking at the gate. Hobart met them, gave them money, rings, watches, and everything the people inside had, trying to ward off the confrontation. But the Chinese were bent on "getting" the foreigners.

All this time the missionaries were praying, hiding, and imploring the Americans to offer no violence to the Chinese. One missionary hid in a bathtub and would not get out of it so that a signalman could climb through the window and use the roof as a vantage point. At least, the missionary would not shift until the sailors turned the shower on him. Then he got out and went elsewhere to hide from the bullets.

The Americans surveyed their position. They were atop a rise called Socony Hill, and this was an advantage. But the Chinese were around them and at the gates, and in a mood for murder, rape, and loot, inspired by the antiforeignism that played a large part in Chiang's appeal to his troops and the people.

Down below, on the Yangtze, the Americans could see the two destroyers, *Noa* and *Preston*. Moreover, they could signal them, because the sailors among them included Signalmen First Class John D. Wilson, Preston Taylor, and H.S. Warren. Aboard the *Noa* the signalman was Chief Quartermaster Charles W. Horn.

Consul Davis, oil man Hobart, and the other Americans who were not hiding or praying reached for the Springfield rifles and cursed the loss of the machine gun once again. The Springfields had been packed in an oil preservative for months to keep them from rusting, and since there was no turpentine or gasoline readily available, the Americans broke into Hobart's supply of Scotch whisky and used this to clean the guns.

Meanwhile Signalman Wilson, with his flags, pushed aside the shivering missionary as that worthy man climbed from his bathtub, and scrambled through the window onto the tiled roof of the house. Below, resting on the quiet water of the Yangtze, he saw *Noa*, and he began wigwagging to establish communication. Below, Quartermaster Horn took notice and replied.

At 1:00 P.M. on March 23 an escapee from a nearby compound arrived at Socony Hill to tell how other houses in the area had been attacked, broken into and looted without regard for the lives or safety of the foreigners. It was clear that the Americans were in immediate danger. They would have to save themselves with what help they could secure from the men of the ships in the river.

There were many ships on the Yangtze—British, American, and Japanese in particular. None of them had any instructions to enter this war; in fact their instructions were very sparse, and in these days of tension the firing of a gun by a gunboat was a matter for the most careful consideration. Chiang Kai-shek was in league with the Soviet Russians, or seemed to be. China, having been for so long in turmoil, had become a tinderbox, and the fuse was right here in Nanking. So the foreign navy men were well aware that by shooting carelessly they might start a real war.

Although the Japanese consulate was looted, the Japanese ships in the river did not open fire on Chiang's men. Nor did the British, nor the Americans—at least not yet. . . .

A day went by, and when the Chinese knocked at the compound gates they were greeted by a show of arms. For a time that kept them off. But only for a time. The night was filled with noises and threats. The next day was worse and more tense. Below in the city, the looting and burning continued. By March 23 the situation of the compound party was critical—unless they could escape or be rescued, eventually the Chinese would break in, and the Westerners need not expect to emerge alive.

The signal log of the men on Socony Hill and the ships on the river tells very succinctly what was happening up on the hill and down on the Yangtze.

24 March 02:00   *Noa* from Socony   We hear heavy rifle and machine gun fire in city but everything quiet here.

02:15 *Noa* from Socony   We do not know for sure just how
much of city is occupied by Cantonese Nationalists but
there seem to be large bodies of soldiers still entering the
city.

24 March 09:45 *Emerald* [British cruiser] from Socony   Party of
officers from British consulate have been cut off from consulate and taken refuge on Socony Hill.

So the Americans had reinforcements. It was a mixed group in the
compound. The American consul and his party were there, as were British officers and American sailors. Over fifty foreigners were together
within these walls—and the Chinese were shooting at them, in preparation for a real attack.

11:15 *Emerald* from Socony   British consulate has been evacuated. All consular officers are now on Socony Hill.

13:10 Socony from *Emerald* . . . preparing to fire with 6-inch
shrapnel in area beyond Socony Hill.

Meanwhile U.S. Consul Davis had sent a flag of truce to the troops
outside and demanded an interview with the senior Chinese officer in
the area. He proposed to warn the general, whoever he might be, of the
presence of American and British officials, and the grave consequences
to China and the revolution of any hostile actions against the Westerners. Hobart went outside to try to placate the troops. They held
cocked guns against his breast and told him he must let them in. Inside
the compound Mrs. Hobart heard the rapid flow of Chinese and was
frightened. She knew what would happen to her and Mrs. Davis if
these unleashed peasants ever gained entrance to the compound.

Captain Hugh T. England, commander of the British cruiser *Emerald*, was the senior allied officer present, and he was damned if he was
going to let the Chinese get away with capturing Socony Hill. He sent a
message:

13:37 Socony from *Emerald*   To American consul. I suggest
for your consideration that you should demand an interview
for me as senior naval officer present with Cantonese commander . . .

But it did no good—none of it. The fact was that the Nationalists
were out of control and freely looting Nanking. They could not admit

this to the foreigners, but the Chinese generals had no authority over their men, and would not have until the lust subsided.

So events proceeded of their own weight.

An hour passed after Captain England's message. He was champing at the bit to land a force—but he knew, too, how desperate and impossible it would be for the men to fight their way up the hill against thousands of Chinese troops and then fight down again. A few might make it, but not all—the Chinese would overwhelm them with sheer numbers.

On the river, the men of the foreign ships became more nervous. From shore, a Chinese sniper began to fire at *Preston*, causing some trouble aboard that destroyer. But a spotter from *Preston* caught the muzzle flash. *Preston* asked the senior ship, *Noa*, for permission to silence the sniper, and it was given. A volley of rifle fire rang out from the destroyer, and a Chinese sniper joined his ancestors.

By two o'clock in the afternoon, the situation at Socony Hill had become desperate. The Chinese parlayed constantly among themselves for an hour, and now they had apparently decided that they would break in the doors of the compound. They began to advance. The guns of the three warships were already trained on the compound area. Now the signalmen notified the ships:

14:52   Commence firing.

But one minute later there seemed to be one last hope of avoiding violence—and the compound countermanded the order. Then . . .

14:53   We are being attacked.   Open fire—
         SOS   SOS   SOS

The Chinese were at the gates, battering.

The men of the compound stood with their rifles, and fired when they had a target.

Aboard *Noa*, Captain Smith had no hesitation. He spoke to his gunnery officer, Lieutenant Benjamin F. Staud:

"We'll either get a court martial or a medal out of this. Let her go, Bennie!"

The guns began to speak, and shells crashed around the compound.

Immediately the Chinese stopped hammering at the door of the compound and ran for cover. Even in the interior, up in the hills, when the Chinese who were besieging the missions there heard the sound of those naval guns in barrage they stopped looting and ran.

On the compound building roof, the Americans and British sighted their rifles and began shooting the Chinese soldiers as they ran. But it was not over yet, not by far. The men and women in the compound had fought back; now they must expect to be treated as enemies if they were captured. It was imperative that they escape.

On the river, the British cruiser was firing salvoes with her 6-inch guns, each projecting a 100-pound shell, while *Noa* and *Preston* fired their 4-inch guns. The British destroyer *Wolsey* arrived on the scene, and her captain started spraying the riverbank with machine-gun fire. The Chinese troops who had massed there melted away.

The Americans and British in the Socony compound now had to plan their escape somehow. It was still impossible to send a landing party.

When the Chinese soldiers ducked for cover and left the walls and gates of the compound, the Westerners inside decided to act fast. They tied sheets into ropes, and went down to the base of the hill, the outer edge of the compound. The men clambered up the sixty-foot wall to the top and then lowered down a handful of the party, who then stood at the base of the wall, arms at the ready, while the women, children, and missionaries were let down. Then came the sailors, and, at the very last, the signalmen.

Before them lay a mile of open country and a canal that must be crossed by forty-eight men, two women and two children.

The naval bombardment was on in earnest now, and the shells were falling all around the compound, keeping the Chinese at bay.

One man aboard *Emerald* was killed by a sniper, and then Captain England set an example for the other ships, turning fire from his small guns and riflemen onto shore. The effect was devastating. The Chinese simply disappeared from the riverbank. Three Chinese gunboats that had been shelling the retreating war lord forces vanished upstream and were not seen again.

The action from the ships made it possible for the refugees to get down from Socony Hill, and soon they were aboard the warships, safe and sound.

Late that afternoon Rear Admiral Henry Hough, commander of the U.S. Yangtze Patrol, arrived from Hankow in his little gunboat flagship, the *Isabel*, and took over as senior officer present. He was very pleased with all that had been done—and well he might be, for had it not been for swift action by Captain England of the *Emerald* and Lieutenant

Commander Smith of the *Noa* all those Americans and Britons might very easily have been killed that afternoon.

Hough turned his attention to the ninety foreign missionaries still at their posts inland, and demanded that the senior Chinese general ashore come and see him. The senior general was Cheng Chien, commander of the Nationalist Sixth Army. He replied that he was too busy fighting a war to bother seeing an American admiral on the river.

All right, then, said the admiral, either send us our people or we shall shell your military headquarters until you do.

Two hours later all the foreigners from inland were either on the waterfront or safely aboard the vessels. Miraculously, one Chinese general had suddenly shown that he could, after all, control his troops.

13

The Wily Chinese

After the fall of Nanking the Nationalists began consolidating their gains. The American and British warships went on downriver with their refugees. They came under some fire from the banks, but by shooting back lustily the sailors managed to stop that annoyance. It was a time of change in Chinese-Western relations: the foreigners sent more gunboats into the rivers and took a tougher line about business concessions; the Chinese interim became more antiforeign.

The United States put six new gunboats on the Yangtze, all constructed in Shanghai. First was the *Guam*. She was christened with the water of the Whangpoo by the young daughter of the American construction engineer in Shanghai, because her father, who was of the old school, felt the ship should be christened by a virgin, and his daughter was the only one he knew in China.

The 150-foot *Guam* was the finest thing America had sent to these waters, carrying four line officers, a ship's doctor, and a crew of fifty. By this time the Americans had "gone Oriental." Chinese messboys did the dirty work in the galleys. Chinese "boatmen" did the dirty work on deck. *Guam* was also an engineering departure—she burned oil instead of coal, which did away with the Chinese black gang and Chinese coal haulers who had filled the old coal burners at every port. But at rest she still needed a sampan armada, crammed with men, women, and children ready to do the warrior's work and scrub down her gleaming white sides every day—in exchange for the ship's garbage.

Soon other new gunboats were commissioned: *Tutuila, Oahu, Panay, Luzon,* and *Mindanao.* Theirs would be the job of convoying American ships through war-lord country and protecting American citizens along the broad reaches of the river or elsewhere in China if they were so dispatched.

Down south, in pirate country, the Americans maintained another ragtag fleet of vessels. The gunboats *Wilmington* and *Helena* drew nine feet of water, so they could not go up the Pearl River farther than Canton. For inland use there was the *Panpanga*, a wheezy old rattletrap built in 1888. Eventually these ships were joined by *Guam*, which made it easier in the south but a bit less difficult on the Yangtze, where American interests were growing all during the late 1920s.

As times changed, Chiang Kai-shek continued to strengthen his consolidation of the new China. In 1929 he held most of northeast China quite firmly and so the U.S. Marines were withdrawn that year from Tientsin as they were no longer needed. This left five hundred marines on guard in Peking and twelve hundred in Shanghai, plus a battalion of the 15th U.S. Infantry at Tientsin.

There were still annoyances. The *Tutuila* had her troubles with stray bullets coming at her from the Yangtze shore just outside Ichang. Lieutenant Commander S.D. Truesdell got tired of being shot at every time he went up or down river, and complained to the Nationalist general at Ichang that this was hardly friendly.

The general laughed. His men were just big overgrown boys, he said, and they could not refrain from celebrating the coming of the beautiful white ship. It was just a game played by exuberant young men, and he hoped the captain would forgive it all.

Yes, said Truesdell, he understood completely. He had that same peculiar problem with the big overgrown boys of his 3-inch gun on the fantail. Every time they went by the general's headquarters they had a shell in the gun, pointed at the general's office. Of course, nothing was likely to happen—almost always the captain remembered to tell the boys they must not do anything rash. And if one of these days when he was off duty somewhere, or if he fell ill with fever and had to stay ashore, the general would understand, and would not blame the captain if the gun was fired.

The general understood.

This life on the river in the late 1920s still had its excitement and its dangers, even though General Chiang's soldiers were off potting at war lords in the interior and theoretically at least controlled the Yangtze Valley heartline into the western interior.

One day the American merchant vessel *I Ling* of the Cox Line swamped a sampan in its wake during a riot near Ichang. When all the excitement was ended, it was discovered that the sampan was carrying the payroll of the local war lord and that the money had gone to join the dragons of the river. The war lord adopted a peculiarly Chinese attitude—he arrested the captain of the *I Ling* and announced that the officer would remain in custody until his company made restitution for the lost sums.

The captain was D.B. Hawley, who happened to be a graduate of the U.S. Naval Academy, although, at present, he was not on active service. The old school tie was involved, and Captain Rush Fay of *Elcano* decided to get his compatriot out of this predicament if he could. Commandeering another Cox steamer, he put forty men of his crew aboard and steamed to the walled city of Kweichow, where Hawley was being held. There he insisted on seeing the Chinese general in person.

Before leaving for the interview, he decided to put on a bit of the "show" that was so important in China: Donning his best formal uniform, with all his medals—not just the ribbons—and donning his sword and .45 revolver off he went accompanied by a small guard.

Four hours later, back he came with Hawley, albeit a bedraggled and stinking Hawley, who had spent the last few days picking lice off his body in the confines of the general's commodious dungeon. When they returned to *Elcano* there were cheers all around, a Lysol bath for Hawley, and even drinks with their British gunboat compatriots.

Fay's confrontation with the general had worked: Helped along by that bit of a "show"—the glittering uniform, the medals, and the forty navy ratings standing by on the river.

The British on the river were a convivial lot, even more hard-drinking than the Americans because they had more time and occasion for it. After Secretary Daniels' edict of 1914 the Americans had no liquor aboard ship, but the British were awash with it. However, certain Anglo-American accommodations were then made that kept everyone on the quarterdeck relatively happy, and well-displayed how the men on the river maintained a true camaradarie.

On a given Sunday morning, it was customary for the British gunboat on station to call on its American counterpart at about nine o'clock in the morning in order to pick up a boarding officer who would be ferried to the British boat to receive or deliver "official dispatches." From time to time there were official messages from one consul to another, or from one naval type to another, concerning the routine business of the river. There was nothing unusual about such visitations.

An American boarding party, consisting of most of the junior officers of the ship, or perhaps all but the officer of the deck, would then take a boat and head over for the British vessel all dressed in Class A uniforms.

They would be received as deliverers, and immediately dispatches would be handed over.

Then it was time for a drink to celebrate traditional British hospitality. The British would have had a particularly liquid Saturday night anyhow aboard the ship or ashore. It was the tradition. But according to British sea practice, the wardroom bar did not open until 11:00 A.M. and by nine o'clock the sufferers were already thick of tongue, choking on their parched throats at table, and dying for an eye-opener. So the American dispatch gatherers served to relax the rules, and the bar was opened with great ceremony, which saved the day for all concerned.

The river men played hard, but they worked hard, too, risking their lives more than once during every tour of duty.

In 1930 the city of Changsha, capital of Hunan Province, south of the Yangtze, was attacked by a war lord—some said he was a Communist—and the missionaries had to be rescued and taken to a safe place. U.S.S. *Palos* was the American gunboat sent to fulfill the mission. She ended up with one man wounded and a hundred bullet holes in her hull, having fired sixty-seven rounds of 3-inch ammunition plus two thousand rounds of machine-gun and rifle bullets.

There was plenty of traffic on the river during these days. The Hankow port control office counted twelve thousand craft entering and clearing in 1930. That did not include thousands of Chinese sampans and junks that neither entered nor cleared officially. Some forty steamers and twenty-five motor vessels operated between Ichang and Chungking, far upriver, and that meant the foreign gunboats had to go too.

The next few years brought increasing difficulties for Nationalist China, largely instigated by the Japanese. In 1931 the Japanese invaded Manchuria, and early next year they temporarily seized Shanghai, occupying Hongkew, the former American settlement that had become a Japanese business and residential area. The attack on Shanghai led to fierce fighting with the 19th Route Army of General Tsai Ting-kai, a Chinese commander with little love for Chiang Kai-shek. By now Chiang's fortunes had ebbed until he really controlled only the lower Yangtze valley and central China. In Nanking his enemies had the government apparatus thoroughly disorganized. In Canton the war lords were breaking away from Chiang, elsewhere the Communists were arousing the people, and confusion reigned.

China's troubles, threatening the safety of foreign business, led to the expansion of the gunboat patrols on the Yangtze by all the powers that could manage to bring in more craft. From Central America came the American gunboat *Sacramento*, and for a time her captain was Lieutenant Commander Fritz Baltzley. His chore, like that of all the foreign captains on the river, was to protect his nation's interests, but at the same time not to allow himself to be bamboozled or victimized by wily Chinese merchants and officials, who liked nothing better than to use a foreigner for their purposes.

One day when upriver, *Sacramento* ran aground on a rock below Ichang. They got her off by backing fiercely, but the hole in her hull endangered the stability of the ship. Of course, being a gunboat on the Yangtze far upriver, *Sacramento* had no timber nor virtually anything else with which to repair the damage. They could plug the hole with mattresses, but then if they went forward, even at reduced speed, the pressure of the water would push the mattress right out and the hold would fill.

At the beginning of the incident, a hundred Chinese appeared out of nowhere and stood on the bank, laughing and in general enjoying the humor of the situation: The mighty foreigners reduced to nothing by the power of the river! Then someone went off and found the mayor of the little nearby town. He came, clucked and worried, smiled and frowned at the proper times, and promised Captain Baltzley that he, the mayor, would save the day. To this end he brought Chinese artisans with bamboo poles aplenty and cement and other materials. Baltzley protested that the bamboo poles and the gauzy cloth and the cement would never hold at the water line. The mayor smiled and went about his repair business.

By God, it held! Next morning Baltzley went below and tapped the repair job. It was firm and sturdy. Another day and it was firm enough for *Sacramento* to move back into the river and head downstream for Shanghai.

About two hundred miles downstream, *Sacramento* was accosted by a Chinese government customs boat. The captain and the customs officer came alongside and began shouting at Baltzley.

Had he picked up any Chinese cargo?

Of course not, said Baltzley. He was a gunboat captain, not a merchant skipper.

Had he been consorting with the Chinese?

What did they mean consorting? Baltzley said he had been upriver to Ichang on his government's business. He had entertained a few generals and some Chinese officials aboard, as he always had.

The customs men were skeptical. Could they come aboard? They had word that *Sacramento* was carrying a load of opium.

That was nonsense, said Commander Baltzley. *Sacramento* was carrying nothing and there was no way any Chinese could have smuggled a quantity of opium aboard. Baltzley was already late; he had been delayed two days and he had no time to play games. No, they could not come aboard.

The customs men were used to dealing with hard-headed gunboat captains who had been made intractable by the recurrent attacks of the war lords and by the exigencies offered by the stubborn Yangtze itself. They did not press their argument. They only asked that Baltzley not allow anyone to come aboard or leave the vessel except the fleet boarding officer until customs was able to inspect the boat down in Shanghai.

That seemed reasonable enough, and with an affable wave, Baltzley was off again, downriver.

In time he arrived in Shanghai and tied up at *Sacramento*'s buoy. The customs officers came aboard and searched the gunboat from stem to stern. They questioned everyone, and finally learned of the incident below Ichang. They tore into the bamboo poles that had repaired the hole in the hull and there found $500,000 worth of opium, neatly packed and cemented in place by the mayor and his friends.

The wily Chinese!

14

"Sewer of the Universe"

For a while in the 1930s things improved for the Chinese Nationalist government. By May 1932 the Japanese had been persuaded to withdraw from Shanghai. Two years later the Communists were driven out of their southern strongholds and forced to take the long march north to Shensi. At Nanking there seemed to be progress in the government, as more and more provinces were brought under control. Several of the powers had given up their extraterritorial rights.

The Chinese were almost ready to build a new railroad system along the Gulf of Chihli to compete with the Japanese-owned south Manchurian system. To help, they had invited the Dutch, who had their fingers deep in this potentially profitable pie. Only in Manchuria were the signs still dark and ominous, as the Japanese consolidated their gains, set up the puppet state of Manchukuo, and plotted the takeover of all China.

It was a time of little activity, and Shanghai was making the most of it. Never had the city been busier, more prosperous, wilder, more sinful, more the open city of the world. Missionaries called it the "sewer of the universe" but foreign sailors called it heaven.

The men of all the fleets spent most of their time ashore in Shanghai simply raising hell. One notable occasion occurred in 1932 when the U.S. submarine tender *Canopus* came up from Manila on the way to Chefoo for the summer. She stopped off in Shanghai, and the British sailors of the submarine tender *Medway* gave a party for her crew, just to prove that there was a true bond among men of the undersea service. The party was a howling success, and somebody had to explain to the Admiralty that considerable cost of replacement of damaged parts of *Medway* was a practical necessity.

The Americans responded with a party at the Hong Kong Hotel, because they could not serve liquor aboard the *Canopus*. This affair ended with the sailors playing football in the hall, rolling marble-topped tables down the hotel stairs, and dropping potted plants into the interior courtyard. Finally someone called the constabulary, and the big, turbanned Sikh policemen of Shanghai's International Settlement arrived to herd the worst offenders off to a quiet place for a few hours. The survivors then headed out to raise hell in the town of Shanghai for the rest of the night.

The enlisted men, on such an occasion as this, would make for the French Concession, the residence area of thousands of White Russians, most of whom seemed to have luscious daughters. The daughters, somewhat restricted in occupation in Shanghai proper, worked here as salesgirls, secretaries, manicurists, bar girls, waitresses, some as *grandes horizontales*, and some as simple ladies of the evening. The cabarets of the concession's "Blood Alley" were full of them.

The junior officers would make for the Palace or the Astor hotels or *Le Cercle Sportif Français*, Shanghai's greatest social club and athletic club. Here the ardent young men ogled the daughters (most of whom were duly virtuous) of the city's wealthy foreign families, or the beautiful, expensive White Russian girls (who were not). They drank martinis and ate beefsteak and *fruits de la mer* and other items from the marvelous *cuisine de France*.

The senior officers went to the Shanghai Club, where they drank pink gins and brandy and sank down in chairs most of the afternoon to discuss high finance, the peculations of the government agencies with whom the foreign businessmen dealt, and the dreadful lowering of international standards that was making all China a land of misery and cutting back on profits. They read the *Shanghai Evening Post*, the *Mercury*, the *China Mail*, and the *London Times*, which came out as fast as the old Peninsula and Oriental steamers could bring it. For news of what was going on in China they read the *China Weekly Review*, published by the American, J.B. Powell.

For the most part the enlisted men were busy with their girls and the bottle, but the younger officers and the ofttimes senior ones too went to the race course during the weekends for amusement, or played tennis at the *Cercle*.

Shanghai could be too hot for anything but swimming in the summer and too bitter and windy for anything at all in the winter.

If the Asiatic Fleet had a theme song in those days, it was an old chant that had been around for years. "Oh, we'll all go back to China in the springtime . . ." it began, and went on from there. There were many verses. It was sung by gunboat men in Manila and submariners at Amoy, and it referred to the happy habit of trying to give every serviceable ship at least a little time at the Chefoo station during the spring and summer months. For Chefoo was to America what Tsingtao had been to the Germans and Weihaiwei to the British—the jewel of the Orient. It was cool and clean and breezy during the months when the China Sea could be dreadful and all a man on the Yangtze could do was sweat and dream.

During the early 1930s, the question of how long it would all continue became problematical even in the optimistic eyes of the old China hands. The Japanese were changing everything. In Hangchow, the old American settlement now overwhelmingly Japanese, they had destroyed the places of amusement for their own reasons: a Japanese whorehouse for fleet or army was strictly a functional affair—nothing like a geisha house in old Japan, but a place where men went for one specific purpose, and which was to be accomplished as efficiently and speedily as possible.

By 1933 the older American gunboats were mostly gone from the China Station. It was just as well. One day the skipper of the *Palos* dropped anchor near the flagship in Shanghai Harbor and went to pay a call on the senior officer. He got on deck, and the admiral took a look at the old tub across the way and asked the young fellow if it was his ship.

Why, yes, said the skipper, with manly pride.

Well, said the admiral, the lieutenant had best get back aboard his ship quickly, because from where the admiral stood it appeared that she was sinking.

Sinking she was not, but decrepit she certainly seemed to be.

So *Monocacy* and *Palos* went to the graveyard of gunboats, and newer vessels undertook their duties. In *Palos'* case the end of the line was reached in 1936, when she started up the Yangtze on her last voyage. She reached Chungking by something of a miracle, those old engines wheezing and grinding all the way, and there, aged twenty-three, she was decommissioned, sold to the Ming Sen Industrial Company for $8,000, and turned into a hulk for the storage of oil.

That was Washington for you—no sentiment at all.

15

War Clouds

In 1937 the Japanese struck hammer blows in China that foretold of the great climacteric of World War II in the Pacific that would begin in December of 1941.

Four events stand out:

JULY 7. The Japanese invade China proper from Manchuria, following an incident at the Marco Polo Bridge. Within the month Peking, the Chinese capital, falls.

AUGUST 11. The Japanese, backed by a massive fleet, land in Shanghai. The Battle of Shanghai begins. The city falls on November 8.

DECEMBER 12. Japanese bombers sink the U.S. gunboat *Panay* and destroy three American tankers on the Yangtze, with American losses of two dead and seventy-four wounded.

DECEMBER 13. The Japanese capture Nanking, the new Chinese capital.

The Chinese then retreated to Hankow and later to Chungking. After the *Panay* incident, the Japanese asked the Americans to remove their naval craft from central China so that there could be no more problems of mistaken identity. Asking such a thing from Admiral Yarnell, commander of the Asiatic Fleet, was like asking an admiral to give up on the night before battle. The Japanese were answered accordingly.

Hankow became the new Chinese capital and to Hankow went the gunboats. The officers spent their time at the Hankow Race and Recreation Club, the men at Ma Jones' International Cabaret. The officers escorted and courted the daughters of the businessmen of the international set; the men enjoyed the favors of the White Russian hostesses.

But the idyll ended all too soon; Hankow was abandoned to the approaching Japanese on October 25, 1938, when the Nationalist government moved up to Chungking. Gunboat *Tutuila* followed to be the official representative of American might on the river, swinging at her mooring in Lung Men Hao lagoon on the south bank of the river, across from the city. She was soon immobile—these were days when the only fuel was coming in by airplane or by truck over the Burma Road, and diesel oil for gunboats was not a high-priority item. So *Tutuila* operated through a wood- and coal-burning tug stationed alongside, which ran her generators to keep the lights bright and the refrigerator cold.

Such overland communication with the world as was possible came through the potency of an armored truck called "Bessie," which made the tortuous trip between Chungking and Haiphong, the port of Hanoi in Indochina, far to the south. "Bessie" took half her carrying capacity for her own fuel but she kept the Americans supplied with cigarettes, whisky, and medical stores.

The fall of Nanking brought the control of most of central China under Japanese troops and the invaders' puppet governments. But back in Japanese-occupied Shanghai life soon settled down to normal. The dog races started up again, and the clubs served as much gin and whisky as a man could hold or want.

Then the foreigners began letting the Japanese push them around. A message from the Japanese command on December 21, 1937, requested foreign warships in Shanghai to clear with the Japanese before they moved. Admiral Yarnell told them to go to hell. But Admiral William A. Glassford, commander of the Yangtze Patrol, was less adamant. He took the view that the Japanese were in charge and had to be respected, despite the British argument that to give in was to lose face and bring open hostilities even closer.

Yarnell's tour ended in 1939 and was not extended, since Secretary of State Cordell Hull did not share Yarnell's view that the best way to deal with the Japanese was to show them a front of steel at all times. He was replaced, and to command the Asiatic Fleet came Admiral Thomas Hart, a peppery little man who had served long and honorably in the United States Navy in preparation for his new position.

Between Hart and Glassford there soon arose the old argument over how best to handle the Japanese. Hart wanted to get tough, but Glassford tended to share the views of the State Department, which sought to temporize. In the crucial period of 1940, as war spread over Europe and tensions rose in the Far East, Admiral Glassford and his views prevailed over Admiral Hart because of the greater needs of American military strength elsewhere.

Glassford wanted a unified command of all American elements in China, including ship and shore units, and he finally persuaded Hart to give it to him. The step was accomplished in October 1940, when Tommy Hart made a trip to Shanghai in cruiser *Houston*, the new flagship of the Asiatic Fleet, from Manila, where he had moved his headquarters. At that meeting, Glassford learned that Hart would not be coming north to Shanghai again—an indication that the clouds of war were very dark indeed.

The darkness was felt in Shanghai that winter of 1940-41, for the cotton mills were working at far less than capacity. The business of the international port was slowed because of the war in Europe and the uncertainty of affairs in the Orient. Shanghai was not the gay, giddy place it had been in the 1920s and 1930s. No matter what the Japanese did to persuade the city that life was going to be as before, few believed them.

A great influx of Jewish refugees from Nazi Europe had swelled Shanghai, bringing new problems of adjustment for the city. Given good times, the Jewish refugees found life very hard and even Shanghai not very pleasurable. Their suffering created an unhappy air that spread across the foreign community. Even the roulette wheel at Joe Farren's did not have the old appeal; nor did the glittering White Russian girls at the Park Hotel's sky terrace.

Early in 1941 Admiral Hart was making what preparations he could for the war he knew to be coming to the Far East. In Asia, there could be no doubt about Japanese intentions; only at home could Americans afford to wear blinkers. In Shanghai the growing arrogance of the Japanese told more swiftly than words what horrors they intended for the Caucasian foreigners and for the Asian peoples over whom they would assume absolute control.

Caucasians were still moving in and out of the jewel city of China, although not as frequently as before.

The summer of 1941 saw a number of young naval officers newly arrived in Shanghai as replacements for the gunboat patrol and for myriad other duties. One of their number was a reservist, Lieutenant Malcolm M. Champlin, who had been assigned to the fleet as legal officer and aide to the admiral in charge of Cavite Navy Yard, near Manila. Champlin had graduated from the naval academy, but had resigned his commission earlier to join the Federal Bureau of Investigation. His experience was typical of a navy man's life in the Far East in those last few months of peace. Going ashore, he made his duty call on Admiral

Glassford and got along so well with that crusty officer that—had Glassford had his way—he might have stayed right there in China. Then Champlin headed into town for a few days' rest and recreation.

He and his friends stopped off at the Pacific Hotel for a beer. Then they went to the Palace Hotel, where they encountered one of the most beautiful girls Champlin had ever seen—a bewitching Eurasian of the type for which the Orient was noted. Engaged to a young American naval officer, she was half French and half Chinese, with pale skin and upturned eyes, a lithe, long figure, and the style of a French lady of breeding. She was coquette, courtesan, financier, and politician all rolled into one—Champlin had never met anyone like her, and he was stunned.

They ate that night at Didi's, the whole gang of Americans, with or without their girlfriends. The food was Russian, from the first bite of *zakuska* to the last sip of special reserve vodka. They then left to go their separate ways.

Next day, Champlin and his friends, who were new to the Orient, went to Wing On's to pick up the pith helmets that were so much a part of the Asiatic Fleet scene, and that day they had their first taste of the real state of affairs. The old hands warned them solemnly that they must not on any account be lured or attracted by *anything* to cross the Hangchow Bridge. On the other side lay the old American settlement— now Japanese—and there had been many incidents—Japanese officers slapping Americans, or trying in other ways to start a quarrel from which an incident could be manufactured. Tension was everywhere in Shanghai.

Lieutenant Champlin then set out for Manila aboard a transport, along with other replacements for the fleet. In a few days they saw the steep hills of Luzon Island, the mountains rising into the fog back of Subic Bay as they approached. Along the coast they passed the little island containing Fort Wint, and then the old naval base at Olangapo.

The fleet in the Philippines was readying for war—no question about it. Outside the minefield guarding Manila Bay they stopped while a harbor patrol vessel came up and exchanged signals, then set out to lead them through. On the left they passed the peninsula of Bataan, a thickly wooded string of land. On the right they saw a rocky little island, Corregidor, and Champlin, who had heard of the impregnable fortifications there, looked in vain for any sign of them.

Soon they were in Manila Harbor, tying up to Pier No. 7, where the transport docked. Then buses came to pick up the recruits and take them to Cavite Navy Yard, miles away. Through the city they drove, along Dewey Boulevard, through the Pasay section, and past Nichols airfield, where they could see the Brewster Buffaloes lined up alongside a handful of more modern planes. Finally Cavite loomed ahead, with its adobe buildings and old world atmosphere.

The housing officer quickly sorted them out. Champlin and four others would share bachelor officers' quarters at Cavite. There was scarcely any other kind of quarters now, since the women and children of the fleet had been removed to the American mainland the year before. So Champlin went to his quarters at Sangley Point, a mile's drive from the yard through Cavite city. And as he went he looked vainly for antiaircraft guns or any other sign of defenses. For everyone about him was tense and ready, but the navy yard still seemed totally unprepared.

That day Lieutenant Champlin paid a duty call at the Commandancia, the graceful old building where the commander of the Cavite Navy Yard lived. The commander was Rear Admiral Francis Rockwell, who was officially commandant of the 16th Naval District, although he wore several other hats as well. Champlin would be his aide and legal officer —a letter had come from Glassford requesting Champlin's services in China but Rockwell had ignored it.

It was as well for Champlin, as it turned out, for the days of the Americans at Shanghai were very definitely numbered.

The same was true for all American navy men in China. For by the summer of 1941 all China had changed. Hankow, now long occupied by the Japanese, was a shadow of her former self; only a handful of consular officials and die-hard businessmen frequented the gloomy halls of the Race and Recreation Club, which had rung with laughter ten years earlier. The White Russian girls were gone from the cafés. Most of the bars and restaurants were closed, their proprietors gone to Shanghai or Habbin, or away from China altogether.

The U.S.S. *Wake* was the only gunboat on the river here, and the forces of other nations were equally notable by their absence.

Even Admiral Glassford was now preparing for war, knowing that it must come, and writing about his intentions in his reports to the fleet. It was hoped, of course, that the Americans and their vessels in China would be able to retreat to the Philippines to fight, but if not, the orders were to blow up the ships and burn them to the water line.

On November 7, 1941, President Roosevelt decided that the gunboats should be withdrawn from China, and also all the marines except a handful who guarded actual American installations. Signs of the coming conflict were everywhere. Someone, it was rumored, had seen Japanese occupation currency printed for the Philippines and other areas.

This could not be explained away to anyone with any sense. At Hankow the Americans began selling off supplies, trying to retreat in an orderly fashion. The Japanese insisted on escorting *Wake* downriver when she left to join *Luzon* and *Oahu* in Shanghai. On November 28 these ships were readied for war.

Next day Admiral Glassford made one quick call on the Municipal Council to announce that the American troops were leaving. He sat in his car and the Japanese admiral came out and stood on the sidewalk as they talked. If there were any doubt about the state of relations between America and Japan, at least there was none on the streets of Shanghai. Both men *knew*.

Glassford prepared to sail from Shanghai and sent a telling radiogram to Admiral Hart.

SHALL MAKE EFFORT TO RUN STRAIGHT MANILA INSIDE PESCADORES ARRIVING IF ALL GOES WELL ABOUT 4 OR 5 DECEMBER. SHOULD WAR CONDITIONS RENDER NECESSARY SHALL FOLLOW COAST AWAIT OPPORTUNITY FINAL LEG MANILAWARD. IF UNABLE MAKE MANILA PROPOSE MAKE FOR HONG KONG IN HOSTILE EMERGENCY.

There it was—all that anyone needed to know about the state of affairs in Asia. At home America was sleeping, and in Washington the diplomats were playing out a game that all of them realized must soon result in disaster.

But in the Asiatic Fleet they *knew* what was in the offing. There was no question at all. It was a matter of days, even hours.

Part Two

THE DEATH OF
THE ASIATIC FLEET

16

The Time Bomb Begins Ticking

In the 1920s and 1930s the basic official American naval thinking was encompassed in what high authorities called the ORANGE plan, a strategy for war against Japan. No one was in any doubt about the necessity for such a plan.

But from the viewpoint of the navy, the supporting elements for OR- ANGE had always been woefully inadequate. Congress was under the impression that America's military forces existed "for defense only" and that "defense" required half the force the admirals wanted; thus the "fleet train," or reserve, was nearly always eliminated from the Navy's budget. In a way, this Congressional blindness was the biggest single factor in the timing of the war that would begin on December 7, 1941. For some time the Japanese military and naval planners had known of the immense industrial strength of the United States, they also knew of the intense distaste Americans had for war, and of the concomitant cut- back in American military forces that had been undertaken throughout the 1920s and 1930s. Japan's generals and admirals knew their country could not win a sustained war with the West, but they counted on a lack of military spirit, bad planning, and an unwillingness to fight that would let them consolidate their first victories and secure the oil of the East Indies before the Westerners could manage a solid counterpunch. By then, entrenched behind a defense line running from Japan through the East Indies to the Burmese-Indian border, they hoped to cut the lines of communication of the Western powers with the East Asian world and with Australia, and thereby force them to sue for peace.

In 1940 and 1941, as world chiefs of state struggled with the prob- lems of war in Europe, the various Western commanders of Asiatic forces met often to try to sort out their own tactical problems, especially that of organizing a defense when—not if—the crisis came.

At Singapore, on April 21, 1941, Air Chief Marshal Sir Robert Brooke-Popham presided over a historic meeting of Western defense commanders. British, Dutch, New Zealand, Australian, and Indian officials attended, as did Captain William R. Purnell, chief of staff to Admiral Tommy Hart. For a week these leaders met and aired their various national views and were concerned with creating a mutual defense arrangement. But it was impossible. Conflicting national interests prevented effective agreement, and the result, called the ADB Plan (American, Dutch, British), amounted to virtually no plan at all. No one was pleased with the result.

For Americans—at least those who had an inkling of the growing tensions between Washington and Tokyo—the handwriting appeared on the wall in the summer of 1941, when President Roosevelt froze Japanese assets in the United States and banned the shipment of petroleum products to Japan. Oil was the key to Japan's military and economic power. Without it, Japanese armies could not move, armament factories would have to shut down, carriers could not sail, planes could not fly, cloth and steel could not be manufactured. In short, Japan could not survive as an industrial power.

As long as the Americans and others sent oil to Japan, the crisis could be avoided, but once the Roosevelt administration stopped the oil shipments, the time bomb began ticking. In Japan everything had to be back dated from the day when the oil shortage assumed critical proportions. If she did not secure or *seize* a supply, Japan would cease to be a power. For this good reason the Japanese cast their eyes south, to the oil-producing Dutch East Indies and Malaya.

The critical oil issue dominated negotiations carried out in Washington before Pearl Harbor by Admiral Kichisaburo Nomura and Secretary Hull. The most serious Japanese demand then was for a resumption of American shipments of oil; the Japanese Supreme War Council was counting every barrel every day.

Thus it was that as Admiral Glassford made ready to sail in his gunboats for the safety of Manila in late November 1941, Japanese fleets were also at sea, bound for the invasion of the East Indies and Malaya.

On November 27, Japanese fleets were sighted at a variety of locations in the Pacific. Admiral Harold R. Stark, the chief of naval operations, dispatched a war warning to Admiral Hart of the Asiatic Fleet. *It also went to Admiral H.F. Kimmel at Pearl Harbor.* The warning was specific about the Far East:

. . . the number and equipment of Japanese troops and the organization of naval task forces indicates an amphibious expedition against either the Philippines, Thai or Kra peninsula or possibly Borneo . . .

After that point, Japanese diplomacy was a sham. The Pearl Harbor timetable had to be observed, which meant that the diplomatic talks in Washington must be kept going until the Japanese fleet could move into striking range. Or, as Samuel Eliot Morison noted in *The Rising Sun in the Pacific*, the Americans could have bought peace for a little while, but only by resuming oil exports to Japan. That was the key. Without such a step, the die was cast.

Admiral Glassford sailed from Shanghai with the gunboats *Luzon* (his flagship) and *Oahu* at twenty-seven minutes after midnight on November 29, after seeing the last of the Fourth Marines off on the U.S.S. *President Harrison* the day before. The sailing was hurried; a seaman, a cook, and four mess attendants were left behind, without prejudice as they got under way—the ships could not wait. The situation was growing grimmer by the moment.

The pair of gunboats, bright in their white and buff paint, cleared Fairway Buoy at seven o'clock the next morning, making 10.5 knots, and headed for the Saddle Islands, beyond the Yangtze estuary. From there they would turn down the Chinese coast. Built solely for river work, they were getting their first taste of open sea, and the hands hoped for a smooth trip. They steamed along without event until just before dark. Then, in defiance of all naval politesse, a Japanese guardship approached within five hundred yards, saw they were Americans, then moved away just as rudely.

Next morning the gunboats changed course to meet the minesweeper *Finch* and salvage vessel *Pigeon*, with which they were to rendezvous and steam in consort to Manila. On December 1, as they approached the Pescadores, off the west coast of Formosa, they sighted Japanese destroyers. The gunboats were trailed by the Japanese from this point for the rest of the day, until midnight. And all day long the Japanese kept harrying them by signal, demanding to know, over and over again, who they were, what they wanted, and why they were invading Japanese Formosan waters without permission.

Of course, the Japanese would have fired on them had they dared— Admiral Glassford was certain of that. The harassment and the trailing indicated the tension; the fact that they hadn't attacked indicated that the Japanese were waiting for something. Glassford had no way of knowing that the "something" was the positioning of carrier forces off Pearl Harbor, or that they had set sail two days before he did.

Tuesday, December 2, was a miserable day—the worst of the voyage. The Japanese no longer threatened, the American vessels were now beyond the island kingdom's influence, but nature threatened more. The wind came up, a monsoon struck them, and they steamed through heavy seas and gale winds all day. Night was worst of all, with the little gunboats pitching and tossing. Admiral Glassford was not at all certain they were going to stay afloat until morning.

But dawn of December 3 brought a clear sky and less turbulent seas, and as they moved down off the west coast of Luzon, the sun came up and the sea became increasingly calm. Some fear was engendered in the morning when they saw shapes in the sky, but it was a flight of American B-17s that flew low and saluted them, making the seamen comfortable with their presence. Later in the day submarine S-36 passed on its way to station, and they exchanged radio gossip for a bit. They were now coming very close to their objective, Manila Bay and the Cavite Navy Yard. That evening Admiral Glassford was relaxed enough to eat dinner in the wardroom with his officers and enjoy it.

17

"Air Raid on Pearl Harbor"

At the beginning of December 1941, most of the Asiatic Fleet was in the Philippines, although scattered about the islands. Admiral Thomas C. Hart, the commander in chief, was in Manila, as was his chief of staff, Rear Admiral Purnell, who had been promoted to flag rank since the ABD defense meeting in Singapore.

As war clouds darkened, Tommy Hart knew what he was up against, and he knew what he would have to do. A wiry little man, sharp of temper and tremendously demanding of his subordinates, he had been superintendent of the naval academy at Annapolis—a fire-eating super—and occasionally some younger officers remarked gloomily that the old man still thought he was on the banks of the Severn.

He was particularly unpopular because of his decision to shift the headquarters of the Asiatic Fleet after he came to take command in 1939. The old headquarters had been Shanghai, but Hart, who read clearly the bellicose message of the *Panay* incident, knew very well that at the moment of war the Japanese could in a matter of hours bottle him up and destroy or capture him right there on the Whangpoo.

So in the autumn of 1940 he had moved his flagship, the cruiser *Houston*, and most of his fleet to Manila Bay, and in the following year he established headquarters there. Deciding against tying up a cruiser by making it fleet headquarters, he set up his HQ in the Marsman Building in Manila.

He took these decisions against the outcries of the younger officers, their wives, amahs, cooks, chauffeurs, and houseboys. Worse, he had ordered all the wives, children, and other dependents to leave the China Station and go home, while the sailors were directed to abandon the fleshpots and return to the sea. There was never a less popular admiral in the history of the China Station.

But Tommy Hart now had the bulk of his fleet where he wanted it. Not that he had any illusions about the future of his command. No one in authority expected the small naval force in the Philippines to be able to stand the brunt of the invasion the Japanese were capable of staging. For years the basic army-navy plan for the defense of the Philippines had shown little change.

The plan called for the Philippine army and the U.S. garrison to fight a delaying action against the Japanese, and then retire to the Bataan Peninsula to hold out as long as possible. This action would prevent the Japanese from making use of Manila Bay, and that was the prime objective—to deprive the enemy of the base until the U.S. Pacific Fleet and the American army could swing into action. Under this plan the Asiatic Fleet's cruisers and destroyers would move to the safety of the Indian Ocean to await the arrival in the Philippines of the Pacific Fleet, while the submarines and motor torpedo (PT) boats—all expendable—would be used in the Philippines for local defense as long as they lasted.

In May 1941 a new war plan took shape that was very much like the old one. Under this plan, General MacArthur and his armies would still fight a delaying action and then retire to the Bataan Peninsula to hold out as long as possible. The larger ships of the Asiatic Fleet would move south to better defensive positions. And at Hart's discretion they could shift to a British or Dutch base where they would help the allied naval forces defend the Malay Barrier—the chain of large, strategic islands running from the Malay Peninsula through the Dutch East Indies to New Guinea.

That summer the planners in Washington suffered from severe myopia. They came to the mistaken belief that the Philippines could be defended with a relatively slight build-up of the army and air force. Hoping to grab a share of the reinforcements of his fleet, Hart asked Secretary of the Navy Frank Knox if he could manipulate the war plan so as to concentrate the Asiatic Fleet in Manila Bay for a combined defense. The message either got lost or Secretary Knox thought about it a lot, for it was weeks before Knox answered—with a flat refusal. By that time Admiral Hart was thinking along his own lines and had most of the submarines and auxiliary ships gathered at the Cavite naval base.

But Hart would now have to make do with what he had—and precious little that was. For the Asiatic Fleet, as the Japanese strategists knew very well, was a paper entity—a mere squadron that was not even to be reinforced.

Hart had received some welcome reinforcements from the China Station. Admiral Glassford had arrived on December 5 with gunboats *Luzon* and *Oahu*. Two more gunboats, *Ashville* and *Tulsa*, also made it from China. And gunboat *Mindanao*, one of the old tubs and a veteran of the Pearl River Patrol, was under orders to move from Hong Kong to Manila.

Hart now knew just about what resources he would have to oppose the Japanese naval juggernaut threatening the Philippines. As his flagship he had the 10,000-ton cruiser *Houston*, with a speed of 32.5 knots. Her armament consisted of nine 8-inch guns plus eight 5-inch antiaircraft guns and a flock of small pompoms for the same purpose. She was a fine flagship but she was still a heavy cruiser and nothing more. The old carrier *Langley* gave an impression of extra muscle, but with her ancient engines she could not keep up with the more modern ships and was a liability as far as fleet operations were concerned. So *Langley* spent most of her time either showing the flag to natives who did not know the difference between a carrier and a cruiser, or acting as a super seaplane tender near the fleet.

The other ships included the light cruisers *Marblehead* and *Boise*. The presence of the latter was largely a matter of luck, for she was really a part of the Pacific Fleet based at Pearl Harbor but happened to be on a cruise to the Philippines.

The rest of the fleet consisted of 12 destroyers, 29 submarines, 3 submarine tenders and 1 rescue vessel, 6 gunboats, a squadron of PT boats, 2 tankers, 6 minesweepers, and 2 yachts. For air operations there were 28 PBY patrol bombers, 10 miscellaneous seaplanes and amphibians, and 3 aircraft tenders, all converted from other types of vessels.

The war called for movement of the ships to the south, and as Hart began to read the signs that war was imminent, he started moving the ships. Some steamed to the Dutch part of Borneo. Thus cruiser *Marblehead* and four destroyers went to Tarakan on the colony's northeast coast, facing the Celebes Sea, while four destroyers and the tender *Black Hawk* moved to Balikapan on the island's southeast coast, facing Makassar Strait. *Houston* was sent to Iloilo on the coast of Panay in the mid-Philippines. There with a group of destroyers she would form Task Force 5, a new command designated for Rear Admiral Glassford.

On December 1 submarine squadrons 2 and 20 were reorganized into Submarines Asiatic Fleet, with Captain W.F. Doyle in command. Soon afterward S-36 was sent off to patrol Lingayén Gulf, and she was moving out when she met Admiral Glassford's little force on its way south from Shanghai. S-39 headed south to patrol San Bernardino Strait, between southern Luzon and Samar islands, and other submarines were also given specific reconnaissance tasks.

About this time, important guests showed up at Cavite, where they were entertained by Admiral Rockwell and other commanders. Clare Booth Luce was there, to ask questions and at the same time show herself to be very well informed. Frank Gervasi, correspondent from *Collier's* magazine, came up from Singapore with the definite opinion that, despite all the efforts of the British, that most highly touted naval base in Asia would collapse like a house of cards when attacked by the Japanese. At least that's what he told Lieutenant Champlin that December day.

Considering the difficulties under which Tommy Hart was laboring, by December 1 the naval defense of the Philippines was as clearly worked out as it could be. Manila Bay and Subic Bay were mined. The ships were being moved to positions of best defense and most effectiveness against the day when the attack would come.

And it was coming: Japanese Vice-Admiral N. Kondo's Second Fleet and Vice-Admiral I. Takahashi's Third Fleet were on the way.

On December 2, the *Houston*, outfitted for war and preceded by scout planes, arrived at Iloilo Harbor, 250 miles south of Manila. Here she awaited Admiral Glassford. Meanwhile, Captain Albert H. Rooks, fearing that a Japanese submarine might be outside just waiting for a signal to loose torpedos, established a nightly antisubmarine patrol. A 50-foot motor launch was unshipped from the *Houston*, and each night at dusk an officer and seven men stepped down into her with carbines and .45 automatics and circled the waters until midnight. Then that crew was relieved by another, which remained on station until dawn.

Carbines against the 5-inch gun or machine guns of a submarine were akin to using popguns on an elephant hunt—but at least they could make noise if need be.

The men of *Houston* were waiting. They were nervous—itchy—and on the morning of December 4 a number of them nearly had heart attacks when the officer of the deck tested the general alarm. The bell brought the whole crew to battle stations, stirred by visions of the Japanese fleet descending upon them.

The waiting was the hard part.

On December 5, Vice-Admiral Sir Tom Phillips of the Royal Navy flew in to Manila from Singapore to confer with Admiral Hart, General MacArthur, and other top aides. Sir Tom was brand new to his station in the big battleship *Prince of Wales*. The commanders talked hopefully about using Manila Bay as the base for future offensive operations against the Japanese, their potential mutual enemy. For the moment Admiral Phillips obtained Tommy Hart's promise to send four destroyers to join the British force that would operate out of Singapore. Hart sent off a message to Commander E.M. Crouch in Destroyer Division 57 to leave Balikpapan and move to Batavia, on the northwest coast of Java, ostensibly for shore leave but actually to be seconded to Admiral Phillips.

As they were meeting, word came that a Japanese convoy had been spotted at sea, heading for the Gulf of Siam. Admiral Phillips called an abrupt halt to the meetings—before he had had a chance to finish business or go sight-seeing—and headed back to Singapore posthaste. It was imperative that he find out whether this Japanese fleet was headed for Singora, a Thai port on the Malay Peninsula, or toward Bangkok.

The conference had not been particularly productive, for there were many suppositions and not very much information. Further, General MacArthur and Admiral Hart were each four-star men, and they did not get along particularly well—something of a social embarrassment. It was said in Manila that Hart and MacArthur would never share a table at the country club or at any hostess's home because of the protocol problem—who was to be in the seat of honor. And although they lived within a few yards of one another in the Manila Hotel, they had virtually no contact except through their aides.

But Hart was so impressed with Sir Tom that he decided, if a joint defense could be worked out, to favor Phillips as overall area commander. General MacArthur was also impressed with Sir Tom, although he firmly intended to be commander of any area he occupied.

MacArthur was also obsessed with the belief that when the Japanese struck they would have no air power to match the B-17s and other planes that the army had assembled in the Philippines. In his orotund style, he said as much to the conferees just as the meeting closed.

And as they left the room, Admiral Hart took Admiral Glassford by the arm and whispered. "Did *you* hear what he *said*?"

For naval intelligence assessments of Japanese air strength had made MacArthur's appraisal ridiculous.

Later in the day, looking out of his window in the Marsman Building, Tommy Hart could see much of what he had to work with here in Manila. *Langley*, the carrier-tender, was thirty years old. Most of the other miscellaneous ships were twenty years old. His destroyers, here and at Cavite, were twenty years old, and over on the east side of the wharf lay one of them, U.S.S. *Peary*, which had collided with destroyer *Pillsbury*. Both, consequently, were presently undergoing repair and were of fractional value to him. So were a pair of his submarines that were in for a refitting. Of all those in the fleet, the most modern ships at Tommy Hart's disposal were the two Yangtze gunboats *Luzon* and *Oahu*, but they were built for warfare against soldiers with rifles and machine guns, not against modern fighting ships and aircraft.

Meanwhile, Japanese ships and planes were moving ever closer. Vice-Admiral Kondo, with the main body of the Japanese attack force for the Philippines, was to strike at dawn on Monday, December 8 (Sunday, December 7, Honolulu time), but he was moving in and out of heavy weather and was ready for emergency changes in the plan. The important thing was to knock out the air force of which General MacArthur was so inordinately proud. The Japanese knew something about that air force, for on November 20 the foreign office had received reports from its agents in the Philippines indicating that there were nine hundred American fighting planes in the islands. So many? It was a surprise that upset the Japanese navy men considerably, so photo-reconnaissance planes were sent out from Formosa on November 24 and 25. The planes reported that the number of aircraft on the fields of the Philippines was more like three hundred (actually it was far less). The admirals breathed a sigh of relief and continued with their plans.

Even so, the Japanese naval air commanders on Formosa expected a very tough round of fighting before the American air forces were knocked out. They knew that the B-17s in Europe were doing an impressive job of bombardment, and that their German allies were much concerned about the strength of these planes—called Flying Fortresses because they had so many well-placed machine guns for protection.

The hours passed as the weekend came on. The gunboats *Tulsa* and *Ashville* patrolled off the Manila Harbor entrance, watching for Japanese submarines. They were ships in the Asiatic Fleet proper now, for the China Yangtze Patrol had been officially dissolved.

Manila at night was already blacked out, except for a handful of lights carelessly left on, and Filipino vigilantes patrolled the streets. By the weekend there was virtually not a merchantman in the harbor— only American vessels committed to the war. The others had headed south and east to escape the impending action.

On Saturday, December 6, a number of staff officers of the fleet set off for Bataan on a wild-boar hunt. Admiral Hart warned them not to overstay. "Be back before Sunday night," he said. "The bubble will burst any time after that."

Hart had no time for hunting: soon enough he would become the hunted, and whatever planning he could do in the next few hours was of paramount importance. He and his staff members on duty continued to work. But in midafternoon of Sunday, December 7, Hart finally slapped the papers down on his desk, got Admiral Purnell, and drove out to the Manila Golf Club at Caloocan for a bit of exercise to take his mind off his troubles and clear his head.

At the end of nine holes they quit, and went back to the office in the Marsman Building to finish up more paper work. They worked until after dark, and it was 9:30 that night before they both returned to the Manila Hotel, where the senior officers lived, and where MacArthur had his penthouse above Admiral Hart's apartment.

Hart had dinner and went to bed. He was awakened at three o'clock on the morning of Monday, December 8, by Lieutenant Colonel William T. Clement, the duty officer at the Marsman Building headquarters, who said he had an urgent message which he would be coming to deliver in a few minutes.

Colonel Clement then went downstairs and across the few hundred yards that separated the buildings. Up in the admiral's apartment, he delivered what he had: not an official message to the command, but an interception by a fleet radio operator of a message sent out from Pearl Harbor.

"Air raid on Pearl Harbor," it said. "This is no drill."

Tommy Hart had called the shot—the morning of December 8 was the time when it all came together. He sat there on the edge of his bed, rubbing the sleep out of his eyes, and drafted a dispatch to warn the fleet. Then he picked up the telephone, and called Chief of Staff Purnell. He dressed, ate a quick breakfast, and was at his desk by four o'clock in the morning. It was not yet dawn.

There had as yet been no official news or radio message, but Admiral Purnell drove to army headquarters in town, and delivered the word from Admiral Hart to General R.K. Sutherland, MacArthur's chief of staff.

The war was on.

18

A "Gift" of Turkeys from
the Japanese

In Hong Kong at the beginning of December everyone was talking about war, but no one really expected it—least of all the people who frequented the clubs and the restaurants of the English city. American businessman Norman Briggs moved about the city and heard people talking about the arrival of H.M. battleship *Prince of Wales* and the battle cruiser *Repulse*, big new ships that would give the Japanese something to think about. In addition, new detachments of Canadian troops had arrived in November to defend this corner of the empire. Hong Kong, everyone knew, was as impregnable as Singapore.

Whatever the security of Hong Kong, Lieutenant Commander Alan R. McCracken of the U.S. Asiatic Fleet was ready and waiting for orders to get the gunboat *Mindanao* to the Philippines.

On December 1 the *Mindanao* lay off Shameen Island, having recently completed a tour up the Pearl River. She had been harried in the last few days by Japanese vessels and planes. The Japanese pilots had taken great pleasure in zooming low over *Mindanao*, whose presence in the area was well known, as though she were a stranger that needed investigation. In another incident a Japanese minelayer came very close to the gunboat's stern. When the captain complained to the senior Japanese naval officer in the area, all he got was a short reply:

"Make big busy with fight."

On December 2 McCracken received orders to get *Mindanao* to Manila posthaste. He moved into Hong Kong Harbor and took his problems to a Chinese shipyard. Because *Mindanao* had only three feet of freeboard—the distance between her waterline and the main deck—

she was not fit for a rendezvous with a typhoon. McCracken needed her topsides boarded up to withstand a battering from the sea. He also needed life rafts. The shipyard supplied both needs overnight. The next question was one of companionship on the long voyage, and luckily the Luzon Stevedoring Company tugboat *Ranger* was in Hong Kong on an errand, so they decided to return together.

It took McCracken a bit of time to iron out the details of the voyage, and there was precious little time left. There was the problem of transporting the spare parts for his engines—some were assigned for shipment aboard *Ranger* and some were lashed to the stern of the gunboat to give her some extra weight and stability. He had eight hundred 3-inch shells and a million rounds of .30-calibre ammunition. These were split between *Ranger* and *Mindanao*. He had six months' supply of provisions. These were divided between the ships and the American officials ashore, the half for the landlubbers being entrusted to American Consul Southard.

On December 4 all was as ready as it would ever be. That night *Mindanao* pulled out and next morning was gone. *Ranger* was undergoing some repairs and would follow later. Everyone knew *Ranger* could easily overtake the gunboat, so Lieutenant Commander McCracken gave her captain his course and speed and set off.

Almost immediately McCracken ran into the heavy seas of the monsoon season. *Mindanao* was pitching and tossing not far outside Hong Kong Harbor when a Japanese cruiser came charging up, passed just under her stern, and disappeared off to the east at high speed, leaving the Americans wondering where in the devil she was headed.

Mindanao, a 580-ton riot gunboat, was not used to the open sea. She rolled and she bucked and she snorted her distaste for the whole procedure. The roll became so serious that McCracken changed course after a few hours to put the wind and sea onto the port bow. This course led them toward Japanese-held Formosa. The radiomen were instructed to reach *Ranger* and tell her of the course change but they never did get through to her, and soon *Mindanao* was on her own in typhoon waters.

After three days of this roughhouse, waiting for an actual typhoon that never quite materialized, there was no abatement of the foul weather. Still something had to be done, lest they run on to a rock off Formosa and be truly stuck, so McCracken changed course, putting the fierce north wind on his starboard bow, which had him heading back to China. The hapless gunboat was rolling to 49 degrees, which the men did not quite believe. The deckhouses began to work loose—in fact, all of *Mindanao* worked loose, and her motion became very strange. "She humped along like a camel," said McCracken.

Back in Hong Kong, businessman Briggs lunched at the American club as usual on Saturday, December 6. The big item of conversation that day was the sailing of *Mindanao* for Manila. It was true—Consul Southard confirmed it. But what does it mean?

Next day, Briggs got up as usual at eight o'clock and his boy served him breakfast half an hour later. The morning paper was filled with British flagwaving and warnings to Japan. He spent this Sunday playing Mozart on the piano, then walking his dog along Languard Road to the top of Victoria Peak and looking down on the harbor. He dined at 7:30 and then settled down to read. His housemate, another businessman, returned from a weekend of sailing with the information that the reserves had been called out. Neither man really believed it meant any more than that some local official "had the wind up."

The next morning, Monday, seemed to dawn as an ordinary day. Breakfast was on the table at 7:30, along with the morning paper. Briggs ate and read—and then the phone rang. It was his office, announcing that Pearl Harbor had been attacked. Their houseboy came in wearing a gas mask and tin hat, and announced that he had to get to his air raid warden's job. The two Americans then caught the 8:00 A.M. Peak Tram and started down to the city. On the way down they saw planes over Kai Tak airfield and antiaircraft guns firing up at them. Hong Kong was at war.

At about that time in Manila Tommy Hart, having just got the news of the Japanese attack on Pearl Harbor, was shaking the sleep out of his eyes. Aboard *Mindanao*, 337 miles off the northwest tip of Luzon, Lieutenant Commander McCracken heard the news by radio. McCracken issued orders quickly. Every man seized a handful of cleaning waste and they broke the black paint out of the lockers. Each man dipped his waste into the paint and then began scrubbing at the white-and-buff skin of the ship until she looked as though she had been through a disastrous fire. Whatever she then appeared to be, it was not a spic and span gunboat. That morning the awnings were pulled down and the paint and other flammables were jettisoned. The awning spreaders were cut off and the bases made into mounts for the twenty-six Browning and Lewis machine guns the boat carried. McCracken began destroying papers, as the regulations provided.

On the morning of December 9 they came across a 60-foot Japanese trawler, with a crew of ten fishermen aboard. They inspected the vessel and found nothing amiss, until one of the officers opened a locker—and discovered military uniforms for the crew. That was enough. They took the men off and made them prisoners of war, the first prisoners of the Asiatic Fleet. They took the trawler under tow, but were unable to maintain it in the rough seas and finally had to cut the trawler adrift, keeping the prisoners as their only booty.

That day many planes passed over them, mostly Japanese, but no one paid them much heed, except one PBY that identified itself and assured them that a nearby merchantman was an American.

The night was uneventful. Next morning they moored off the Cavite Navy Yard, which was ablaze from Japanese bombing. The end of a remarkable voyage.

After arriving in Manila from Shanghai aboard the *Luzon*, Admiral Glassford went immediately to the headquarters of the Asiatic Fleet to confer with Admiral Hart. The first thing Hart gave him was a folder of correspondence, and in reading it over, Glassford at once realized that he faced a serious problem. Washington had been asking Hart who should succeed him as commander of the fleet when he was to retire in 1942. Specifically, the personnel men had wanted to know if Glassford would be a good choice, since he was next senior officer in the fleet. Hart, the correspondence showed, did not think so. He believed Glassford was doing a good job in China, he said—a political job. But he did not feel that Glassford "knew the fleet."

This kind of recommendation was likely to wreck a career. Hart was even less complimentary on another matter: he did not want Glassford as commander of Task Force 5, the fleet's fighting unit. But here Hart had been overruled. As long as he was with the fleet, Glassford was entitled to the appointment under American naval tradition.

Glassford conferred with Hart for a few hours, and prepared to leave that same day to join Task Force 5 and his new flagship, cruiser *Houston*, at Iloilo. The parting of the two admirals was anything but happy. As Glassford put it, going off to fight his country's enemies: "Needless to say, I was happy to get away from pessimistic and uncongenial Manila and on my own again."

Even if he was going down to a task force of ships "hoary with age, tradition and pride," and strong in little else, even if he could see that his chances of success and even survival were limited, Glassford was glad to go.

He *was* a bit worried about the trip. For he and two aides were to be flown alone by a single PBY down to the rendezvous on Panay Island to join *Houston*. Since the Japanese controlled the air, Glassford had a right to be uneasy; under similar conditions, the Japanese were to lose half a dozen of their top officers a few months later. It was never good policy for a transport plane to have to fly in enemy air without escort.

Tommy Hart sent Glassford in a barge to the middle of the harbor, where he boarded the *Luzon* for a moment to say good-bye to his men. Then Glassford jumped back into the barge and hastened to the seaplane tender, where Captain Wagner, the commander of Patrol Wing 10, met him wearing a tin hat—one of the first Glassford had seen—an apt reminder that there was "a hell of a war" on. As they came up, Glassford jumped at the "damnest racket" he had heard in months—it sounded as though the whole Japanese air force was pounding down on them. But it was nothing more than Lieutenant Commander John Bulkeley and his force of PT boats revving up for a run into the sea.

Within an hour the PBY was moving, and Glassford was on his way, leaving behind a Manila that to him seemed small and already insignificant.

On the morning of December 7 in Shanghai, Lieutenant Commander Columbus D. Smith went aboard his ship, the gunboat *Wake*, which was being left in the sinful city to function as a radio communications vessel for the U.S. Consulate.

Smith was not regular navy, but an old China hand, a river pilot who had kept his commission—and was now to be a sacrificial lamb. He had a crew of eight radiomen to maintain the consulate's communications and six seamen. That was enough; Commander Smith knew that he was not going anywhere and neither was *Wake*; they were waiting for the Japanese. That day Smith was puzzling over an odd telephone call he had received the night before. A Japanese naval officer friend had called him to offer a pair of turkeys.

Where could they be delivered to him next morning at about eleven o'clock? asked the Japanese.

"Why, aboard *Wake*, as usual," said Lieutenant Commander Smith.

"So good," said the Japanese friend, and hung up.

At four o'clock on the morning of December 8, it all came to light. The telephone in Smith's apartment ashore woke him. It was his quartermaster, and he was very excited. Pearl Harbor had just been bombed, said the sailor. It was no joke.

Lieutenant Commander Smith dressed in seconds, and rushed to the waterfront in his uniform, ready to board his ship. For his instructions were to blow the bottom out of her, and the detonation charges had all been laid. All it would take was a few minutes and an order.

Smith had a terrible time getting through to the pier, for he was stopped half a dozen times in the darkness by Japanese patrols, soldiers carrying rifles with fixed bayonets, who would not let him pass. But eventually he reached the pier, where he was stopped again. He could not board, said the Japanese.

Smith stood on the shore then and learned that his vessel had been taken by the Japanese. They already had a new name for her. She was now the H.I.J.M.S. *Tatara*. There was nothing to be done. All he could hope was that his sailors aboard had managed to jump over the side and escape to shore before they were imprisoned by the Japanese.

As Smith stood there, in the waning darkness before dawn, he could see shooting not far away on the river. The Japanese were sinking the British gunboat *Peterel*, whose skipper, Lieutenant Polkinghorn, had been aboard that night and had refused to surrender his vessel. The Japanese had boarded, said it was their gunboat now, and Polkinghorn at gunpoint had ordered them off the ship. The Japanese departed, but soon the shore batteries opened up and the ship went down. Polkinghorn and half a dozen of his men, almost all wounded, managed to swim ashore, but the rest of his crew were lost.

Smith spent the next few hours destroying records and radio equipment ashore. He was then captured by the Japanese and imprisoned in the old municipal jail on Ward Road. (Later he escaped, along with a British commander and a U.S. marine, and they traveled seven hundred miles on foot to safe territory.)

With the loss of the *Wake*, the end of the U.S. gunboat saga on the Yangtze was at hand. Gunboat *Tutuila*, last of the fleet to be left upriver, did not have enough oil to make the run down the Yangtze, even if she could have beaten her way through the Japanese blockade. So she was turned over to the Chinese navy at Chungking. There was now little naval force anywhere on the great old river that could offer any resistance to the Japanese.

The Sino-Japanese war had become largely a land war, and in many ways a stalemate. But domination of China was no longer the only aim of the Imperial Japanese forces. Their movement was now south and east across blue water to control Southeast Asia and make their Greater East Asia Co-Prosperity Sphere into a huge Japanese economic empire that would eclipse the British imperium of the nineteenth century.

19

Attack on the Philippines

The first important Japanese landing was directed against the British in Malaya. Those ships that had sent Admiral Sir Tom Phillips hightailing it back to Singapore had feinted toward Bangkok on December 6, then headed for Singora, Thailand, on the Malay Peninsula. They anchored just before midnight, and began landing troops before dawn on D-Day —December 8. There was virtually no opposition—they were already halfway down the peninsula to Singapore.

After sending news of the Japanese landings to Tommy Hart, Sir Tom Phillips set off on the evening of December 8 in his battleship *Prince of Wales*, with the battle cruiser *Repulse* and four British destroyers, to challenge the Japanese invaders. One destroyer suffered engine trouble and had to turn back. But the rest moved on.

Next morning Sir Tom learned that it was highly doubtful he would receive any air support in an engagement with the Japanese. He was well aware of those Japanese airfields scattered about the Asiatic mainland. That day, December 9, the British force was shadowed by three Japanese planes, and Sir Tom knew that on the morrow he might well have to face air attack. Still he searched for the Japanese ships but did not find them.

On December 9 Sir Tom headed back for Singapore, but he was diverted by a report of an enemy landing at Kuantan, on the east coast of British Malaga. It was a false report, but it kept him out at sea when he should have been behind the aerial defenses of Singapore. Just before noon the next day, Japanese bombers from Indochina found him. Within an hour they had sunk both big ships, the pride of the British in the Far East, settling once and for all the old argument over whether airplanes *could* sink battleships.

Too late to be of any real assistance, an American unit reached the scene. In compliance with his promise to Phillips at the allied conference at Manila on December 5, Admiral Hart had ordered Destroyer Division 57 to come up from East Borneo to Singapore. The division arrived on the day the Japanese attacked the British ships, and on hearing the bad news the flotilla rushed out to help find survivors. But British destroyers had already rescued two thousand of the ill-fated battleships' crewmen. Sir Tom Phillips and hundreds of others were lost. So the American ships turned about and came back. Two days later Admiral Hart had them heading for Surabaya.

While the Japanese were moving rapidly in Malaya, bad weather stalled them for a few hours in their assault on the Philippines. Vice-Admiral Kondo, in the early morning of December 8, was ready to launch his first air strike against the Philippines. The emphasis was to be on the airfields, to knock out those threatening American bombers before they could strike and possibly delay the carefully constructed Imperial Japanese timetable.

The principal weapon was to be the Eleventh Air Fleet, based on Formosa, about five hours' flying time from Manila. Four hundred planes were available there for this attack. The plan called for an attack on the Philippine airfields at daybreak, but on the night of December 7 the weather in Formosa was stormy and the low ceiling delayed the operation.

The fighting opened that day with an attack by twenty-two planes on the seaplane tender *William B. Preston* in Davao Gulf in the northern Philippines. These planes came from the carrier *Ryujo*, operating east of Davao. Several of the tender's seaplanes were destroyed, and one Japanese plane was shot down; *William B. Preston* then got under way to escape further attack.

Word of this action reached Manila soon enough, where General MacArthur and Admiral Hart were waiting for the Japanese plans to further unveil.

When and where would the Japanese attempt their landings?

As the weather on Formosa cleared at dawn, the Japanese heavy bombers set out, and at 9:30 that morning Admiral Hart received word that they were striking military targets at Baguio in northern Luzon. A little while later another report indicated that small bombers had hit Tugogarao airfield in northern Luzon.

But this was not an attack: it was harassment. Given the lesson of Pearl Harbor, it was apparent that something much bigger must be coming.

Admiral Hart waited.

In midmorning the Japanese launched their major air strike from Formosa. Eleventh Air Fleet sent nearly two hundred planes to hit Clark and Nichols fields, where the B-17s were lined up like clay pigeons on the runways and aprons—an invitation to disaster.

Why?

Were the American air force men such fools?

Earlier that morning the sirens had screeched out their air raid warnings. At 8:30 American planes had gone aloft to meet the apparent threat, but nothing materialized. The army men at Clark and Nichols fields never learned of the attacks on Baguio and Tugogarao, so in an hour and a half the American fliers were back on the field, certainly not as they had been earlier. The crews went to lunch, and then back to the planes to tinker with their engines and make sure all was shipshape, while the commanders met to consider a reconnaissance mission over Formosa to check on the Japanese airfields there. It was all very relaxed.

Meanwhile the Japanese air armada had crossed the coastline, officially unseen, and was heading toward the airfields. They arrived at 12:45. Only two American planes were in the air when the enemy air fleet arrived. It was like bombing practice, with all those Curtiss P-40 fighters lined up on the grass, and all those Flying Fortresses sitting there, big silver propellers quiet. In a few minutes the attack was over; twelve B-17s were burning and five more were severely damaged; while thirty fighters were out of action for good. The Japanese lost seven planes, knocked out by the fighters in the air and the antiaircraft guns on the ground.

The vaunted air force of which General MacArthur had boasted now consisted of only seventeen bombers and forty fighters, many of them damaged severely. The only other land planes in the islands were some old navy Brewster Buffaloes, which had been scheduled to be sent to the Thais. Tommy Hart immediately diverted these to the army air force, but the Buffaloes were overage by at least five years and obsolete by any standards. They would be pitted against the Japanese Zero, at that time very nearly the best fighter plane in the world, and certainly the finest in the whole Pacific.

Thus, on December 8, 1941, with American strength severely diminished, the challenge to the Asiatic Fleet had finally come: The ships of the fleet were all that stood between the Philippines and a quick Japanese invasion and victory.

The Japanese were seriously concerned about this fleet, small as it was. They were mindful of the power of the submarines, and respectful

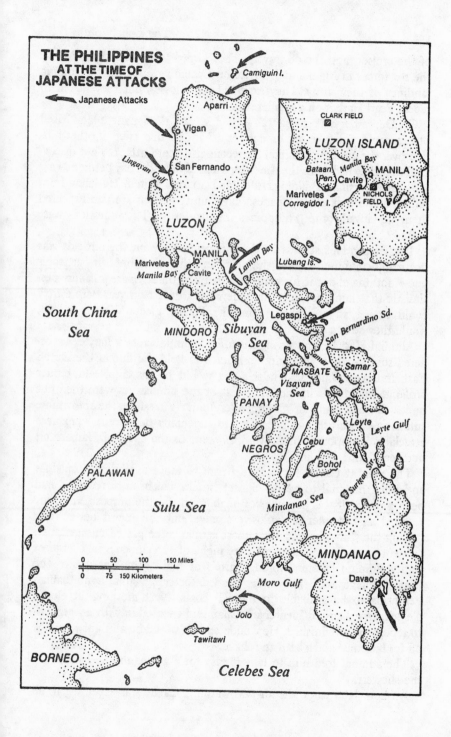

THE PHILIPPINES
AT THE TIME OF
JAPANESE ATTACKS

◄━ Japanese Attacks

Camiguin I.

Aparri

Vigan

Lingayan Gulf San Fernando

LUZON

Mariveles MANILA
Manila Bay Cavite

South China Sea

MINDORO

Sibuyan Sea

Lamon Bay

Legaspi

San Bernardino Sd.

MASBATE *Samar Sea* Samar

Visayan Sea

PANAY

Leyte

Leyte Gulf

NEGROS Cebu

Bohol

PALAWAN

Mindanao Sea *Surigao Str.*

Sulu Sea

MINDANAO

Davao

Moro Gulf

Jolo

Tawitawi

BORNEO

Celebes Sea

0   50   100   150 Miles
0   75   150 Kilometers

CLARK FIELD

LUZON ISLAND

Bataan Pen. *Manila Bay* MANILA

Cavite

Mariveles
Corregidor I. NICHOLS FIELD

Lubang Is.

of the cruisers and the destroyers. They hoped to strike a hard blow at the sea forces in Manila and Cavite on December 9, before the coming landings of their army. They expected some losses, but they hoped to repeat Pearl Harbor on a smaller scale.

On December 9 Formosa was socked in, and the Japanese land-based planes could not take off, except for a handful that tried another mission over the airfields, as much for reconnaissance as attack. They discovered that they had dealt the Americans a hard blow the day before.

In the Marsman Building, Admiral Hart still waited. He knew from radio reports that other Japanese naval units were at sea. He expected them to invade the Philippines momentarily. The question was: Where?

The tremendous success of the Japanese attack on the airfields was not really communicated to the navy, and the submarines in particular knew nothing about it for many hours. But Tommy Hart was very pessimistic that morning, since he believed it would be a year before they could expect any real help from the Pacific Fleet. Where, indeed, would they be in a year?

Admiral Hart began moving his force around. Captain Doyle was ordered south with a submarine task force to hold the line in the Dutch East Indies. Submarine tender *Otus* would be his ship, and tender *Holland* would go with her. The rest of the submarines were then put under the command of Commander John Wilkes. In the meantime, submarine *Spearfish* had been sent to Indochina to harry the Japanese attacking Singapore, while *Swordfish* went to the coast of Hainan, off northern China, to hunt.

The men at Cavite Navy Yard began to move explosives, torpedoes and other material to nearby Sunset Beach, which, until recently, had been a resort. It was hardly a reasonable spot for the purpose, and they violated all the rules of explosive storage, but still it was better than leaving the stuff where it was almost certain to be pasted momentarily.

Lieutenant Champlin spent that night of December 9 in charge of eighty Filipino laborers, rolling barrels of high-octane gas out of the Cavite storage area. They were headed for supply dumps on Bataan Peninsula to be available to the PT boats. Next morning, at eleven o'clock, an exhausted Lieutenant Champlin checked in with his admiral to report the job finished. He wondered if it would be all right to knock off for breakfast and a bath and shave.

The admiral told him to take it easy for a while, and he headed for the showers.

An hour later came the air raid warning. Cavite was expecting it, although one could hardly say that the naval base was *prepared*. The sirens began to sound at 12:10, and fifteen minutes later fifty-four bombers, escorted by fighters, came into view. From the decks of the ships moored alongside the wharf, they looked like German Junkers—although they were Japanese two-engined medium bombers of the *Betty* class.

With virtually no opposition from the remnants of the American air force the planes sailed in at fifteen thousand feet. Lazily, they broke into groups of twenty-seven, then split further into flights of nine.

Below, in Cavite, the Americans did what little they could. For example, the minesweepers *Bittern* and *Quail* were moored on the west side of Machera Wharf at the navy yard, along with submarines *Seadragon* and *Sealion*, submarine tender *Otus*, and salvage ship *Pigeon*. *Bittern* was armed with a number of .50-calibre machine guns, but in her overhaul they were unmounted. All that could be brought into action were two .50s on the boat deck and two twin .30s in the bow.

The first stick of bombs came down at 1:05 P.M. One struck the water south of *Otus*. Then came a hit right on the conning tower of *Sealion*. *Bittern* got it next, and in a minute she was afire. One splinter went through the port side of the fire room, smashed across the ship, and lodged in the starboard bulkhead, very nearly penetrating the ship on both sides. Two men in the mess hall were killed by a direct hit.

Other bombs fell with deadly accuracy around the yard. The power station was hit, and no water pressure was available for fire fighting. Aboard *Bittern* the officers organized a bucket brigade to try to keep the flames under control. They tried to start the ship's portable gasoline engine, but it would not function.

Soon the dock was in flames and the torpedo workshop was burning. *Pigeon* and *Quail* moved out, and soon *Seadragon* also moved out. Captain T.G. Warfield kept on fighting the fires aboard *Bittern*, but it was obvious from the punishment she had taken that she was not going to be saved.

The U.S.S. *Peary*, the destroyer which had collided with the *Pillsbury* a few days earlier, was moored on the east side of Central Wharf. One of the Japanese planes plunged a 250-pound bomb onto her, smashing the foremast between the fire-control platform and the crow's nest. Several men were hurt, including Lieutenant Commander H.H. Keith, the commanding officer. Lieutenant John M. Bermingham took command, and every man turned-to so the ship could be made ready for sea.

When the sirens sounded, Lieutenant Champlin was trying to clean himself up after his night's work. He got into uniform and rushed to the Commandancia, or tried to. At the bridge he encountered two trucks that had locked bumpers as the Filipino drivers tried to cross, one behind the other. Now the trucks were stuck and the bridge was firmly blocked. He ordered the drivers to move—one to back and the other to go forward. Then they all tried to free the bumpers, but could not.

One truck had fourteen wounded men aboard, all bound for the hospital. Champlin leaped aboard and ordered the wounded transferred to cars so they could be rushed to the hospital. He picked up one young Filipino whose left eye was gone and whose face was covered with blood. The man tried to speak as Champlin bent over him.

"Thank you, sir," said the Filipino. He smiled and then he died.

Around the Commandancia the 3-inch defense guns were firing, and in the harbor so were the guns of the ships that could be trained on the enemy. The bombs were dropping still, and the smoke and flame was growing thick as more buildings caught fire.

Champlin made his way to the Commandancia. There he found Admiral Rockwell, commander of the navy yard, clambering out of the slit trench athwart the building, his hat missing, in his shirt sleeves. His shirt front covered with the blood of wounded men.

The powerhouse was ablaze. No help there. In fact the whole fire-fighting system was out. The Cavite telephone system was still working, however, and Champlin managed to get through to Manila to call for pumpers and fire trucks to rush to the scene. They covered the eleven miles in record time, but it was still too late.

The fire coursed through the marine barracks and threatened the whole yard. Admiral Rockwell pulled his men together in front of the ammunition depot. Champlin was sent to an adjacent building that was threatened to pick up the supply of gas masks and remove them to safety. The building was burning, but he had a crew of men who worked like demons—only later did he learn that they were all prisoners from the brig who had been released when the bombs began falling. They requested that he testify that they had been helpful—it might mitigate the punishment for their various crimes.

By five o'clock Champlin had the definite feeling that the fires could be controlled. Then Cavite was rocked by new explosions and new fires began. They spread to the lumberyard, which burned fast. Two hours later Admiral Rockwell sent Lieutenant Champlin to Manila to inform Admiral Hart that Cavite had been completely destroyed as a working base.

Champlin set out by staff car through the crowded, shattered streets.

He was stopped half a dozen times by Filipinos armed with rifles and shotguns. These loyal citizens had been given arms when war broke out and the possibility of invasion by Japanese paratroops was recognized. Having to explain his mission time after time, Champlin was hours in getting to the Marsman Building, and when he arrived Admiral Hart was fast asleep. He had watched from the rooftop as Cavite burned, and he must have known. Champlin left a message and headed back to the base. Admiral Hart would have it in an hour, having left orders to be awakened then.

As far as Cavite was concerned that day, it was mostly "sit there and take it," but elsewhere elements of the Asiatic Fleet were in action against the enemy. Patrol Wing 10 put up five PBY patrol bombers at Mariveles, on southern Bataan at the entrance to Manila Bay, at 9:45 in the morning. They soon sighted an enemy force that was thought to consist of a pair of battleships, a cruiser, and two destroyers. They moved in from 11,500 feet, and attacked with their bombs—each plane carrying four 500-pounders. They were greeted by antiaircraft fire but managed to drop all twenty bombs, and the leader of the flight was sure one bomb had hit the stern of a *Kongo*-class battleship. Others missed, some narrowly. The battleship made a sharp turn and the planes moved off, to return to base and report. They found one small hole in the elevator of Patrol Bomber No. 5. As for the report about the Japanese—no *Kongo*-class battleships were destroyed that day. But at least Patrol Wing 10 was fighting back.

And fighting back was what it was going to take, as every man in the Asiatic Fleet very well knew. Total war had come to the fleet that day.

20

The Fleet Moves South

One of the key men at battered Cavite on the morning of December 11 was Commander Thomas K. Bowers, the inspector of ordnance. He was not inspecting this day, but instead was supervising the movement of torpedoes and parts to Sunset Beach. The destruction of some 230 torpedoes had severely crippled the fleet. Now the torpedo shop was to be moved to Corregidor, where it would be safer in the tunnels, while other explosives were to be moved to various places around the island. Commander Bowers gave the orders and then, with the help of Mrs. Hawout, his secretary, and Miss Carlson, his stenographer, began destroying the records that might be useful to the Japanese. The civilian personnel at Cavite were strong and resilient—none but the chief clerk ran away from the destruction and the battle, even though the base was a wreck without power or other facilities.

Bowers' job was also to get guns and mounts to shore and working. They moved the spare 1-inch gun and 17,000 rounds of ammunition from *Houston* to Bataan. That was at least one antiaircraft installation! In all this moving, they had the help of big trucks that said on their sides: *Luzon Stevedoring Company*. It was everybody's war, and everyone knew it.

As Admiral Hart soon learned, the initial Japanese bombings would have all kinds of repercussions. They had just about finished the army air force, knocked out Cavite, and destroyed a transmitter that was being used to keep in touch with submerged submarines. From now on, submarine operations would be seriously hampered.

That would make it more difficult for Hart to do one of his main jobs: to protect installations and logistics for the army forces that had the task of defending the Philippines. There could be no surface fleet activity in the Philippines as such; the most General MacArthur could count on was some help from the submarines, for the other fighting units were being moved south to coordinate with the British and Dutch. Perhaps their combined efforts would afford a chance of stopping the Japanese. There was no chance in the Philippines.

But Admiral Hart also intended to remain in the Philippines himself as long as he could assist the army and make effective use of his submarine force against the enemy landings and supply lines. He soon learned it was not going to be for long.

With Cavite in ruins, Admiral Rockwell went to Manila on December 11 for a meeting with Admiral Hart. They decided to evacuate the hospital from the navy yard, move what was left of the supply department, and to concentrate the arms at Mariveles and Corregidor. There was nothing left at Cavite to save except odds and ends. The submarine *Sealion* had been so badly damaged by the bombing that she would soon have to be destroyed lest the enemy capture her.

The Japanese had taken Bataan Island, north of Luzon in Bishi Channel. On December 10, they landed at Aparri on the north coast of Luzon in order to capture the airfield located there. Here the army air force staged one of its few satisfactory attacks of the campaign, sinking a minesweeper and interrupting landing operations. But the Japanese gained a foothold and the airfield. On December 12 the enemy landed at Legaspi, at the southern end of Luzon, near San Bernardino Strait. Admiral Hart knew a much larger force was at sea and heading for Lingayén Gulf.

The submarine tender *Canopus* had been held in Manila Harbor, with staff and enlisted men living in the old navy enlisted men's club, while communications were handled through fleet headquarters in the Marsman Building. Now *Canopus* was covered with fishnet and her outlines obliterated in an attempt to fool the Japanese pilots. She was surrounded by torpedo netting brought up from Mariveles, and her torpedo shop was moved to the caves of Corregidor, for that was the last repair service in Asia.

Off in Moro Gulf, on the southern coast of Mindanao, the seaplane tender *William B. Preston* was standing in Polloc Harbor when Filipino friends reported that the Japanese forced a landing on the island's northern coast and were marching on Polloc. The tender sent planes out to patrol the Celebes Sea, and got under way to Tutu Bay in Jolo Island, far to the northwest. But the planes found nothing.

Still, Admiral Hart was worried. The Japanese had established such complete air control by this time that he decided to send the tender and its planes to an area still farther south. *William B. Preston* was ordered to hoist her two Kingfisher float planes aboard, and to fly her bigger PBYs out to Tarakan in Borneo.

The order was understandable, but not easy to execute. *William B. Preston* was a converted ship, and she did not have any proper cranes for hoisting Kingfishers, nor a place to store more than one of them. But she managed to hoist one and put it astern to be cradled between the two motor launches, and took the second under tow in what was, luckily, a smooth sea. They managed a speed of 15 knots that day, heading south. They steamed through the night, and next day came upon two shapes that worried them; they executed a 180-degree turn to get away, but the shapes stayed with them. Fortunately, they were friendlies and not enemies: the Dutch destroyers *Kortenaer* and *Witte de With*, which then escorted the tender into the Dutch Borneo port of Balikpapan.

By this time Admiral Tommy Hart was seeing the handwriting writ very large on the wall of his office in the Marsman Building. One-third of his submarines were patrolling off enemy-occupied harbors, one-third had been sent out to intercept Japanese vessels off the Philippines, and one-third were held in reserve. But the first two-thirds of the force had really been outguessed—the enemy had moved too quickly and there were virtually no results from the submarines.

Admiral Hart was also disturbed in those first days by the number of reports of sightings of enemy forces—when there was actually nothing at the sighting points. This erroneous information, made through fear and carelessness, caused him to dissipate his forces, for every sighting mentioned either transports or battleships—prime targets.

By December 10, Admiral Hart was speeding up the schedule of departure for his ships from the Philippines, for the islands were lost, no matter how much wishful thinking was going on in the clubs. On that day he ordered a sailing. Submarine tenders *Holland* and *Otus* and the yacht *Isabel* left for the south, accompanied by two destroyers. Gunboats *Tulsa* and *Ashville* sailed with another pair of destroyers. All headed south to join Admiral Glassford's Task Force 5. Also, Hart began moving out the merchant ships, some forty of which had fled to the refuge of Manila's spacious harbor. They were no longer safe there. On December 11 he called a conference of masters, explained the problem, and sent them on their way. All but one of these ships escaped the Japanese.

By December 12 the Japanese were trying to extend their control of the Philippine seas; Admiral Kobayashi's minelayers were placing their mines in Surigao and San Bernardino straits, in the mid-Philippines, which made these "home" waters very dangerous. The submarines were not performing well. S-39 had a chance at these minelayers but sank nothing and was vigorously depth-charged.

For the next few days the planes that remained to the army and navy in the Philippines fought as hard as they could, suffering a slow attrition against the apparently inexhaustible Japanese force. On December 12 Admiral Rockwell gave up on Cavite altogether and moved 800 shore-based personnel to Sangley Point. A few burial parties were left. The town of Cavite was still burning, as they placed 122 bodies in the slit trench before the Commandancia and covered them.

On December 13 the army could put only a handful of fighters and bombers in the air. And Admiral Hart's air arm suffered a heavy blow when the Japanese knocked out half of Patrol Wing 10's remaining force in a single strike. The planes had gone out on patrol. They had come back safely but they had been shadowed, and as soon as they were down and defenseless the Japanese had swooped in and destroyed them in the water. Hart thereupon decided that the surviving planes should also move out. So on December 14, Patrol Wing 10 was ordered to the Dutch East Indies, and off they went, taking three tenders and all personnel except a handful. They left behind four PBYs that were too badly damaged to fly at the moment. There was no time to disassemble them or wait and repair them.

On December 14 the Americans' communications in the Philippines were threatened. The cable to Guam had suddenly been broken. The Japanese were bombing the radio towers near Manila to knock them out. That day the French steamer *Maréchal Joffre* was seized by men of the U.S.S. *Gem*, for Admiral Hart was very uneasy about the loyalties of the French captain and officers of the ship. She was manned by Americans and sent on her way to Surabaya on Java's northeast coast.

Meanwhile, Admiral Glassford was moving his growing force southward to join the Dutch. The old carrier *Langley* had been ordered to join him, along with the tankers *Pecos* and *Trinity* and several destroyers and submarines. These ships had quite a time getting through the minefield off Manila. They were helped by *Langley*, which picked out the entrance buoy in the darkness by flashlight and led them safely into open water.

Langley reported being the target of a pair of torpedoes en route, and did much firing around the compass. Her report that she had been attacked received support next day when the pilot of a Dutch patrol plane that picked the ships up warned that the carrier was being shadowed by a submarine. He also reported that he had sent it below the surface twice with diving attacks.

Langley and her escort of little ships met Glassford's force on December 13, and in consort they continued to Balikpapan. There they lay in the harbor but went to Condition 2—one hour's readiness—and there was no shore leave.

In mid-December Admiral Purnell, Hart's chief of staff, joined Task Force 5. With the dispatch of much of the fleet southward, Admiral Hart was moving its staff to Glassford, too. Preparations were now begun to make Task Force 5 effective as a fighting force, operating from an advanced command post set up at Surabaya by Glassford. Quarters were sought ashore for the admiral and staff in order to free flagship *Houston* of the administrative burden. The office was to be located at 15 Reiniersz Boulevard, and the officers would live at 118 Darmo Boulevard. They got to work, installing a radio transmitter in a small building so that they could be in touch with Hart and Pearl Harbor.

Admirals Glassford and Purnell made trips from Surabaya to Batavia, the Dutch East Indies capital on Java's northwest coast, to meet with Vice-Admiral C.E.L. Helfrich, the Dutch commander, and Commodore John Collins, the British senior officer. Within a week the joint defense was taking shape. The four officers worked out a general plan that called for the Americans to protect the area between Borneo and the Celebes Islands, including Makassar Strait and Molucca Strait, and east into the Banda Sea, west of New Guinea.

The British would work between Singapore and Sarawak, on the northern fringe of Borneo, and the Dutch had the whole Java Sea to patrol.

So the Americans undertook to defend 1,300 miles of foreign coastline, without adequate charts or knowledge of the area. The British and Dutch helped remedy this lack—they had far better charts than the Asiatic Fleet had ever possessed, but they had so few that each had to be hand-traced for copies. It was not the easiest way to fight a war.

On December 13, Admiral Hart wrote in his diary that the Japanese enemy "was already meeting success" in his efforts to conquer the Philippines. That was the day he sent off Purnell to Task Force 5. He assessed his own forces in the Manila area: 2 destroyers, 6 PT boats, 27 submarines, the submarine tender *Canopus*, the salvage ship *Pigeon*, 3 river gunboats, 3 minesweepers, and 1 fleet tug.

North Manila Bay was badly bombed the next day, and it seemed that the Japanese could see right through that fishnet on *Canopus*, so plans had to be made to move her out.

The air raids, coming every day now, thoroughly disorganized the services of Manila, and many Filipinos left the city so as not to be identified with the Americans. At least one Japanese agent was nabbed —a woman who had maintained a radio station right in the middle of Cavite naval base. She lived in a house in an ancient Spanish shipyard that had never been investigated because it had been there so long. In general security was poor—there was no censorship, nor administrative order, nor even many services offered by the disorganized government. The Manila Club, the Yacht Club and other spots were going full blast —tennis matches were still being played on the courts between air raids. The city was living out a charade, and waiting.

The Japanese moved everywhere. In the first days of the war they landed almost simultaneously in the Philippines, Malay Peninsula, Hong Kong, Borneo, and Guam, attacked Wake, and invaded Thailand and the International Settlement in Shanghai. The American marine detachment at Peking surrendered—there was little else they could do.

The Japanese had their own rumors, and a few setbacks. The *Langley* was erroneously reported sunk on December 9 by a Japanese submarine —this was evidently the same attack reported by the carrier tender, with supporting evidence from the Dutch flying boat. But there was more truth than fiction in the Japanese accounts. Wake was captured on December 22 after a gallant American defense—although two Japanese destroyers, *Hayate* and *Kisaragi*, were lost in the battle. This was bad news for the Japanese, but it was countered by the fact that Guam was occupied—so were Makin and Tarawa in the Gilbert Islands. The juggernaut moved forward.

For a while it seemed easy, except in the Philippines, where the Americans and the Philippine guard fought with vigor. On December 16, when the Japanese invaded Dutch Borneo in a high wind, their landing craft tipped crazily and some capsized. Although there was no enemy to oppose them, twenty men drowned. Ensign Toshiro Nakamura, who was there, watching, was moved to poetry by the sadness of it all:

> The force made a tragic landing
> Which moved even the Gods to tears,
> But the blood-surging brave warriors of
>   the Imperial Army

> Did not know what to do,
> For the enemy was not in sight.

The Americans were not the only ones fumbling in these early days of war.

21

Christmas Party, 1941

As the year progressed toward its end, the fighting grew more grim. In the Philippines the Japanese land forces moved forward, through jungles and across the plains, and the main Lingayén force put its heels into the Luzon soil far sooner than anyone expected. But there was a reason: The Japanese had expected heavy air, submarine, and surface opposition. They had none. The opposition came on the ground, and then only when it was almost too late.

In the middle of December Admiral Rockwell had Lieutenant Champlin assigned to half a dozen tasks. He interrogated the Japanese woman agent captured at the Cavite naval base and investigated the broken-up radio set they found there. Because of his FBI background, Champlin was supposed to know the ropes of investigation. But what could be done with her? She was turned over to the civil authorities and when the Japanese moved in she would be "liberated" and made a heroine.

The Japanese bombed the supply dumps at Sangley Point, Cavite. On one raid, as Champlin took shelter in a ditch, he watched with awe as a bomber dropped a missile that blew a huge hole in the road. He later measured it: 18 feet deep and 23 feet in diameter.

The Japanese also went after the radio towers near Manila daily, and, finally, with a mass of small bombs they did what they could not do with the big ones and succeeded in knocking the towers off their legs. By now much of the fuel cache was gone. So were the heavy ships. All that was left for Admiral Hart to do now was to attempt to help General MacArthur, and though the two headquarters had little contact with each other, they were both carrying out their responsibilities as best they could.

On December 19, Sangley Point got hit again, and badly; the oil dumps there took a pasting, and twelve marines were killed. Next day, the water supply was wrecked. Admiral Rockwell communicated with Admiral Hart, and the decision was made to move naval operations to Corregidor, into Queen Tunnel.

This desertion of the old naval areas made it essential that all the loose ends be tied up. *Sealion* was blown up with three depth charges. Other depth charges were set off at Cavite, and soon the fires at the base were burning fiercely. But when all seemed done, and the officers and men were in the Corregidor tunnels, they suddenly discovered that the officer who had been in charge of destruction of the mines at Sangley had not done the job. The explosives were important, but far more so was the secret detonation device, which must not be allowed to fall into the hands of the Japanese.

Lieutenant Champlin decided to volunteer for the mission to destroy the mines, and Admiral Rockwell let him call for volunteers. Forty men responded, among them many of the "chain gang" who had been instrumental in putting out fires and working at Cavite after they were let out of the brig.

Champlin picked twenty-five of the men, along with Lieutenant (j.g.) Henry, and in the evening took a motor launch out into the bay to the salvage ship *Pigeon*. As darkness fell, they headed for Sangley Point. In the *Pigeon*, Champlin called for men who knew something about cars and car repair, and hands went up. All right, he said, they would be the auto gang. After the landing, they would go find some cars that were running or almost running and bring them to the point for use in moving men and matériel. One detachment would start moving mines. Champlin and a signalman would investigate what could be done to dispose of the mines. The boat's crew would remain with the *Pigeon*.

At Sangley Point Champlin ran into an American civil engineer who had a hundred Filipino laborers with him. Here was his labor force. The auto crew found a Buick and Ford with flat tires—but they ran. He went into Cavite City to find Colonel Natividad, the mayor. With tears in his eyes, the mayor announced that the Japanese had come—and left. They had brought a tank right up the street to the Cavite base, and then made a complete about face. They had discovered, obviously, that the base was deserted. Apparently they had thought that it was also mined.

While Champlin and his crew were at Sangley they decided to take on some additional tasks. They would blow up the gasoline dumps, destroy the airplane engines in the Pan-American shop, and finish off the damaged PBYs that had been left behind by Patrol Wing 10.

They got one dockside crane working, and the auto gang brought up some trucks that were loaded with mines. At the dock they found the telephones in the area were still operable, and on a hunch, Champlin called "Chick" Parsons, the manager of the Luzon Stevedoring Company office and asked for his help. Parsons replied that he could not do anything right then, but if they would wait until the next night he would have a lighter alongside the wharf, and they could load their mines aboard it.

By this time it was nearly dawn, and the skies belonged to the Japanese in the daylight hours—as did the sea. Champlin took *Pigeon* back to Corregidor. Next night the crew and ship were back again, and sure enough, the lighter was there, manned by *the office force* of Luzon Stevedoring! By dint of hard work, they had the lighter laden with mines before dawn. They then towed it out into the middle of the harbor, and at 8 knots the tug flipped the lighter, which capsized, sending the mines down into the mud of Manila Bay.

Back in Manila, in these last days of 1941, even Admiral Tommy Hart was beginning to have doubts about his own past judgments, for some of the men he had counted on were failing him, while men he had despised were conducting themselves valiantly. Lieutenant Champlin's "sad sacks" out of the brig at Cavite, many of whom were in confinement for breaking most of the fleet's peacetime regulations, were performing like heroes every day. One of Hart's most trusted captains—a full captain, mind you—had simply abandoned his post and responsibility in a cruiser.

And as the end of the fleet's effectiveness in the Philippines drew near, Tommy Hart, in the privacy of his room in the Marsman Building, sat down to philosophize a bit about the war.

American military training was rotten, in his view. The American system of building and supplying and maintaining a military force was next to impossible. But most important of all was what he had recently rediscovered about his fleet. As he put it:

> The personnel were long-service and experienced in peacetime training but—like everyone else—were not experienced in the kind of war that they found. Only war proves what is correct and what is not, who is effective and who is not.

Tommy Hart ought to know. This was his second major war, and in any list of those responsible for the development of the submarine—a new weapon in World War I—Tommy Hart's name must be mentioned. And yet the very qualities that made him a fine peacetime commander—sticky in rulebook discipline and sharp on the golf course—were not the qualities most needed to serve his country now. Tommy Hart was sixty-four years old—retirement age—and he still had not picked a successor because he did not like the logical man, Admiral Glassford, and his ego kept him going. In the Glassford matter, he had already created confusion. He would create more.

But now it was time to leave the Philippine capital. By December 23 it became apparent that the Japanese were not going to be stopped short of Manila. General MacArthur decided to move down to Corregidor and defend Bataan, as the plans called for him to do, and to declare Manila an open city—not subject, under international law, to enemy bombardments. The navy learned about this decision only hours before it went into effect, and Admiral Hart made his plans to leave the Marsman Building and go to Corregidor himself. Admiral Rockwell was already there, and Captain J.H.S. Dessez, his second-in-command, was ordered to the island, evacuating Sangley Point.

Before leaving Manila Admiral Hart ordered his staff to mine Subic Bay, and the men drove 130 miles in a 12-ton dump truck, carrying the detonators in pillows on their laps. Subic Bay was mined, using a wheezy broken-down tug and a leaky barge.

The submarines were moved to hideouts on the Bataan Peninsula, for the Japanese photo planes and reconnaissance aircraft were out every day, and not far behind were flotillas of fighters and bombers that could be quickly moved into action.

Finally Admiral Hart boarded a PT boat at the Manila wharf and, escorted by the diesel yacht *Maryanne*, made his way to Corregidor. In a matter of hours, the Marsman Building would be in the hands of the Japanese.

Thus on Christmas Eve the defense force was strung out along Bataan and at Corregidor, the Rock.

That day, Lieutenant Champlin was in Manila dealing with a problem that had been largely forgotten until the last moment. There were enough caches of oil products in and around Manila to operate the whole Asiatic Fleet for the next two years, he learned from an oil company executive. They must be destroyed, lest the Japanese get the oil—after all, this was one of the things the war was being fought over. It was particularly important that the supplies of alcoholate be destroyed, for there was enough of this chemical compound in Manila to create 2.5 million gallons of aviation gasoline from ordinary gasoline.

And so Champlin stood Scotches at the Yacht Club and drank brandy at the University Club, and cajoled and pleaded until the Americans finally agreed to destroy their supplies. The British said they had no option to do so—they were the servants of higher executives. So the Americans lit the matches, as the British executives stood by in their tennis clothes and watched the oil supplies, American and British, go up in flames.

So it was on Christmas Eve, 1941, in the Asiatic Fleet.

22

The PBY Castaways

It was apparent on Christmas Day that the American naval position in the Philippines was totally untenable, and had Admiral Hart and General MacArthur been the closest of friends there would have been no need for Hart to stay on, to direct a vehicle that was going nowhere.

As Tommy Hart prepared to go south himself, he was considerably troubled by the performance of his submarines. The Asiatic Fleet was just beginning to discover that instead of having the best torpedoes in the world they possibly had the worst. Not only were the depth-regulation and exploding devices faulty but the missiles were far inferior to the enemy's in speed and range. This was not something that could be corrected easily, but was the result of twenty years of Congressional restrictions on military budgeting that had caused the navy to cut back on its weapons research.

The submarines inside Lingayén Gulf had performed very poorly in intercepting the Japanese. Lieutenant W.G. "Moon" Chapple managed to bring little S-38 into the shallow water inshore and sink the transport *Hayo Maru*, and *Seal* sank the small 850-ton freighter *Hayataka Maru* off the province of Ilocos Sur, on Luzon's northwest coast, but that was all. The Japanese reported they were bothered more by the weather than by the American navy.

Admiral Hart had little confidence in Admiral Glassford and immense confidence in himself, so he was eager to be down in Java, where he had already sent most of the fleet. The submarine problem could be looked into and possibly straightened out down there. The cruisers and destroyers could be used to advantage. Two PBYs of Patrol Wing 10 had been assigned to fly the admiral and his staff south, and he was ready to depart on Christmas afternoon. But the flying boats were found by an enemy observation plane, and bombers came in and destroyed them. On the night of December 25, then, Admiral Hart and his staff boarded the submarine *Shark* and headed south.

That same day submarine *Sturgeon* was nearly sunk in Manila Bay, straddled by a pair of bombs. She got away, but it was apparent that there was no place to hide in the Philippines where supplies and maintenance would be available.

As Admiral Hart headed south, so would the submarines as they finished their patrols or as they needed service. General MacArthur's men were moving down on Bataan. The Japanese were coming at a leisurely pace to occupy Manila. The general himself was making ready to take over the caves of Corregidor. Admiral Rockwell was left to direct the naval remnants, and the focus of the Asiatic Fleet moved to the Dutch East Indies.

In the first two and a half weeks of the war, the Japanese had conducted nine different amphibious invasions of the Philippines, the ease with which they moved about the islands was humiliating. The last of these was on Christmas Eve at Jolo, an island at the eastern end of the Sulu Archipelago, between the Sulu and Celebes seas.

Patrol Wing 10 had been sent south to Borneo waters and was functioning again. The pilots got word of the Japanese landing at Jolo Island, and on the night of December 26 they were ordered to make a bombing raid on the enemy ship concentration there. Six PBYs would make the raid, led by Lieutenant (j.g.) J.B. Dawley, of Squadron 101. He and the other pilots were briefed: They would carry 1.5 tons of demolition bombs, they would attack the enemy, and they would return to report. They had sixteen hours' supply of gas, which should easily get them there and back. That night, the briefing officer wished them good luck, and at 11:00 P.M. they were in the air.

Lieutenant Dawley's plane carried seven men. Dawley was captain and first pilot. Ensign Ira W. Brown was second pilot. The rest of the crew included: Aviation Machinist's Mate First Class Dave W. Bounds, third pilot and bow gunner; Radioman First Class N.T. Whitford, tunnel gunner; Aviation Machinist Mate Second Class Evren C. McLawhorn, flight engineer; Aviation Machinist Mate Second Class Earle B. Hall, port waist gunner; and Radioman Third Class James M. Scribner, starboard waist gunner. It was a big crew, but the PBY was a big plane, very much like the Pan-American flying boats that ranged the Pacific in those years.

As the six planes rose from the water, they circled and formed into two V's for their long flight. The attack was scheduled for the precise moment of dawn, when they would be able to see the enemy ships below them at Jolo but the enemy would not have had a chance to send out planes of his own. The Japanese had no radar; they were dependent on spotters and on their own eyes and ears. Here the Americans had an advantage. If they used it wisely, they would be coming from the east with the sun, and would not be betrayed.

The two sections maintained radio silence, and in a way this was the cause of later difficulty, for the second section moved out ahead of the first, and also ahead of schedule. As a result, these bombers arrived over the Japanese ship concentration *before* dawn, were unable to find the targets, had to circle, and by the time they were in bombing position, the Japanese were alert. They were also prepared for action, for the island was already militarily secure—a naval aviation force had arrived and the carriers *Ryujo* and *Chitose* were not far away.

As the second section of PBYs peeled off to launch the attack, the planes were met by heavy antiaircraft fire, and Japanese float planes began taking off to contest them. One of the PBYs was shot down. The other two managed to escape and get home. But by the time the first section arrived to bomb, the Japanese were thoroughly aroused, and planes were buzzing about the island and the transports.

Even before Lieutenant Dawley could begin his bombing run, his plane was hit by an antiaircraft shell. He checked. No one was hit. The controls responded—so there was no vital structural damage. He went on in.

But now, in addition to the gray and black and white puffs of ack-ack fire, six fighters came boring in on the PBY, and in their first pass with cannon and machine-gun fire they killed both port waist gunner Hall and starboard gunner Scribner.

Flight engineer McLawhorn then climbed down into the waist and manned both guns. In a few moments he was hit—a fragment of a shell or a bullet struck him in the eye, and he was wounded in both arms and legs. Yet with one good eye, he kept the two guns firing, shooting off burst after burst as the enemy flashed into the sights of one or the other.

Lieutenant Dawley nosed the PBY down and dropped three bombs, aimed at an enemy cruiser. He had no idea whether or not any of them was even a near miss, because all the way down these six fighters were still working him over, wrecking the plane with their accurate cannon and machine-gun fire. Gas was streaming out of both engines. The control cables to the rudder were cut and he had no rudder control. The starboard engine was hit by a cannon shell or an antiaircraft burst, and went out.

Dawley decided he must land while he still had enough control. If the ailerons went out, the PBY would not have a chance and would definitely crash. He headed for the south side of Jolo Island, moving into shore as close as he dared, waiting as long as possible to gain distance. The moment the plane hit the water, the crew began to abandon her, for she was already beginning to burn and the gas tanks might go up at any moment. So the bodies of Hall and Scribner were left in the fuselage, and the other five scrambled out the hatches, just as the plane began to sink. Even as they came out, they could see and feel the impact of the Japanese fighter strafing the burning plane.

Lieutenant Dawley had managed to put them down in the warm water only two hundred yards from the beach, and they swam, pulling McLawhorn along, until they reached the shore. As they waded in, out came natives, armed with spears and bolo knives. They saw the men in the water and Dawley began to shout.

"Hello, Joe," he cried. That was the American war cry in the Philippines, and thus the natives could identify them. A good thing, too, for, as these men of the village of Lapa told Dawley and the others later, if they had been Japanese, they would have been killed.

Ashore, Dawley checked his crew. Tunnel gunner Whitford had been nicked twice by bullets, but it was nothing serious—minor wounds of the back and wrists. McLawhorn was badly hurt, with that fragment in the eye and three other wounds, the most serious of which was a bullet in the leg. The natives had a first-aid kit, which they offered, and Dawley and Ensign Brown dressed the wounds of the men.

But the first-aid kit was all the islanders offered. These natives evidently belonged to the Muslim Moro people found throughout the southern Philippines, and as Dawley looked around him, he was not quite sure how friendly they really were, particularly when they stripped the Americans of some of their clothing and possessions. Dawley lost his watch, twenty American dollars, his knife, and some papers he was carrying. The others were robbed as well, and the Moros took all their .45-calibre automatics.

Speaking rapidly in Tagalog or a dialect, two of the Moros now took charge and brusquely ordered the Americans up and moving. Were they friends? With shaved heads, filed teeth, and those curved krises waving about, Dawley and his men were not quite sure. Carrying McLawhorn, they moved on for about a quarter of a mile until they came to a nipa hut, where the Moros said they might stop.

By this time it was 7:30 in the morning and broad daylight. The Japanese were nowhere in sight, and the Moros told them they were safe for the moment. As for the future of the Americans, this must be decided by the authorities, and that meant the provincial government. They would have to wait.

While they waited, the Moros offered them some native clothing and fed them a meal of rice and boiled chicken. Dawley had been in the Philippines long enough to know that a chicken was not killed except on a special occasion and that this was another sign of the friendliness of the natives. However, the Americans still had difficulty in communicating with the Moro warriors, who were about the fiercest-looking men they had ever seen.

Many villagers came to grin and talk and encourage the Americans and make ugly signs and threats against the Japanese. Namii Indongi, an English-speaking schoolteacher from some place near the village, suddenly appeared to talk to them, and told them the Japanese had appeared on Christmas Eve and landed to take control of Jolo. But they were far away, he assured the Americans. What they had to do now, he said, was get to the government center of Siasi, on Siasi Island farther south, by boat and then they could find the governor, who would know what to do.

At just about that time, a shout went up from the natives: "The Mundos are coming!"

And all the natives ducked back up the hill. For the Mundos were the local hill men who preyed on the people of the shore, and robbed and pillaged them to support themselves. This was a war that had been going on for generations—the struggle with the Japanese was only a passing matter. But this time the cry was a false alarm—at least, no Mundos appeared to bother the Americans.

On the shore, a friendly native put the Americans in touch with a visiting fruit peddler who lived at Siasi and who agreed to take them there. They boarded his *vinta*—a long outboard canoe with a sail—and they set out at dusk, for they did not want to be in the gulf in daylight hours when the Japanese might stop them.

The next morning was December 28. As dawn came up the Americans found they were about twenty miles from Jolo, no farther, and their captain and his two boys were doing nothing to move the *vinta*. So the Americans began to paddle—and soon discovered that they might as well drift, for they were getting virtually nowhere. When the current and the wind and the tide adjusted themselves, they moved on. They stopped at another island, and here they found Ensign Christman, from one of the other PBYs, who had also survived and had spent thirty hours in the water. He was badly sunburned, and they tried to treat him but did not have medical supplies. It was decided they must all go to Laminusa Island, where a doctor lived. There were also officials on Laminusa who would know how to shelter the Americans from the Japanese.

On their travels they met Arasad Alpad, a first lieutenant in the Philippine army, and several other Filipinos who befriended them. One who helped them most was the American wife of Assemblyman H. Gulamn Rasul, although they never did learn her own name. She fed them a meal of rice, eggs, and mangoes, and doctored Ensign Christman's sunburn. Then the Americans moved on toward Siasi, which, they discovered, was indeed the headquarters village. The three most important men in the area lived here: Dr. Isaoni Chance, Judge Yusup Abubakhar, and Mayor Iman Lkibul.

They learned at Siasi of other survivors, and picked one of them up, Machinist Mate Don Lurvey. His plane had landed twenty-five miles out at sea and burned. He thought there were two other survivors on one of the smaller islands.

Dr. Chance took a look at McLawhorn's eye, but decided that he did not have the facilities to treat it. He might make it worse. That night two more *Americanos* came in, Ensign Gough and Radioman Third Class Paul Landers. And the elders of the island and the Americans held a conference. It was decided that they must now go on to the town of Bato Bato on Tawi Tawi Island. That would put them beyond the reach of the Japanese; they could move on to Borneo from there. Hopefully, they could then get more planes and come back and bomb the Japanese again.

Once that was decided, the word spread through the place and its effect was electric. They were presented with gifts of food and Moro clothing. Their hands were shaken and smiles were bestowed on them. Lieutenant Brillantes of the Philippine constabulary offered to transport them, and procured a big sailboat. Mr. Jesus, the local Protestant clergyman, insisted that they sail past a certain point, and later, as they left the island by moonlight, they saw bright lights on the point and heard people singing English hymns, accompanied by a trumpet.

It was New Year's Eve, and they sailed along in the night air, until the moon above the mast told them it must be around midnight. Then Lieutenant Brillantes brought forth four bottles of native brandy he had "squeezed" from a Chinese storekeeper, and, as Lieutenant Dawley put it, "we dropped the hook for 1941 and weighed anchor in 1942."

At Bato Bato, the Americans were out of the immediate sphere of the Japanese influence, although still far from safety. They met Father C.B. Billman here, a Roman Catholic priest and a man Ensign Brown knew from happier days in the Philippines. There was a hospital here, where they could treat McLawhorn's eye and the bad sunburns of four of the Americans. The injured went to hospital.

Here they also met the governor of the province, Major Alejandro Suarez of the Philippine constabulary—a man of considerable local power. They went hunting with .22 rifles for pigeons. They stayed with the priest and had a fine dinner. And more important, or so it appeared, the governor found a sailor who promised to take them by boat to Borneo for 150 pesos. Unfortunately, that did not work out.

Finally, there arrived on the scene a certain Mr. Stratton, an American soldier of Spanish-American war vintage, who had stayed in the islands and had married a Filipino girl. He went off to a small nearby island where his wife's family lived and came back with a boatman and his sailboat.

It was now January 3, and the Americans were itching to get to Borneo and its relative safety. Laden with pigs and chickens and fish, they made ready to sail on the next leg of the long voyage. A Chinese storekeeper supplied them with goods: cigars, cigarettes, bully beef—and a whole case of Pabst Blue Ribbon beer!

Finally, it was time to go. Father Billman gave each American a little cross and promised to pray for them daily for the next thirty days. Their boatman, a wizened little fellow, settled them down in the big sailing craft, and then stood before the mast and talked to the gods. He went forward and kicked the bow. He went aft and kicked the stern. He sat down and took the tiller and prayed for a long time. And then he shoved off and set sail straight for the north end of Sibutu Island—and although they sailed out of sight of land and in total darkness, they reached the landfall of Sitankai, a neighboring island, at dawn, just as he said they would.

It was January 4. They had come here because someone thought the government launch might take them across the water to Borneo.

At this place Deputy Governor Amirkamja Japal assured them that there was such a boat, adding, with some chagrin, that unfortunately it did not work. The craft, they were told, was a 50-foot diesel-powered customs launch. They hastened to look at it—the description was correct, but had failed to mention its age. This was possibly the first 50-foot diesel-powered customs launch ever built; dry rot had consumed the bottom, and worse, its pressure tanks had holes in them.

But Dawley and the others realized that this launch represented their very best hope of getting to Borneo—they had the feeling that they must move quickly because the Japanese might be close behind. So they repaired the diesel launch, discovering, by trial and error, a technique of filling the holes with wooden plugs and holding the plugs against the pressure tanks with steel bands wired around the tanks. An engineer would have scoffed, but they built up the pressure—100 pounds, 110, 120, 150—and the plugs held. So the launch was as good as new—or almost.

This repair had taken two days of thought and work, and it wasn't until the night of January 5 that they set out, using the governor's charts to determine a course for Tawao in British North Borneo.

They made it. On January 6, the party arrived at Tawao and was greeted by Dr. Krantz, a German refugee, who patched up the wounded again, and by Mr. Adams and Mr. Johns, rubber plantation owners who gave them food, comfort, and told them how to get to Tarakan, farther down the coast of Dutch Borneo.

These fellow Caucasians did not seem eager for them to stay, and Dawley soon found out why: A Japanese landing party was expected at any moment—the "bamboo telegraph" had warned of it—in fact they were already overdue.

So the Americans hastened away for Tarakan.

They set out on the night of January 6, with a native crew and Lieutenant Dawley as captain of their vessel. The current was strong and running against them so they anchored at seven o'clock that night and decided to sleep until midnight. Dawley took the first watch and then put a native boatman on watch and took a nap. He was to be awakened at midnight.

He woke up at 3:00 in the morning and found his watchman fast asleep. They were high and dry on the seabed, and the tide was out. Now they had to wait, and wait they did. It was midmorning before the tide rose and they could get off the bottom and to sea once more. It was almost noon before they sighted the Dutch lightship at Tarakan Harbor and glided in to shore. At Tarakan they were greeted by a smiling Commander O. Verneuler, who gave them hot food and clean Western clothes to replace the Moro garments they had been wearing throughout their odyssey.

The next day, January 8, saw the arrival at Tarakan of a truly lovely sight—a Dutch Dornier flying boat, which took them all to Balikpapan and a joyous reunion with the men of the Asiatic Fleet.

They had spent the most adventurous two weeks of their lives; they had been under the noses of the Japanese almost continually; they had been befriended by scores of people; and hundreds more had known of their existence and whereabouts. And in all that time, not one person had betrayed them.

23

Running the Japanese Air Gauntlet

Admiral Glassford always referred to the period from December 8, when he left the stifling air of Manila, until January 1, when Admiral Hart arrived in Surabaya as "the first phase" of the campaign to defend the Malay Barrier—the chain of big islands stretching from the Malay Peninsula through the Dutch East Indies to New Guinea. It was easy for him to think in those terms, because for these brief three weeks he had, in a tactical sense, been his own boss without Hart's disapproving stares.

Glassford knew precisely what he faced in the Dutch East Indies. Interviewed by the Columbia Broadcasting System at his headquarters, the admiral first set down some ground rules for what should be stated publicly: The interviewers must be optimistic in their appraisal of the situation, and they must indicate that there was the closest cooperation possible between the United States Army and Navy and the Dutch. Then he added his private opinion, not for publication. There had never been a blacker day for America. The crisis would last for five or ten years, barring the collapse of Germany, the admiral said in a momentary lapse into bitter conjecture.

For from where Admiral Glassford sat, there was very little to be optimistic about in this war. Behind him stood a commander-in-chief of the Asiatic Fleet who did not like him; beyond that the chief of naval operations in Washington, Admiral Ernest J. King, was already pressing for action to stop the Japanese to improve American morale at home. Before Glassford loomed a well-organized Japanese military and naval machine that was still fifteen hundred miles away from the Dutch East

Indies and thus impossible to engage except by air or by submarine. However the submarines carried torpedoes that were now known to be faulty; what was left of Patrol Wing 10 was being rapidly decimated by enemy bombers and fighters. Beside him sat a Dutch ally who had developed a sharp contempt for the American navy after Pearl Harbor, and a British ally who was concerned only with the preservation of the British Empire.

As for Admiral King's pressures for action against the Japanese, Glassford still hoped that reinforcements, especially in air strength, would soon bring that possibility closer to reality. And at about this time his hopes were raised—and then dashed.

Down in Townsville, on Australia's northeastern coast, there was an American army air force installation which boasted of a whole new squadron of twenty-one American fighter planes. The planes were still in crates on the ships that had brought them from America. The pilots were brand-new trainees out of America, green as grass, with only their flight training and a brief bit of home practice behind them. But to Glassford, these planes seemed to be the ideal answer to his need for fighter craft to protect his patrol bombers. In Townsville, the harried air corps command uncrated the planes and agreed to risk them on the journey north. That would mean sending the untrained fliers on a long island-hopping voyage.

Soon the whole squadron took off from Townsville. At each stop one or two planes crashed on landing, or, worse, were lost at sea. Island after island demanded its tribute from the untrained pilots, and finally five planes arrived in Java—in such dreadful condition that not one of them ever flew in combat.

So much for last-ditch methods of supply. The Americans were learning what the Japanese had to learn late in the war: there was no substitute for a well-oiled, well-trained military machine.

It was a wonder that Admiral Glassford was not totally discouraged.

But in the blackness of the hour, there emerged small elements of the brightness of the human spirit that proved all could not be lost. If the Dutch admirals and governors were contemptuous, the Dutch people on a personal level were generous and could be helpful and friendly. If the campaign in East Asia was already lost, and the road back was to be hard and bloody, at least the American fighting men did not think so, and they exhibited a show of bravery in the Philippines and the waters beyond that was to become legendary.

This was quickly demonstrated as the ships of the Asiatic Fleet moved south through the enemy-controlled waters of the Philippines.

By the end of December it had become apparent that the skies above Manila Bay belonged to the Japanese, and that every vessel left in those waters was in danger. So before leaving the Philippines Admiral Hart had begun releasing the secondary elements of his fleet. He had kept destroyers *Pillsbury* and *Peary* back for odd jobs. Specifically they were assigned to Admiral Rockwell's 16th Naval District to help the offshore patrol. But on the afternoon of December 26 the destroyers were attacked by nearly fifty Japanese planes—it was amazing they were not sunk then and there. It would be even more remarkable if they could survive another week in this environment. Admiral Hart thereupon released the destroyers, sending them to join Admiral Glassford's Task Force 5.

Pillsbury sailed to Balikpapan and arrived without incident. *Peary's* story was somewhat different.

U.S.S. *Peary* was already a battle-scarred veteran, having been damaged in the first Cavite bombing of December 10, when her captain, Lieutenant Commander Keith, was injured and the ship was taken over by Lieutenant John L. Bermingham. Subsequently Bermingham was posted to official command of the ship and was quickly promoted a half stripe. But he had not supervised the maneuvering of the ship during the big Japanese raid of December 26—he had been ashore for a conference with Admiral Rockwell, and Lieutenant M.M. Koivisto had performed the job superbly. So if Bermingham, back from his conference, had nothing but an old tin can to take him south, he also had men of battle experience and real enthusiasm to support him.

Bermingham already had his sailing orders, and at 8:30 that night *Peary* headed south to join Admiral Glassford's task force. She moved through the minefield beyond Maudn Harbor, and next morning at 8:30 anchored at Campomanes Bay on Negros, midway down the Philippine archipelago. There Bermingham stopped to camouflage his ship as best he could. Crews went ashore to pick up palm branches, and they scrounged enough green paint from the army to confuse the slender lines of the destroyer.

Minutes after the hook dropped, five enemy bombers passed over Negros, bound north. This was a bad break, and Lieutenant Commander Bermingham began to sweat, for there was no reason in the world why the ship would not have been sighted by these planes and no more reason why the planes would not have radioed Formosa to launch a strike. Perhaps there was even a carrier in the area, which would make matters worse.

Either these planes had dropped their bombs or they did not see

Peary, for they continued without a pause over the ship and beyond. In an hour *Peary* was moving along the shore to Asia Bay to hide again and hopefully to complete the camouflage. She anchored in the bay at 10:30 that morning. Four hours later, as the job progressed, five more Japanese bombers passed by, but again they did not give the *Peary* a second glance.

Three and a half hours later, Bermingham was ready to set out into the broad sea. He charted a course for Pilas Strait, off western Mindanao, ordered the anchor up, and rang up a speed of 25 knots.

At eight o'clock in the morning of December 28 the ship had passed Jolo and was in the Celebes Sea, which seemed to be safer country. To save fuel, the captain cut the running speed to 18 knots. Ten minutes later a bomber was after them, one of the big four-engined flying boats that would come to be called Kawanishis. The bomber began maneuvering for an approach, but each time her pilot headed in, Captain Bermingham radically made course changes. He succeeded so well that after a few passes the Kawanishi moved back to a position near the sun, and from there floated along, shadowing the *Peary* for the rest of the day.

Peary was reading the radio traffic from Task Force 5 with great care. One dispatch reported an enemy minelaying submarine in Makassar Strait, and an enemy cruiser off North Borneo. *Peary* changed course so as not to intercept that cruiser, ran the speed back up to 25 knots, and tried frantically to report the presence of the Japanese shadower. Every man knew it would be only a matter of time before the shadower was joined by friends.

Task Force 5 did not respond.

The radiomen increased their efforts, using every frequency assigned. No response.

The ship sped along through the sunny sea, a gray-green shadow back in the sun following them. At 2:00 P.M. two PBYs were sighted, but neither by radio nor by blinker could the *Peary* attract their attention. They must have been Dutch patrol bombers. The Dutch did have some PBYs but the liaison between Dutch and American commands was in its infancy.

The inevitable occurred twenty minutes after the PBYs headed off into the horizon—three more big Kawanishis joined the shadow, and the planes began to peel off one at a time. The first plane came in and dropped two 500-pound bombs. They missed. Then came the second plane, and the third, and the fourth. . . .

On the bridge Lieutenant Commander Bermingham played a dangerous guessing game with the Japanese. A plane on the port quarter—full left rudder, turn into him and out. A plane to starboard cut a circle and reverse, making a figure eight. Reversing, stopping, changing speed, boxing the compass, the captain kept the ship moving and shooting continually for the next two hours. After each of the four planes had made an attack, three of them made a second attack—then up came a single-wing torpedo plane on the port bow. He was coming in at fifty feet above the water, ready to drop, and about five hundred yards out he did drop—two torpedoes.

Captain Bermingham moved his ship. "Full astern, starboard engine," was the command, and *Peary* slowed and turned, and the torpedoes passed ahead of the bow, their wakes trailing off into the distance.

Hardly a man watched them, for ten seconds later a second torpedo plane was upon them, coming in on the port quarter in the same drop pattern as the first. Five hundred yards out, two fish went into the water and splashed, then began their deadly runs.

A sharp turn to starboard swung the ship's stern clear and the two torpedoes passed along the starboard beam, about ten yards off the ship —it was that close.

During these torpedo plane attacks, the fourth Kawanishi came in astern to launch her second attack, hoping to catch the ship off balance while attention was directed to the torpedo planes. That sharp maneuver, swinging the stern around to miss the second pair of torpedoes, had cost *Peary* her forward movement, but the captain rang up emergency speed and the engine room responded beautifully. The ship went from a standing start to 15 knots between the time the enemy released his bombs and the time they hit—the whole stick struck a hundred yards astern.

No sooner was this emergency ended than the men of the *Peary* were dodging and fending off strafing attacks by the torpedo planes. Through all this they had been training and firing their .50- and .30-calibre machine guns, their antiaircraft guns, and even the destroyer's 4-inch guns had come into play.

All this time Bermingham was on the bridge, along with Lieutenant W.J. Catlett, Jr., who helped him spot the planes coming in and maneuver the ship so as to avoid the attackers.

Outside the bridge, Lieutenant (j.g.) A.L. Gustafson, the gunnery officer, was standing on the fire-control platform, in full view of the enemy pilots and gunners, directing the fire of the antiaircraft guns and the 4-inch battery. All around him bullets were plowing into the sea and bouncing off the steel upper works, while pieces of shrapnel were tearing at the ship.

Then the attack ended, the two torpedo planes swung off to the northeast, the Kawanishis followed ponderously, and the *Peary* was left alone on the sea.

Lieutenant Commander Bermingham set his course to pass through Banka Strait, at the northeastern tip of Celebes. He had considered taking shelter at Menado, a nearby port, but fortunately he changed his mind. The Japanese were then pushing landing forces into Menado and *Peary* would have most certainly been in among the enemy. She passed that area just after 5:30 in the evening and used her searchlight to blink a question to the Dutch.

"Is the strait mined?"

There was no answer. The shore light was not functioning—the Japanese were all about, and it was a very ticklish time.

Worse was yet to come.

Half an hour later, as the darkness grew, three Lockheed Hudsons moved in from astern. The men of the *Peary* recognized them—they were British planes. They came in right and properly, crossing the ship's course from starboard to port. The *Peary* gave the proper international challenge. One pilot waved. All was well.

But not with the second pilot, who in his concern over the Menado landings, considered all destroyers to be his enemies. He executed a glide-bombing attack.

Those white and blue wing circles might mean he was British, but a bomb attack was an enemy action, and the men of the *Peary* were not putting up with any more without fighting back. They opened up with ack-ack fire as the Hudson dropped its bomb, which missed a hundred yards to port.

As the captain came hard right to miss that bomb, the force of the turn knocked Seaman First Class Billy Green overboard from his post at the No. 4 .50-calibre machine gun. His mates saw him hit the water and go under and then bob up. Someone threw him a life jacket. The last they saw of him, as the destroyer maneuvered to escape the British, Seaman Green was swimming toward the life jacket. They hoped he could reach the island of Bunakang, about a mile away. They could only hope; they could not stop.

All three Lockheed planes made two runs on the American destroyer, dropping a single 250-pound bomb each time. Not one scored a hit, but the last was a near miss, about ten yards off the port propeller guard.

Shrapnel spattered the ship. One piece pierced the shell plating of the after engine room. Twenty pieces went into the steering room and cut the wheel ropes to the bridge. One piece cut the steam supply line to the steering engine. A 4-inch shell was set afire topside, and burned for several seconds before Fireman Third Class Glenn Fryman seized it and threw it overboard.

One large piece of shrapnel smashed through the mount of the .30-calibre machine gun on the fire-control platform, and hit Seaman First Class Kenneth Quinaux, who was manning the gun. It killed him instantly, even as he fired at the diving plane. Other bits of shrapnel did further damage—from cutting wiring to piercing three depth charges so that they had to be jettisoned.

What the Japanese enemy could not do, British allies nearly managed to do. But having missed, and used up all their ammunition, they headed home. When they got there and learned what they had done, their explanation was that in spite of the recognition signals and the American flag, the ship looked like a Japanese destroyer. And had they not seen it earlier in the day, *convoyed* by those Kawanishi flying boats? What more proof did a pilot need?

That night the exhausted crew of *Peary* examined their ship and notified Admiral Glassford of all that had occurred. The ship was short of fuel and water, and headed east for sanctuary toward the Halmahera group, where she made for Maitara Island near Ternate. She went in, a bow line was strung to trees on shore, and there she rested, with about two fathoms under the keel.

Here the men found more palm fronds, leaves, and branches, and during the night they festooned the ship as if a Christmas party were about to be staged. The executive officer and the men began making repairs, hoisting a foremast to replace the one that had been shot away. Captain Bermingham went to Ternate to make a formal call on the Dutch military commandant and the assistant resident. Supplies began to come to the ship: good water, ice, bread, native fruits.

Checking carefully, the engineers discovered they had 19,000 gallons of fuel, enough to get them to Ambon, farther south. And at sunset on December 30, they steamed off, a little uncertainly but once again ready for action if need be. The whole passage was made on the port engine, for the starboard was out of commission, thanks to the British bombs. *Peary* reached Ambon on December 31, at noon, got more aid and more fuel, and staggered on—until she made Port Darwin, Australia, on January 3.

Captain Bermingham had at least one slight consolation. His friends were damned sight better shots than his enemies.

24

The Admiral Arrives
by Submarine

When seaplane tender *Heron* got the word that she was released from Philippines' duty because there were no more seaplanes to tend and the men could very well get their heads shot off to no avail, Lieutenant W.I. Kabler, her skipper, set course for the south. He, too, hoped to join the ships of the Asiatic Fleet.

No table of organization was likely to call a seaplane tender a first-line fighting ship, and under normal conditions she would not travel other than in the company of a couple of destroyers.

But as 1941 drew to a close, conditions in the fleet made it unwise, even if it had been possible, for ships to travel in consort. The Japanese had assembled what they called the Eastern Force, under Vice-Admiral I. Takahashi. It included, among other ships, eight carriers and a dozen cruisers, with a battleship or two that could be called upon for assistance. This force would support the occupation of Menado, Kandari, Ambon, Tarakan, Palembang, and Bali in the not-too-distant future. Units were assembling and moving about the waters of the south all the time. And *Heron*, like all the other American ships, had to run for cover and be sure to get there before the enemy caught up with her.

She was steaming along on her southern run at 9:30 on the morning of December 31 when a big 4-engined flying boat was sighted, almost on the approach pattern that recognition rules required—but not quite. She approached low, and then the gunners realized that she was nothing they had ever seen before, and was indeed Japanese—a Kawanishi to be specific. They opened up with the .50-calibre antiaircraft machine guns.

Then began almost the same battle pattern that had been experienced by destroyer *Peary*.

Satisfied that the ship was American, the Kawanishi climbed and made a high bombing approach, then dropped a pair of 100-pound bombs, both of which went into the sea fifteen hundred yards short of the ship. It did not seem there was much to worry about.

Twenty minutes later the plane was back again, dropping another pair of bombs—this time they were only three hundred yards off the starboard bow.

Heron's course took her into a squall, which she steamed through for more than half an hour—but when she emerged, there was the Kawanishi, trailing. The flying boat came in again, this time low on the starboard beam, apparently to determine if this was the same vessel he had attacked twice before. This time the gunners were ready for her and they poured on a stream of .30-calibre and .50-calibre machine-gun fire that drove the Kawanishi into as quick a climb as the pilot could manage. But he did not go away. With the snoopiness of a neighborhood gossip, he sat back on their starboard quarter, well aft, at about 1,500 feet, and trailed them. Lieutenant Kabler knew they were in for more trouble. "Charlie" up there was waiting for friends.

At 3:20 in the afternoon they arrived—three more flying boats—and they made their passes. All missed.

Ten minutes passed, three more Kawanishis came up on the starboard beam, dropped their bombs and missed—but this time *Heron*'s gunners hit one of the flying boats. It began to smoke, faltered, turned away, and then seemed to get the fire under control. It then retired from the scene so that *Heron*'s men never could tell what actually happened to it.

Two of the Kawanishis attacked again, and missed. Then along came five twin-engined level bombers of the kind the sailors would soon be calling Bettys. They made a medium-level attack without scoring any hits, circled and came back again fifteen minutes later. This time one bomb hit the *Heron*'s mainmast and smashed it, while three hit the water fifteen yards off the port bow, knocking out the port 3-inch gun and injuring some men. Fire broke out in the forward storeroom and the executive officer went below to supervise damage control.

By this time it was 4:45 in the afternoon—*Heron* had been under attack and surveillance since 9:30 in the morning. Her men were very nearly exhausted, but they fought on. Another Kawanishi appeared, and another, and a third—these each launched torpedoes in an anvil attack, one plane coming in toward each side of the bow, and one on the port quarter. Captain Kabler maneuvered like a snake and evaded all three fish as they came boring in. The gunners kept their guns hot, trained on the enemy, and they hit one of the flying boats hard enough so that it had to make a forced landing off the port bow. The other two planes launched a strafing attack to protect their friend, but they were driven off by the .50-calibre machine guns.

Lieutenant Kabler ordered the 3-inch gun turned on the Kawanishi, and after a few rounds Kawanishi 0-35, squadron unknown, blew apart and sank. Eight survivors splashed about in the water, but when the *Heron* steamed slowly past them to throw out lines, the Japanese refused to take them.

That was the end of those Japanese, for Kabler could not wait and would not risk the lives of his men by sending them out in a boat. So the ship steamed away, and the Kawanishis flew off northward, their castaway comrades keeping the code of Bushido, placing honor above death.

Lieutenant Kabler then began sorting out the day's work. The ship was on her base course, heading for safety—he hoped. There was fire in the forward storeroom which burned until seven o'clock that night, when he ordered the room flooded. The Japanese bombs had punched twenty-five different-sized holes in the *Heron*'s skin, ranging from one to ten inches in diameter. The emergency radio generator was out—that could be tough if they got into real trouble. The aircraft boom was wrecked, and all three of the ship's boats were holed by fragments.

That damage did not sound too severe. But the real test of the fight they had been in came in the head count. Coxswain Michael Borodenko had been hit by the bomb that smashed the mainmast—he was killed instantly. Chief Quartermaster Dennis Allmond had been wounded in the shoulder and back—he died late that night.

Another twenty-five men, or nearly 50 percent of the ship's complement, had been wounded more or less seriously in the all-day battle. But on balance, *Heron*, which completed her voyage safely, had won— one of the first American naval victories of the war.

There were certainly few enough of these. By the end of the month *all* allied air power had been lost or evacuated from the Philippines, and the Japanese control of the skies made everything else in the islands a last-ditch defense operation.

General MacArthur was holding on stubbornly, ready to use his U.S. Army forces and the Philippine army and constabulary, as well as marines and sailors, to fight for every foot of ground on Bataan Peninsula. But anyone with an outside view could see that all he was doing was playing for time—and giving the lie to the notion that Westerners were indeed an effete people, incapable of sacrifice and death in the manner of the Japanese.

Until now, the tasks of the Americans in the Philippines had been largely to recover from surprise, to round up the usable resources, to fight and fall back, and make ready to bring as unified a group as possible to the Bataan Peninsula. All this had been done. General MacArthur was ready to continue the fight. He was calling daily on Washington for reinforcements of men, ammunition, and planes, and he was holding firm. Perhaps more than any other man, MacArthur understood human psychology and what must be the international effect of these easy Japanese victories of the opening days of the war.

Tommy Hart, on his way to Surabaya, fretted over the delays in resuming active command of his fleet. Admiral Rockwell, in his tunnel in Corregidor, had precious little to command. His office consisted of a desk, another for his chief of staff, Captain Dessez, and one for a single yeoman who did the typing, plus a stack of canned goods on which were spread all the available charts of the combat area.

On December 26 Admiral Rockwell and his chief of staff buttoned up their jackets and paid an official call on General MacArthur up in Topside Barracks on Corregidor; that took care of army-navy social formalities. Then it was back down into Queen Tunnel to work. That day Captain Dessez was ordered to move everything on Bataan to Mariveles, at the foot of the peninsula, and Corregidor. Next day all vessels were ordered inshore to the lee of Monkey Point, on the southeast shore of Corregidor. Farther away they could not be protected at all from Japanese air attack. All but one company of marines was brought to Corregidor that day as well, as the consolidation began.

On December 28 the American designation of Manila as an open city was finally announced, placing the city under international law and beyond the scope of enemy attack. But this did not seem to interest the Japanese, who continued to bomb and shell the city anyhow. Submarine tender *Canopus*, despite her camouflage, was hit in an air raid and eight men were killed.

Next day, Corregidor received its first pasting from the air. From 11:30 in the morning until 4:00 in the afternoon, the bombers were overhead, flying lazily at 22,000 feet, and dropping bombs with the slow care that might have signified practice runs. Topside Barracks took a number of bombs that did considerable damage. Queen Tunnel was unhurt, but *Canopus* was hit again and twenty-five more men were killed.

On December 30 Mariveles was bombed and set afire. That day, Lieutenant John Bulkeley, the commander of the PT squadron, moved his boats to nearby Sisiman Cove, where high cliffs gave them some slight protection from bombers. Bulkeley was in and out of Queen Tunnel, sporting a pair of handguns, somehow managing in his naval uniform to look more like a pirate from the Caribbean than a beleaguered small-boat officer.

December 31 was the day that the army forces finally consolidated their position on Bataan. It was the beginning of the long siege, and they would go it alone. For now, at the year's end, the ships of the Asiatic Fleet were almost all gone.

Even the submarines were dispersing southward. Captain Wilkes, their commander, headed in *Swordfish* for Surabaya to set up a tactical command there alongside fleet headquarters. Commander James Fife, Jr., was ordered to Darwin to establish another submarine base, and *Seawolf* took him.

Tender *Canopus* and salvage ship *Pigeon*, the subs' own ships, were declared expendable and left at Corregidor to an uncertain fate. One by one the submarines moved southward as they ran out of torpedoes or food or fuel. *Searaven* headed out, and then *S-40* and *S-41*. On January 1, *Tarpon* ran into a storm in her patrol area so severe that she suffered real trouble in the pump room and was in danger of foundering. But the crew got her enough to rights to head south for safety and repairs, thus taking another warship out of potential action against the fast-moving enemy.

Meanwhile things were looking up a bit for Admiral Glassford in the air war. After the disastrous attempt to reinforce the fighter potential of Java with the green American air corps men from Townsville, Glassford did manage to persuade the Dutch to turn over a few PBYs for which they had no pilots, and thus augmented the force of Captain Wagner's Patrol Wing 10. Even better news followed. Coming down from China, air corps Lieutenant General G.H. Brett stopped off in Surabaya, and in the course of talks with Glassford promised to try to do something about the plane situation. He went on to Australia and produced quick results, for almost immediately the Surabaya command was reinforced by a whole squadron of B-17s under Lieutenant Colonel Eugene L. Eubank.

Eubank moved in quickly, under abominable supply and maintenance conditions, and was soon flying almost daily strikes against Japanese targets that grew closer and closer. For parts he cannibalized damaged bombers—there were no other supplies. His pilots grew crafty and successful. And luckily, because of the tremendous fire power of the Flying Fortress, they were effective: even the Japanese Zeros quickly learned to leave the dangerous big bombers alone.

There was a good deal of confusion and time lag in the last days of December as Admiral Glassford set up operational headquarters at Surabaya. Besides keeping Task Force 5, his striking force, in top readiness for action, Glassford had to maintain relations in Batavia with Admiral Helfrich, the Dutch commander, as well as with the governor general of the Dutch East Indies. Glassford solved that problem by sending Chief of Staff Admiral Purnell to do the diplomatic work while he stayed with the striking force.

During this period, the Japanese were moving with considerable strength to secure fuel oil supplies. They sent invasion forces against the British protectorate of Sarawak, in northwestern Borneo, landing there in the third week of December at Miri, south of Brunei Bay. The British and Dutch troops soon retired to the capital and seaport of Kuching, and the Japanese launched an assault on the city by land and sea.

But the Japanese way was not as easy as their successes indicated. On December 26, the day they took Kuching and raised the Rising Sun flag above the city, the Japanese lost the destroyer *Sagiri* to a Dutch submarine. Minesweeper No. 6 went down. And up in Takao, Formosa, the destroyer *Murasame* collided with the minesweeper No. 20.

Next day the ship *Nojima* went aground. Two days later the submarine RO 60 hit a submerged reef. One trouble was the coral reefs, for even if the Japanese had the best charts in the world, those coral reefs were still a problem. They could grow upward at the rate of six inches a year, and if a chart was ten years old, the difference between listed and true depth might be two fathoms.

These were not serious capital losses, but the Japanese certainly knew they were in a war. If in Tokyo the admirals plotting the movement of their ships and troops around the board were pleasantly surprised at the ease with which they won their victories, still to the men of the ships and the soldiers slogging through the bush there was ever-present danger and death. They were winning victories, but Japanese soldiers and sailors were dying, too.

The speed and ease of the Japanese victory had no better attestation than the manner in which Admiral Thomas Hart, commander of the U.S. Asiatic Fleet, arrived in Surabaya Harbor on the drizzly afternoon of January 1, 1942. Never before had a four-star admiral come to a new post in a submarine. Tommy Hart had been reduced to this ridiculous transportation by the course of events and Japanese air power. He was, in fact, lucky even to have a submarine to travel in, the way the war was going in the Philippines. But now he was here, tired, irritable, and annoyed at the world in general and Admiral Glassford in particular.

Phase One of the defense of the Malay Barrier had ended.

25

An Order to Destroyers: ATTACK!

If a table of organization could win a war, then the command that the Western Allies set up at Lembang in the pleasant hills of West Java in January 1942 could certainly not be beaten by the Japanese. The European powers' chief representative was a field marshal, and the other officers included an air chief marshal, a full general, a full admiral, and two lieutenant generals. To face all these brass hats, the Japanese had only a couple of mere vice-admirals. The difference lay in what the two commands had to work with.

Field Marshal Sir Archibald Wavell was supreme commander of the American-British-Dutch-Australian (ABDA) forces which were trying to stop the Japanese at the Malay Barrier, thus preventing the occupation of Australia and New Zealand and the total collapse of Western power in the Indies and Malaya. The chief of staff was a British general, the chief of air was a British air marshal, and Admiral Hart was chief of the sea forces.

As for the Japanese, Vice-Admiral Nobutake Kondo was in charge as commander of the Second Fleet, which had overall supervision of the Southwest Pacific Operations in 1941 and the beginning of 1942. Vice-Admiral Takahashi commanded the Third Fleet, which included the Philippines area, and Vice-Admiral Ozawa led the Southern Expeditionary Force, which was penetrating Malaya and the East Indies.

But a comparison of the ships available to each side showed where the power lay:

The Westerners had 2 cruisers, 5 light cruisers, and 22 destroyers at their disposal, plus a handful of PBYs, various support ships such as tenders and oilers, and some 40 submarines.

The Japanese had 2 battleships, 7 carriers, 13 cruisers, 6 light cruisers, more than 50 destroyers, and dozens of submarines, plus scores of support craft and hundreds of fighter planes and bombers based on Formosa and other more forward fields. Besides this, the invading armies had their own planes, which might occasionally attack Allied vessels.

So from the beginning, all that could be expected from the Western naval forces was a holding action: to serve while the powers at home got their wits about them, examined their resources, and decided what their priorities must be. All the while the men in the field fought the Japanese, destroyed the resources they could not protect, and retreated with as much cost to the enemy as they could exact.

The overlapping of gold braid did not help much from the beginning. Admiral Glassford had been sent south to establish Task Force 5 with the understanding that Admiral Hart was going to stay put in Manila for a good long time. Suddenly, less than a month later, the two were face to face again. There were just too many admirals for the work to be done efficiently.

When Hart had sent Glassford south, he also sent some of his staff to keep an eye on things. At the time it seemed a fine idea: Hart trusted Admiral Purnell implicitly, so Purnell was assigned as Glassford's chief of staff. Being a fine, easygoing officer, Admiral Purnell managed to get on well with Glassford. Suddenly, with the return of Hart to command on the scene, Purnell went back to being Hart's chief of staff and became Glassford's boss. The muddle did nothing to improve relations in the naval service, or the calibre of the decisions being made.

It was the same in the international field. Admiral Hart was chief of all the naval forces in the Asian sphere. Vice-Admiral Helfrich, the Dutch commander, was not even on the ABDA command staff—and here they were, all these other Western chiefs, sitting on the verandas of the big houses in Java, Helfrich's own backyard, sipping Geneva gin and telling him what to do. It did not go down well with the Dutch ego. So more trouble brewed.

Furthermore, the American naval effort was now being fouled up by Washington. Sitting at his desk in Main Navy, Admiral King considered Port Darwin to be the most suitable place of all to maintain the American Asiatic Fleet service base. But the trouble was that transportation facilities to Darwin were dreadful, the town itself was half frontier post, and the port was so deep that a bombing attack on a moored vessel could cause it to sink almost below the retrievable level. Furthermore, the port facilities were slight and the tides were very strong.

One thing Glassford and Hart found themselves immediately able to agree upon was the pigheadedness of the decision to put service headquarters at Darwin, so far away from operations. But there it was, and a good share of the Asiatic Fleet was either in Darwin, operating from there or on the way there, when Tommy Hart arrived at Surabaya.

From the first day, Admiral Hart's stay in the Dutch East Indies was unhappy. The weather was foul, and he found the quarters inadequate and the radio service totally incapable of meeting his needs. To cap it all, when the time came for him to travel to Batavia to pay his duty calls on the Dutch, there was no air service of any kind, and he had to take the train. On his arrival in Batavia on January 4, Hart was thrust knee-deep into the international political tar pit when Field Marshal Wavell's supercommand was created by the powers.

The first thing to do, from Hart's point of view, was to get Admiral Glassford as far from the scene as he could, and this he managed by reorganizing Task Force 5 and making *Boise* Glassford's flagship. With the striking force at sea, that meant Purnell would be in charge in Surabaya, while Hart was coping with international policy at Lembang. Two days later Hart ordered Captain Wilkes, the fleet's submarine commander, who had just arrived in *Swordfish*, to begin his submarine operations forthwith.

A lot of demands were floating through the air that week. On the day that Wilkes arrived from Corregidor, Admiral Rockwell learned that Admiral Hart had gotten to Surabaya and informed General MacArthur, whereupon MacArthur stepped up his demands on Washington for help, ammunition, and reinforcement.

Thus the first week of January ended with very little progress, except that Glassford was afloat in *Boise* and getting ready for action, Wilkes was issuing orders to his submarines, Captain Wagner's Patrol Wing 10 was out every day snooping the skies, and the service force at Darwin was trying to put together a repair and supply station.

But all the elements of a major naval clash were building up in the area of Makassar Strait, between Borneo and Celebes Island. When *Peary* had run that gamut of British planes on her way south on December 28, one reason she had been attacked was the British nervousness about what was happening at Menado on Celebes Island. The Japanese had just staged a hit-and-run attack, and the British believed an invasion would follow immediately. They were right except for the timing: The invasion of the Menado Peninsula came by paratroops on January 11, and that same day a Japanese naval and amphibious force took Tarakan Island, off the east coast of Borneo.

This pair of invasions gave the Japanese control of the northern approaches to Makassar Strait. That was perfect for their purposes, for what they wanted was the oil-field region around Balikpapan, three hundred miles farther south.

At this time, Admiral Hart's main plan was to stop the Japanese before they could eliminate the bases the United States would need for the reconquest of the Philippines. On January 13, most of the submarines operating northward were pulled back. Tommy Hart was not at all happy with the results of the submarine operations. *Swordfish,* the most successful of the American undersea craft, had sunk three transports and a tender in the past month and damaged another ship, but she was almost alone in her success. S-38 had sunk two ships, and five other submarines had claimed one. It was not much of a record, with all the Japanese shipping moving about the China Sea and the Pacific. On top of that, S-36, one of the handful of submarines that had managed to sink at least one enemy vessel in the past month, ran aground at the south end of Makassar Strait and had to be abandoned.

On January 15, Admiral Hart learned of a concentration of Japanese shipping at Kema, in the northern Celebes, and he decided that he would make an attempt to destroy it. He assigned Glassford the task, stipulating that *Marblehead* be brought up for it, with four destroyers, and that *Boise* would cover the other ships.

The American ships assembled, but on January 17 came the word: The Japanese ships had already left Kema and gone on. So Admiral Glassford headed for Kupang on southwest Timor Island, where he would refuel at the oil depot there.

On January 19, the submarine force became aware of a stirring in Makassar Strait area—an obvious presage to action. There were various signs—too many Japanese Kawanishis prowling about, too many patrol craft going here and there, and too many reports of too many ships sighted in too many places. It meant something was about to happen. The question was: Where?

Half a dozen of Captain Wilkes's Surabaya submarine force were out on the prowl, and they kept reporting back sightings. They were right: Admiral Takahashi had expected to be a month or more in the conquest of the northern approaches to the Makassar Strait, but they had fallen like pins before a master bowler. He had therefore advanced to the next step in the Japanese southern operation—the conquest of Balikpapan. Control there would not only give the Japanese the oil fields and domination of the strait, but also a good jumping off place for an assault on Surabaya.

On January 19, submarine *Pickerel* spotted a Japanese destroyer "going somewhere," steaming down the middle of Makassar Strait with a bone in her teeth. That raised suspicion: Where was she going, and why?

No one ever answered that question satisfactorily, but the Americans and the Dutch had the wind up. Captain Wagner's planes were out every day, looking for evidence of enemy movement. Captain Wilkes's submarines continued searching, day and night.

The Dutch did not help a great deal by throwing out a handful of rumors and false reports. On January 20 they insisted they saw a convoy en route to Balikpapan. The instinct was right but the timing was off: The convoy did indeed sail the next day, in two sections, out of Tarakan for Balikpapan.

On the night of January 22, *Porpoise* and *Pickerel* found the Japanese convoy, but could not get off any shots. *Sturgeon* did better: Lieutenant Commander W.L. Wright fired four torpedoes at one target and claimed two hits on a carrier or a light cruiser. He never got any better look than that quick one through the periscope, because after the firing the Japanese antisubmarine patrol was on him. He was depthcharged, chased, and had to stay down until the convoy was long gone. But Wright survived and was pleased to be able to surface and send a report: "*Sturgeon* no longer virgin," it began, playing on a popular ditty of the 1930s.

Admiral Glassford, anchored with *Boise*, *Marblehead*, and the four destroyers at Koepang, was not so lucky.

Marblehead should actually have been in a repair yard, for one turbine was out and she was cut down to about half speed. On hearing that the Japanese assault force was on the move, Glassford moved out to attack, and *Boise* promptly ran aground on an uncharted rock in Sape Strait, northwest of Koepang. The Americans were feeling the absence of reliable charts; the grounding was no one's fault—just plain bad luck.

Now both cruisers were out of action. Admiral Hart was furious if for no other reason than that Glassford, in his view, was in the wrong place, too far away from the potential scenes of action to do any good. The implication was clear that Glassford had made a bad decision in going to Koepang in the first place.

Admiral Glassford transferred his flag to *Marblehead* and sent *Boise* back to Surabaya for repairs.

Tommy Hart was dismayed, but not discouraged. He ordered the attack operation to proceed without either cruiser. So Admiral Glassford moved *Marblehead* toward a point south of Balikpapan where he could at least cover the withdrawal of the four destroyers.

Commander Paul Talbot of Destroyer Division 59 would lead the assault. Talbot, in destroyer *John D. Ford,* was very much aware of one salient fact: This was the first chance Asiatic Fleet had to make up for the punishment the Japanese had been dealing out since December 8. So the four old four-piper destroyers—*Ford, Pope, Parrott,* and *Paul Jones*—poured on the coal and headed toward Makassar Strait, passing through Sape Strait and then by the Postillon Islands en route to Balikpapan.

Up to this point, the Americans had been treading water. Tommy Hart was having trouble up in Lembang keeping the British from withdrawing their naval forces to protect Colombo, in Ceylon, and the Indian Ocean. He was also assembling his old staff and making ready to dig in in Java and defend the Malay Barrier. Captain Felix Stump, for example, had been relieved of command of the carrier *Langley* and brought to headquarters as an air intelligence officer.

Hart was chopping at red tape, listening to MacArthur's insistent demands back at Corregidor for the use of warships as supply vessels, and still trying to fight. Here, he sensed, was his first opportunity to strike a real blow at the enemy, and although deprived of his cruisers this time, he was not going to lose it.

From headquarters to Commander Talbot of Destroyer Division 59 went out the simple, specific order: ATTACK!

26

The Battle of Balikpapan

Riding in *John D. Ford*, Commander Talbot surveyed the force he had at his disposal this day, when he was ordered in to Balikpapan to break up the Japanese landing. The command destroyer and her three companions—*Pope, Parrott,* and *Paul Jones*—were all old coal-burners that should have been retired and replaced by diesel-burning destroyers years before. But they were all he had. And on the afternoon of January 23, with *Ford* in the lead and the others following in column, they steamed through the sunlight, heading up along the coast of Celebes Island at more than 20 knots.

Officers checked their guns and torpedoes. The torpedoes were given more than usual care, particularly after Commander Talbot issued his orders to the force that afternoon:

Initial weapons will be torpedoes. Transports chief objective. Cruisers as required to accomplish mission. Launch torpedoes at close range if unsighted by enemy. Attack independently. If necessary when all torpedoes fired, close with all guns. Use initiative and determination.

If ever there was a call for heroism, it came here. The commander promised them he would try to avoid action en route with any lesser or protective force, for the object of the attack was to battle the enemy ship concentration at Balikpapan and thus put a crimp in Japanese expansion through the East Indian islands. It would be romantic for destroyer to engage destroyer, or to take on a heavy cruiser, but it would also be foolhardy. If Talbot wanted his men to be heroes, he wanted them also to be useful heroes, and he was determined to lead them in among the transports and hit the enemy hard.

Steaming up along the coast of Celebes, Talbot hoped to convince those snooping Kawanishis that he was on some mission unconnected with the landings. Luckily, no Kawanishi appeared; the only plane they saw was a PBY from Captain Wagner's Patrol Wing 10.

It was quiet on the sea. The men heard the swish of the water, the clink of the coal shovels, the hum of the engines, and the clicking and snapping sounds on deck as the crew moved ammunition and worked with the weapons.

That evening, as the destroyer column moved along, the radio room reported that Dutch PBYs had attacked ships in Balikpapan and destroyed several of them. Patrol Wing 10 reported much shipping headed in that direction. So Commander Talbot was going to have a target and some light to shoot by, for Balikpapan was aflame with fires set by the Dutch, who had burned their refineries and oil-storage facilities to deny them to the Japanese.

After sunset, the destroyers approached Cape Mandar on Celebes, the point at which the island thickens, and turned to port, which meant toward Balikpapan. Orders were issued to the four ships for a night torpedo attack; speed was changed to 26 knots and the course was 336 degrees, heading straight for Balikpapan lightship. Shortly after eight o'clock that night the speed was upped to 27 knots, just about all they could manage. That speed was to be maintained all through the fight.

Four hours passed. A spotter saw a light dead ahead, stabbing up into the sky. But it disappeared. Another spotter saw orange fires on the water, again dead ahead. And these fires persisted, so that Commander Talbot began studying them through his glasses. Figuring course and speed, Talbot deduced that they were some twenty miles distant; they must be the ships the Dutch had set aflame that day. His calculations became conviction as the fires flared and died and flared again, particularly one of them, which appeared to be a burning tanker.

At two o'clock in the morning the column was at last coming within range. The tension was almost unbearable. Men checked and rechecked weapons that had been worked over to perfection hours earlier. They stood at their battle stations, showing nervousness in their own ways, as Commander Talbot led them in on an oblique approach to the outer line of Japanese transports anchored neatly in a row about five miles outside the harbor.

Then, out of the blackness, came blue signal lights flashing—and a Japanese cruiser loomed ahead. Commander Talbot changed course to head for this ship and moved in, maintaining that 27-knot speed that left just a little margin for emergency.

The ships passed each other swiftly, traveling at high speed in opposite directions, and there was no indication that the Japanese thought the destroyers were anything but Japanese ships. Why should they? Except for the encounter with the *Repulse* and *Prince of Wales* off British Malaga, the Japanese had not found the Westerners looking for a fight. They were used to having the seas to themselves.

The port was active that night. A division of Japanese destroyers passed by, blinking lights again, but unperturbed when the four-pipers did not answer their calls.

The torpedo tubes had long been trained outboard, and the torpedomen were at their posts. Each tube was set for normal spreads of torpedoes.

Parrott launched first, her captain unable to stand the strain, and the spread of three fish all missed. She veered to port and fired again at another target, five torpedoes this time. Again all of them missed or misfired. *Ford* fired one, and then so did *Paul Jones*, but the vessel they were after, which turned out to be a minesweeper, was under way and managed to avoid all the torpedoes.

Commander Talbot now headed south to come in for another attack. *Parrott* was traveling on a line parallel to the anchored transports, and she fired another spread of three torpedoes from the port tubes. They clinked and swished and splashed along, and then there was a tremendous explosion as the ship they hit went up in the air. She was evidently carrying high explosives. The *Sumanoura Maru* was gone with all hands.

If there had been any question about the presence of an enemy before, the Japanese now knew they were being hit. Rear Admiral Nishimura was traveling in the light cruiser *Naka*, and had with him nine destroyers, a handful of minesweepers, and a subchaser. He led them out into the strait—in precisely the wrong direction—looking for submarines, which was exactly what Commander Talbot would have asked him to do. With the Japanese defenders out of the way, the American destroyers were in the position of foxes in the henhouse—with the farmer gone away.

Admiral Nishimura, later destined to go down to disaster and death in the Battle of Leyte Gulf, has not been treated well by naval historians. Small wonder, for his charge into the open water seemed aimless, except that there was a Dutch submarine in the area. Three hours before the Americans arrived on the scene, the submarine *K-14* sank the transport *Jukka Maru*, and might have stayed to sink more enemy ships that night. But with the coming of the American destroyers it would have been hard to tell friend from foe, so K-14 withdrew, and Admiral Nishimura, knowing of her attack and seeing ships going up from torpedoes, jumped to the wrong conclusion and sped off after a submarine contact.

Destroyer *Pope* now rushed in, and Lieutenant Commander W.C. Blinn ordered the firing of a spread of five torpedoes. Off they went. The other three destroyers also fired, and at least one torpedo struck *Tatsukami Maru*, which blew up and sank.

The division was running out of torpedoes at this point, but there were a few left. Talbot ordered a turn of 90 degrees and headed back toward the ships at anchor, and, spotting what he thought was a destroyer, led the column to attack. *Pope* and *Parrott* between them fired five torpedoes at the vessel. She was, in fact, a 750-ton torpedo boat, converted to a patrol craft and hardly worth so much explosive. Three of these torpedoes hit and literally blew her out of the water.

By this time the harbor was full of activity and light from burning ships and searchlights from living ones. The Japanese transports were getting their anchors up and beginning to move. *Ford* and *Paul Jones* fired more torpedoes, and the transport at which they aimed, off to port of the column, was able to maneuver and get away, but as she turned *Paul Jones* fired again, and hit this ship in the starboard bow. She was also evidently a munitions ship, for that one torpedo blew her up, and she sank. She was later identified as *Kuretake Maru*.

In the darkness and the confusion, the column of destroyers came apart. *Ford* led and turned northwest, toward the inner line of ships. *Pope* followed and then lost the leader as the lights and the movement in the harbor distracted her. *Parrott* was out of torpedoes and retired, and *Paul Jones* followed her south and out of the action.

Pope was out of torpedoes but not out of shells. She began firing tracers, and then *Ford* opened up on a merchantman with her 4-inch gun. The Japanese were now firing back, and one small shell hit the port side of *Ford*'s torpedo workshop two feet above the deck. It exploded and wounded four men.

Another fragment hit a gasoline tank and started a fire on deck. The men began dumping drums of gasoline and kerosene over the side. Meanwhile *Ford*'s guns punished the Japanese ship that was firing at them, and in a few moments the enemy battery was put out of action.

Commander Talbot had one more torpedo, and he intended to use it wisely. He turned in toward the shore, where the lights from the burning oil fires lit up another big transport off to port. He gave the order to fire, and the gunnery officer fired the last fish. It ran hot and true and exploded against the transport, which began to list. Then *Ford* was speeding away, and no one saw the transport later. Somehow she managed to survive, damaged though she was.

Now, with no more torpedoes, *Ford* headed out and south to join *Marblehead* at the rendezvous point. As dawn came up, so did the other three destroyers, all of them safe and relatively sound, their crews immensely pleased with themselves for having run through the Japanese safely and for having inflicted a tremendous amount of damage.

They had sunk three transports out of the twelve anchored at Balikpapan, as well as a patrol craft, and had battered several other ships. Perhaps this was not a great deal to boast about from an attack that lasted more than an hour and in which they had had little opposition. But Commander Talbot offered no excuses. The 27-knot speed might have made it more difficult to aim torpedoes accurately but, in his opinion, it was what saved them from effective counterattack. The confusion and visibility problems of a night attack added to the difficulties.

There was also the usual nagging doubts about the efficiency of the torpedoes. Asiatic Fleet still did not know what was wrong with its torpedoes, but the fact was that the warheads sometimes did not go off at all, and that the torpedoes often functioned erratically and missed their targets.

It was a victory nevertheless, and the Americans were pleased to have fought successfully in their first surface action of the war. Their cachet with the Dutch was much improved. Even Tommy Hart was happy, although he was upset because so many torpedoes—so hard to replace—had been expended.

The men of the fleet were immensely heartened. Aboard cruiser *Houston*, on escort duty between Darwin and Singapore, the crew heard of the affair and cheered and cheered again. In the Indies, in Australia, and at home the story of victory did much to overcome the dreadful feeling of despair that was almost endemic in these first few weeks of war.

No matter what else those four destroyers had done, they had given American morale a very badly needed shot in the arm.

27

The Hopeless Garrison

Like a giant amoeba, the Japanese Empire was eating up its neighbors in the winter and spring of 1941-42. Hong Kong fell on Christmas Day. By the end of January, Malaya was almost entirely under Japanese control. Indochina and Thailand had accepted Japanese conditions of survival; the Dutch East Indies were threatened with invasion. And in the Philippines, the Americans and the Philippine army were making their last desperate stand on the Bataan Peninsula.

Slowly but steadily the American and Philippine forces were being compressed along the peninsula as the Japanese brought in more planes and more soldiers to do the job. Major General Jonathan Wainwright was in charge of the left flank, which would last the longest, for the right flank was taking the pressure as the enemy pushed relentlessly toward Corregidor.

After Admiral Hart moved out on December 26, so did all the fighting ships that could be used in defense of the Malay Barrier. This left in the Philippines a handful of small craft and decrepit larger vessels that, in the staff's opinion, could not make the trip south.

With the small forces available to him, Admiral Rockwell did his best to coordinate his naval activities with those of the army forces. It was not easy, for the coldness between Admiral Hart and General MacArthur had spilled over to the staff. Consequently, although MacArthur and Rockwell were on Corregidor, the admiral was seldom called to the daily staff conferences and so had to get his information about the changing situation as best he could.

With the evacuation of Cavite and Manila, the naval forces moved to Mariveles and Corregidor.

On Corregidor, the navy men were distributed in several tunnels. Admiral Rockwell's headquarters, Queen Tunnel, housed 50 officers and 50 men. Tunnel Afirm held 20 naval officers and 100 men. Tunnels Seven, Eight, and Nine each housed 100 men. And the estimate was that on the beach, fighting in one way or another, there were 100 officers and 1,000 men—marines and sailors, plus the Inshore Patrol of 80 officers and 1,000 men. Later the majority of the Fourth Marine Regiment would be ordered to Corregidor.

The "Rock" began taking it with the New Year. On January 2 Japanese bombers came over in their leisurely way and hit Corregidor. They returned on the third, the fourth, the fifth, and the sixth. Then there was respite. But not for Bataan, where Japanese planes were overhead daily and might come at any time to bomb and strafe. In the harbor, President Quezon's yacht, *Casiana*, was sunk.

As for the navy men on Bataan, they were ready to pitch in on the land defense. Some of them worked with the marines; some went to school to learn combat. In the earliest days of the siege both marines and navy men got busy setting up and manning antiaircraft guns. There soon emerged a colorful group of warriors, known as the Naval Battalion.

This group was organized by Commander Francis J. Bridget, of the aviation arm, from the ragtag elements left to him. Six companies were formed from several hundred supply and aviation men and marines, and each company was given a defense area.

By January 15 the naval companies were strung out across the southern area of Bataan. Lieutenant Commander Bowers, the supply man from Cavite, first camped down with his company near a small stream close to the old Pacific Naval Air Contractors Barracks. Then he went over to Talaga Bay, an inlet west of Los Cochinas Point, on the sea side of Mariveles Harbor.

This camp was a two-hour hike over the mountains to Lieutenant Hogaboom's marine company, the next battalion unit, but that inconvenience was soon put to rights by the installation of field telephone service. It was not easy—telephone wire was a really precious item of supply these days—but it was done. Gunner Hoyt, who had earlier distinguished himself by blowing up half of the Cavite Navy Yard, now again won praise by establishing a fresh-water system for the camp. He located springs, someone found some pipe, and presto—they had running water. Not only that, but in the afternoon it was hot water, after the sun had baked the pipes for a few hours. Someone else volunteered to be baker and set up an oven. Other men scrounged and traded for supplies, and for a time they had fritters and doughnuts and biscuits in addition to the basic ration of rice, coffee, and cigarettes.

But it was no happy dream world. The Japanese were all around them; they saw the evidence every day in the bombing and strafing, and they were on half rations, which meant two meals a day when their "bakery" items ran out. The men lost weight, and it took tremendous surges of enthusiasm to replace the energy they were not getting in their diet. The two-mile hike to Lieutenant Hogaboom's company across the hills seemed almost interminable. But they were surviving, and one night they even had wild boar—Torpedoman's Mate First Class T.R. Knipperberg shot the beast in the dark by mistake, thinking it was an infiltrating Japanese.

After their arrival in the area, Lieutenant Commander Bowers's men tried to set up the best defense they could. They put two .50-calibre machine guns on top of Los Cochinas Point, and a set of .30-calibre Lewis guns at the head of Apatot Bay, the next inlet. And they kept them manned. Since each place was a forty-five-minute hike from camp, the men spent a lot of time on the trail.

The slowness of the rollback of the defending forces on Bataan did not satisfy the Japanese, and around January 22 they decided to speed up matters by landing an infiltration force of several hundred soldiers at Longoskawayan Point, west of Mariveles Harbor. They made the landing unopposed and unseen at night, and the first the Americans knew about it was when the Naval Battalion lost contact with its lookouts up on Pucot Mountain. A search party went out to find the men, and discovered them at the base of the mountain, with the news that they had been attacked by Japanese earlier in the morning.

A squad of marines found the Japanese landing point. Doctrine would have had them wait below, but for some reason they decided to go up the mountain after the enemy. They shot two Japanese, but one marine was killed in the brief action.

The Americans fell back to report at least a platoon of Japanese were in the hills above Longoskawayan Point. They called back to Corregidor to Admiral Rockwell to get the marines to lay down a barrage of heavy mortar fire, and this was done. A marine unit with a pair of smaller mortars was sent out to join the troops at Longoskawayan.

Then came several days of jungle fighting, the Americans attacking, being ambushed, and ambushing. Soon they realized the enemy force was much larger than anyone had realized—it was estimated at three hundred troops. The navy men were simply not equipped by training or organization to dislodge them. So the Fifty-seventh Regiment of Filipino Scouts was called in—little men dressed in khaki all splotched with green and yellow, and wearing bushes in their helmet.

It took a week to move the Japanese out of the hills. Then they retreated into caves on the cliffs of the bay and had to be routed out by dynamite, sea attack, and starvation. The sea attacks were conducted by the three motor launches of the submarine tender *Canopus*, which were armored with boiler plate and sent in to spray the caves with machine-gun fire. The first threat of the enemy landing had been cut down, and the road that led from General Wainwright's corps headquarters had been protected.

Offensively, the sea war was being carried on actively by Lieutenant John D. Bulkeley and his squadron of PT boats. Night after night in those early days of January they were out looking for game, but without much luck.

Then one night, as the marines and navy men battled in the Bataan mountains, Bulkeley encountered a ship west of Sampaloc Point—a 4,000-ton transport that was lying-to. Bulkeley took *PT-41* in to a point eight hundred yards off the vessel, turned, fired the after torpedo, and watched it run "straight hot and normal" and explode against the side of the ship.

PT-41 sped off, very nearly smashing another PT boat as she went, and enemy ship and shore batteries began to open up on her. That night *PT-41* was very nearly wrecked on an antisubmarine net as she returned to base, but she got away, and Bulkeley swaggered over to Corregidor to report his success to Admiral Rockwell.

On another occasion at Corregidor, Bulkeley talked to Lieutenant Champlin, Admiral Rockwell's aide, and they got into a discussion of the good that could accrue from having someone ashore spotting targets for the PT boats and then relaying the information to them. This meant navy signalmen and a watcher's post high on the cliffs overlooking the bay. Soon Champlin had an opportunity to put the plan into effect. For at about this time, in the last days of January, the lack of liaison between the military branches was worrying various commanders. Admiral Rockwell was fretting over the Longoskawayan incident and the lack of coordination it revealed between army and navy men. So was General Wainwright on Bataan.

Every day Lieutenant Commander Mike Cheek, district intelligence officer on Corregidor, made the tortuous sea-and-land journey to Bataan and its defenders. It was his task to keep the admiral informed of the activities of those navy men. Since MacArthur did not give them information, Rockwell sent Cheek after it. But it was a grueling and exhausting job that could not be kept up forever.

One day near the end of January, an army colonel appeared in Queen Tunnel and asked Admiral Rockwell if he could send a liaison officer to join the Wainwright staff for a while. Rockwell thought about it, turned a speculative eye on Captain Ray, his second-in-command, and on Lieutenant Champlin.

"Champ," said the Admiral to his aide, "do you think you could handle that job?"

Champlin had been itching to get into action ever since the day he left Manila after arranging for the destruction of the Philippines oil supply dumps—his eyes sparkled.

"Look at that gleam in his eye, Captain," said Rockwell, turning to Captain Ray. And so Champlin was dispatched to the dusty hills of Bataan.

Somewhere he found a musette bag. He traded his bulky .45 auto-

matic, which tended to jam, for a .38-calibre revolver, which did not. He found a Springfield rifle and persuaded an enlisted man to clean it up for him in a hurry as he scurried about getting ready. He got a map of Bataan from the pile on the cases of tomatoes. He found a navy signalman who wanted to go with him, and he rummaged through the tunnels until he came upon a book of Japanese ship identification pictures. That he sent to Bulkeley.

That old veteran of the Bataan trip, Mike Cheek, led Champlin and the signalman on their voyage. They slept that night until sometime before dawn. They had to be up and out then, for while the seas around Corregidor belonged to the American Inshore Patrol at night, they belonged to the Japanese air force after dawn, and any craft, large or small, caught in the open in daylight hours was almost certain to be bombed and strafed.

By 4:45 their small boat was making its way through the minefields toward the sea side of Mariveles Bay. They pulled in near the old Philippines Quarantine Building. A battered staff car met them there, and they started up the rocky road to Wainwright's headquarters, four miles away. As they went along they saw parties of soldiers and Filipino workmen dumping rock along the road—a precaution against the rainy season, when the roads would turn to mud unless reinforced by rock.

About halfway along, the driver seemed to become suddenly alert, and then Champlin heard the noise of airplane engines. The car stopped and ran off the road; the planes passed over and bombed the bridge they were approaching. This time the planes missed.

The men went on. Farther along the road they were stopped by a Filipino soldier who wanted to know who they were and where they were going. The information that they were going to General Wainwright brought directions to the headquarters, which they found three hundred yards off the road. It consisted of a handful of tents surrounding some split bamboo tables—and there was Wainwright.

Champlin first delivered a bottle of Scotch from Admiral Rockwell.

Wainwright took the bottle and held it to the light reverently. "This is the best Scotch liquor there is. And I haven't had a drink in three months," he announced, putting it away.

Then Champlin began to settle into life with the army.

Every day Wainwright went to the front line, and while others jumped into foxholes when they heard the sharp bark of the Japanese .25-calibre rifles, Wainwright sat and exposed himself, showing the men by example that courage was the watchword of Bataan.

The men were short on ammunition, on food, on every supply.

Wainwright had nothing to give them but courage, and that he gave hour after hour. He only complained once. That was on the night he recognized the sound of a high-powered Japanese rifle barking near his trailer—he got up to complain to his aides.

"Goddammit," he said. "I don't mind being shot at all day long, but if I am going to get up to the front tomorrow, I've got to get some sleep."

Whereupon the aides went out and captured the "enemy"—a Filipino rifleman who had been out hunting monkeys to augment his slender diet, and had used a captured Japanese rifle so he would not waste government issue ammunition. He offered to share the monkey he had bagged with the aides, but they sent him away and the general went back to sleep.

One of Lieutenant Champlin's first jobs was to establish a lookout post high on the cliffs above Manila Bay where the signalman could send his information down to Bulkeley and the PT boats. This was done. Thereafter there was direct contact between the spotters and the PT squadron.

Another of Champlin's duties was to discover what was happening with the various naval units still on Bataan. He found Commander Sackett's men of *Canopus* pouring foundations for gun mounts and using guns no one thought could be employed. He visited Nurse Anne Bernatitus and navy doctors Smith and Nelson, and got the word back to Rockwell that they were performing gloriously. After Longoskawayan, the placement of guns went on apace, and another half-dozen old 3-inch navy guns were found and mounted and manned by gunners' mates dredged from the command.

One day Lieutenant Champlin went down to Commander Bridget's headquarters and found the leader of the ground troops of the navy in his cot, hollow-eyed and shaking. He was suffering from a bout of malaria and was nearly out of quinine, for the medical people had so little it had to be rationed. He was down to his last ten pills and was taking only a few a day—not enough to knock out the bugs. So Champlin shared his bottle of fifty quinine pills with Bridget and went away hoping the commander would shake the fever.

There were more Japanese landing attempts. One night they came in with a cruiser to Moron Bay, on Bataan's southwest coast, and brought twenty-four landing barges. The last three P-40 planes in the Philippines were called up that night to fly and they strafed nearby Quinauan Point for an hour, knocking out barges and shooting at men struggling in the water. Bulkeley arrived with his PT boats and began sinking barges. The Japanese had a force of about eight hundred men. Some got ashore with food and ammunition and made their way into caves again.

Once more it was a question of routing them out, for the Japanese, like those Kawanishi flying-boat men out in the sea, were not inclined to surrender. Once in a while a patrol took a prisoner. Usually he was wounded or suffering from shock, for the typical Japanese trick was to pretend surrender or to play dead and then blow up the Americans who approached them with a self-destructing hand grenade.

As the American perimeter on Bataan shrank, so did the need for the navy men. At the end of January most of Bridget's naval aviators were called out and sent back to Corregidor for shipment south, where trained aviators were badly needed. No sense in letting them die in the trenches or on the beaches of Bataan.

Submarines were the usual means of transport. At the end of January *Seawolf* arrived with thirty-seven tons of antiaircraft ammunition for General MacArthur's men, and took out with her sixteen torpedoes and twenty-five army air corps men and navy pilots.

On the night of February 3, *Trout* arrived from Pearl Harbor, bringing the first material support the Pacific Fleet had been able to send. The cargo consisted chiefly of 3-inch antiaircraft ammunition, which was unloaded that night. *Trout* then submerged and lay on the bottom during the daylight hours, returning that night after dark.

In the interim, Philippine officials and the Americans had conferred and decided to send out the government's gold and silver treasure for safekeeping. It was loaded aboard *Trout*, and there was so much of it that she could only take on three torpedoes and a supply of fuel. As she left, *Seadragon* arrived with more supplies. *Seadragon* picked up twenty-three torpedoes and twenty-two passengers, mostly radiomen, and then departed.

Bit by bit, the specialists of the fleet were being brought out of Corregidor to fight again.

28

The Waiting Game

If the Battle of Balikpapan was a welcome victory, it did nothing to improve relations between Admirals Hart and Glassford. Admiral Glassford was particularly incensed at Hart's disregard of his command function in giving Commander Talbot direct orders to attack the Japanese—almost as if Glassford would not have had the courage or the sense to do it.

Glassford wrote in his diary that affairs had gotten to the point where either he or Admiral Hart had to leave the Indies because of the conflicts between them. Admiral Purnell, placed in the impossible position of middleman, managed to placate them both, but he could do nothing to stop the spread of dislike and difficulty.

As for the attack at Balikpapan, the fact was that Glassford had carried on a long conversation with Talbot about the tactics to be employed and had convinced the destroyer commander to follow a pattern Glassford had learned from an incident in World War I. In this action, a British skipper named Evans had taken destroyers into enemy waters, and by relying solely on torpedo attack had created complete surprise and confusion among the Germans. Talbot's high-speed torpedo attack had been a version of the Evans plan, and Glassford was proud of himself for offering it and of Talbot for carrying it out. His displeasure with Admiral Hart now approximated Hart's dislike of Glassford.

Even as Glassford steamed back to Surabaya, a counterpart of this drama was being played out in Washington. Admiral King had indicated that Hart must give up his command of the Asiatic Fleet when he took over as commander of all sea forces for the American-British-Dutch-Australian (ABDA) command. Hart had simply not done so, working out his own way of organizing forces. Now Tommy Hart received a direct order to divest himself of operational fleet command—one he could not misunderstand or circumvent.

Glassford arrived at Surabaya with his little fleet on January 25, and sent the destroyers in to Holland Pier, while *Marblehead* took refuge in the Dutch naval base in the hope that she could secure the repair of her defective shaft. Glassford left his ship that day to go to navy headquarters, and then, when he learned from his staff what was in the offing in the command department, he put up at the Oranjie Hotel and that night gave a party for the staff at the Simpang Club.

Next day down from Bandoeng to Surabaya came a privately furious Admiral Hart for conferences with Glassford and Purnell and the hated task of officially turning over command of the Asiatic Fleet to Glassford.

The formalities were observed, the message was prepared, and then, like a pair of tomcats, Admirals Hart and Glassford went back to Batavia to confer with British and Dutch authorities about future operations. Next day Glassford was back again in Surabaya. For the next two days he was involved in many conferences with Admiral Purnell and others. Purnell had to change his hat again—instead of being Glassford's boss, he was now once more Glassford's second-in-command. Purnell accepted the change without a raised eyebrow; he was the most level-headed of the three American admirals in the Indies.

On January 31, Glassford received official word of his promotion from rear admiral to vice-admiral, and the word was passed about his command job. He was commander of all American naval forces in the Southwest Pacific, while Admiral Hart was commander of ABDA's naval forces—a somewhat confusing and ambiguous situation. Nevertheless, that night Vice-Admiral Glassford celebrated his new star with a bottle of champagne.

Tommy Hart had not given in an inch. "The American fleet was decidedly embarrassed at this time," he wrote later, "by having to change the command status of its most senior officers at the Navy Department's insistence." Hart still could not accept the idea that he no longer had direct command of the Asiatic Fleet, and he continued to behave as if he were in charge of operations.

All those conferences at the end of the month between Hart, Glassford, and Purnell concerned Hart's estimate that they had a good chance to hit the Japanese again in Makassar Strait, for the attack of January 24 at Balikpapan had certainly slowed the enemy down. In Batavia, meanwhile, Hart was trying to secure a commitment from the Dutch, who he believed had some warships available for another strike.

But he got nowhere with Admiral Helfrich when he asked for five fighting ships.

So on January 29, alerted by submarines and patrol planes of Japanese shipping movements, the American commanders sent *Marblehead* and the four destroyers off on another attack. But the approaching Americans were "spooked" by a Japanese patrol bomber that began shadowing them at night. The leader of the force thereupon decided that without the element of surprise the expedition was not a good risk, so the ships turned back.

One of the Americans' biggest problems at this time was the worsening condition of the Asiatic Fleet by attrition. The ships and submarines had been at sea far too long without overhaul or refit or shore leave for the men. How they operated as well as they did under the conditions was a minor miracle, a tribute to the staying power of the human spirit. For the crews were tired, if not exhausted, and some of the men were ill.

There was further bad news from the submarine force. *S-36*, which had been one of the more aggressive boats, grounded on a rock thirty miles west of the city of Makassar. The crew was taken off in a Dutch coastal steamer, but the submarine could not be saved. She had to be scratched from a force that was growing ever smaller. Then on January 22, *Seawolf* knocked out her fathometer by scraping a rock, and there was nothing that could be done to make repairs outside a navy yard. A week later a gasket in her flood-valve control system gave out, and she had to operate with her buoyancy tanks fully flooded all the time. It could be done and it was, but this was not the way a submarine should be working.

In spite of such problems Admiral Hart had to rely on the submarines as the bastion of the ABDA fighting force. The submarine tenders *Holland* and *Otus* were brought to Tuilatjap, on Java's south coast, from Darwin at the end of January, for Darwin simply was not working out as a base for operations. Yet within a week they were moved back. Sometimes it was hard to keep track of what was going on.

As for the rest of the submarines, they were reporting more activity all the time, with more enemy ships spotted and more tracked and attacked—but with very poor results. At this time Admiral Hart tended to consider most of the fleet's problems as personnel failures and the result of too much time at sea. The big submarines had been at sea an average of fifty days and the smaller S-class boats an average of forty days since the war began. It was way too much.

But that question kept Hart's mind off others. He believed the submarine arm was taking time to shake down to war conditions. So he did not give as much attention as he might have to the continual complaints about ineffective torpedo warheads and torpedoes that acted erratically. It would not have made much difference anyhow. The torpedoes the boats were using were all still coming from the Southwest Pacific area—there were no other supplies available—and the change in the torpedoes that would render them more effective was still months away.

The Asiatic Fleet was suffering from another problem—the control of the air by the Japanese. The trouble was that the PBY was always a sitting duck for a Zero. The big boat could hide in the clouds, and if there were enough clouds it had a pretty good chance to get away. But there were not always clouds. So the odds were always heavily with the Zero.

But on one notable occasion, the pattern was upset. On January 17, Ensign J.F. Davis in PBY No. 5 encountered a Zero at ten thousand feet. He was out on patrol at 00°15' South and 124° East when he was jumped. In came the Zero on the port quarter and one of the crew spotted it and let out a yelp over the intercom. Captain Davis called for the attention of all hands and began to maneuver. As the plane turned he slipped left, and the Zero then turned right to the starboard quarter, did a wingover, reversing his flight direction, and came in lazily as if this was going to be the easiest kill in the world. The starboard waist gunner began to fire. So did the Zero.

Ensign Davis was really putting his heart into that slip—the PBY was losing altitude at 200 knots. The Zero slid underneath, came up in front, and started another wingover—the pilot could fly rings around the PBY at will. Davis slipped right, and the port waist gunner now came into position. He began firing and, marvel of marvels, the Zero took fire, slid off on one wing, and went down in flames.

When Ensign Davis and his crew got back to PBY tender *William B. Preston* that night and told their happy story, there had to be a celebration. So there was a party, lots of laughter and the best chow on the ship, and plenty of warm Coca-Cola.

William B. Preston was safe that night, anchored in a little nook off Alor Island, in the eastern Dutch Indies. She would be there four or five days, heavily camouflaged with branches and paint and anything else possible to break her outlines. The Japanese would come searching for her, so five days were about maximum for one operational area; then she would move.

She had started this tour at Boeton, on Moena Island in the Celebes, then moved on when the Japanese got the word; they bombed the place just after she left it. After moving, she got more PBYs from Surabaya—gifts from the Dutch. She then lost three planes. After she left Alor Island, it was bombed. *Preston* then steamed south to Timor, and then to Darwin, and then was ordered back to Alor, but the Japanese beat her to it, so she went back to Darwin.

It was a matter of constantly dodging the Japanese. The flagship tender *Childs* of the Asiatic Fleet Aircraft—as Patrol Wing 10 was now known—was another successful dodger. She was actually in Kendari, in southeast Celebes Island, when the enemy invaded there on January 24, the same day that Commander Talbot was attacking at Balikpapan. At five o'clock in the morning, in came the Japanese occupation force, but they were followed by a rain squall, and *Childs*—taking cover under the squall—made a miraculous escape, avoiding half a dozen destroyers and six Zeros that spotted her and attacked.

In the air war, the Dutch were as helpful as they could be with their limited air resources, but the British were not as amenable. Air Chief Marshal Sir Richard Peirse was not a good listener. Hart had hoped for close cooperation between the air and naval units, but he did not get it. "The new air marshal," he commented, "had not been trained for such cooperation."

By this time, the British army, navy, and Royal Air Force were being pushed out of Malaya, and ABDA Supreme Commander Sir Archibald Wavell decided they were to give up lesser tasks and concentrate on the preservation of Singapore, which he believed could hold out indefinitely. British air power was being used heavily to this end. And British and Dutch naval forces were escorting convoys to Singapore, making them unavailable to help stop the Japanese advance toward the Dutch East Indies.

And the Japanese were moving rapidly, and with ridiculous ease. Kendari, at the foot of that strange octopus island of Celebes, fell with the invasion of January 24. Next, Admiral Hart expected an invasion of Ambon Island, on the other side of the Molucca Sea, which would give the Japanese control of that body of water. Sure enough, in the last week of January, heavy Japanese naval forces, supported by carriers, began attacking Ambon. The Japanese then staged a well-timed and well-executed amphibious invasion, and by February 3 Ambon was occupied.

Meanwhile Admiral Hart had finally persuaded the Dutch to give him naval support, and he promptly, for political reasons, appointed Dutch Rear Admiral Karel W.F.M. Doorman as head of the ABDA Striking Force, thus eliminating Admiral Glassford from operations. He tried to solve his fighter-plane problems by sending the carrier tender *Langley* to Fremantle to pick up a whole shipload of newly assembled P-40 fighters. Things seemed to be looking up.

Plans for the ABDA Striking Force were discussed by the American, Dutch, and British naval commanders at meetings on February 2 at Lembang. With Doorman in command, Purnell, Hart's old chief of staff, would be chief of staff. Again, Glassford was very neatly boxed out.

On February 3 the plans were approved by Field Marshal Wavell. Admiral Doorman was to go out next day and track down the Japanese in Makassar Strait and hit them with the combined Striking Force.

The decision came none too soon. For now two events spotlighted the urgent need for action against the enemy. On that day, February 3, the Japanese made their first air raid on Surabaya. And Allied spotting planes reported a large Japanese expeditionary force heading down Makassar Strait for a new landing.

29

The Ordeal of Marblehead

On February 3, 1942, the cruiser *De Ruyter*, Admiral Doorman's flagship, was anchored at Bunda Roads, a few miles from Surabaya near Madura island, which separates Surabaya Harbor from the Java Sea. Assembled here were four other Dutch warships. In addition, there were the American cruisers *Marblehead* and *Houston* and nine four-stack American destroyers—the cream of the Asiatic Fleet. The Americans knew something was up at nine o'clock that morning when a PBY pulled up alongside *De Ruyter* and Admiral Purnell disembarked. All commanding officers assembled on the Dutch flagship.

During that conference the ships were suddenly alerted by a general alarm—the call to battle stations—and through the ships ran the bugled warning: AIR DEFENSE. Some fifty Japanese fighters and bombers were reported airborne and heading for Surabaya.

The four float planes of the American cruisers got off the water, assumed a diamond formation, and stayed out of the way. They were hardly good for much else; these old Kingfisher scout bombers that carried only 170 gallons of gasoline and a pair of 100-pound bombs. Usually they were catapulted into air, but at anchor this was impossible, and their margin of performance was almost nil. If the Japanese ever caught sight of them, a lone Zero could polish off all four in ten minutes.

The Japanese bombers came in that day, with their typical insouciance, and hit Surabaya hard. Paying particular attention to the seaplanes and airfield, they knocked out a good part of the Dutch air force. They then returned to base. But they would be back—that much was certain—and if they were now able to reach Surabaya with land-based air, the place was in for constant bombardment. For years the admirals had been quarreling about air power and its real effects on naval warfare. Now there was no argument at all: All naval vessels were extremely vulnerable to air power.

As the Japanese were battering Surabaya, Admiral Purnell was getting ready to leave the Striking Force at Bunda Roads and return to headquarters. A PBY came to pick him up, and was spotted by a Zero returning from the Surabaya raid. The PBY was making a low approach, the Japanese plane swooped down on him—and the PBY gunners shot it down—the second victory of a PBY over a Zero in three weeks. That victory was an auspicious if illusory beginning for what was soon to come.

Up in Lembang, Admiral Hart was already kicking himself because he had not moved the Striking Force into action sooner. He might have been able to prevent the Kendari takeover. At least he could have hit the Japanese another hard blow at Balikpapan, for the evidence he had from the South China Sea indicated this was the time to strike. But his destroyers had come back from that first raid on January 24 with all their torpedoes expended, and by delaying further action, as he had, Hart had given them time to rearm.

Then Allied spotter planes located a large Japanese concentration—including cruisers, destroyers, and transports—that was steaming for a landing at some place in the southern area of Makassar Strait. At Bunda Roads Admiral Doorman and his Combined Striking Force were poised for action. Hart and Doorman decided on an immediate attack. Here was a chance to strike a damaging blow at the invaders. True, the Allied force still lacked air support. That meant the enemy could throw bombers into the fray without air opposition but it was a risk that must be taken.

The ships of the Striking Force sailed at midnight. Later they assumed battle line: the flagship *De Ruyter* in the lead, with *Houston* behind her, then *Marblehead*, and finally the Dutch cruiser *Tromp*, with seven hundred yards separating each ship. The American destroyers *Stewart* and *Edwards* were sent out to starboard bow and beam as a submarine screen. *Bulmer* and *Barker* had the same position and same task on the port bow and beam. The Dutch destroyers *Van Ghent*, *Piet Hein*, and *Banckert* covered the rear.

The column traveled slowly and carefully, following a zigzag pattern to throw off the enemy submarines, and headed northeast. At 9:35 the warning flashed from *De Ruyter* to the force that thirty-seven Japanese bombers had been sighted—heading for Surabaya. At least that was what Admiral Doorman hoped.

Aboard *Marblehead*, Captain A.G. Robinson had ordered Condition III, which meant that five of the eight antiaircraft guns were manned, and down below the engine room had power to make 27 knots, but not all the boilers were lit.

The wind was coming from the southwest at 15 knots. The sea was moderate that morning, and visibility was good, with cloud cover ranging from 80 percent in the early morning to about 40 percent as the day wore on. In the north they could see the low mountains of Kangean Island, and off to the side the high peaks of Bali and Lombok.

At 9:49 that morning of February 4 *Houston* raised a signal: STRANGE AIRCRAFT SIGHTED

Marblehead prepared for action. Four groups of nine planes each were coming in on an eastern course at seventeen thousand feet.

AIR DEFENSE was the signal that rang through the ship, and the men scurried for their helmets and their action stations.

Captain Robinson ordered the ship closed up to the maximum watertight condition and gave the command for general quarters. Heels clanged on the deck as they ran to damage-control stations, repair stations, boiler stations. On deck the aviators dumped 4,200 gallons of aviation fuel stored near the after single gun mounts. The magazines were opened and the train of ammunition started to the guns. The six remaining boilers were lighted and preparations were made to give the ship full power in twenty minutes.

American air defense at this time was as primitive as the rest of the air doctrine. It called for the ships to scatter to provide smaller targets, rather than to concentrate to provide intensity of fire on planes coming in. So they scattered—their first mistake.

At 9:53 twin-engined planes were over the dispersed fleet, and a minute later they were peeling off by groups, each group taking a cruiser for its own.

The group making for *Marblehead* assumed a shallow V formation at seventeen thousand feet and then came down in a lower glide to fourteen thousand feet. As the bombers moved in, the guns of *Marblehead* began to bark.

The Japanese did not bomb on their first run. *Marblehead* was maneuvering radically, full left rudder, full right rudder, full speed.

The planes flew over, turned, and flew back—still no bombs. Another formation of eight planes flew over. No bombs.

At 10:08 the gunners of *Marblehead* hit one Japanese plane, which began to smoke and pull away.

Eleven minutes later the Japanese came over again, and dropped a stick of seven bombs on *Marblehead*. The bombs missed, fifty to a hundred yards off the port bow. But in the lower compartments the men could hear a sound like the rattling of pebbles on the hull as the shrapnel from the exploding bombs spattered the ship. The ship was now making 29 knots.

The Japanese came in again, and this time the gunners of *Marblehead* got a direct hit with a 3-inch shell, and one bomber disintegrated before their eyes. Another was hit and started a maneuver that American ships would later grow to watch with dismay. The pilot swung in, in a slow spiral, obviously aiming his wrecked plane for *Marblehead*, determined, if possible, to use it as a flying bomb—a forerunner of the Kamikazes of 1944-45. As he came in, the .50-calibre machine gunners concentrated their fire on the plane and may have killed the pilot, for the Japanese bomber turned lazily away and splashed into the sea amid the cheers of the gunners, missing the ship by a thousand yards.

At 10:26 another flight came over, this one of single-engined bombers. Captain Robinson swung hard left to evade their attack. But seven bombs straddled the *Marblehead*, two hit her squarely, and one near miss did almost as much damage.

The first bomb smashed the starboard motor launch on the boat deck. It then sliced through to the main deck, killing a number of officers and men in and around the wardroom, wrecking the officers' staterooms, pantry, post office, canteen, barber shop, and tailor shop, and then crashing through to the next deck, demolishing water and steam and telephone lines as it went. It blew a hole six feet by six feet in the main deck and completely demolished the sick bay.

The second bomb landed squarely on the fantail, four feet in from the port side of the ship, and exploded in the hand-steering room, killing everyone in the area. It destroyed the chief petty officer's quarters and killed a number of men there. It demolished the nearby engineering living space. Worst of all for the ship, it jammed the rudder hard left, which meant she could steam only in circles.

The third bomb, the near miss, buckled the bow plates so that *Marblehead* began going down by the head.

In a few moments the damage reports began to come in. The executive officer came to the bridge, badly burned and suffering from a head wound. He could not continue to function, and had to be taken to the conning tower for first aid. The gunnery officer, Lieutenant Commander N.B. Van Gergen, took over the exec's duties, while Lieutenant E.S.L. Marshall took over as gunnery officer. The ship continued to fight back.

Down below in damage control, the ship's first lieutenant, Lieutenant Commander M.J. Drury, was moving from one compartment to another, making sure that his men's efforts were being concentrated in the right places. They were. The ship had fires and was taking a good deal of water, but as far as possible every bit of damage was getting attention.

At 10:30 *Marblehead* was going in circles at 25 knots, the rudder still jammed hard aport, and she was settling by the head so much that *Tromp* moved in with the apparent intention of rescuing survivors when the ship went down. Van Gergen ordered men operating forward to move aft to change the ship's center of gravity.

Down in the engine room there was much damage, but the chief engineer reported that he could give the captain 22 knots. His report was made by voice tube to the bridge, because the ship's communications were out, except for sound-powered and battery-powered units.

The next hour in the life of *Marblehead* was critical. What the officers and men did to save this ship, still steaming in circles, her rudder jammed, would tell the tale:

11:00   The first lieutenant reported the fires on the ship were under control.

11:04   More bombers overhead. The ship steamed in circles at 20 knots.

11:06   The antiaircraft guns ceased firing, and the men began tossing shell cases over the side. The Japanese planes were gone.

11:11   More Japanese planes overhead. The report was final: Hand-steering was totally out of the question. Captain Robinson began experimenting with steering by engine. The captain stopped the starboard engine and moved full ahead on port. Like a crab, the ship began to move forward.

11:26   Another flight of Japanese planes appeared overhead. The antiaircraft guns opened up again.

11:28   *De Ruyter* asked for a report on *Marblehead*'s condition. It was given. Captain Robinson indicated that *Marblehead* was hard hit and needed assistance. Admiral Doorman suggested she head for Tjilatjap, on Java's south coast, the new American advanced base created by Admiral Hart. *De Ruyter* would convoy her part of the way.

11:38   Seven Japanese planes came in high, and dropped another
          stick of bombs. They landed two thousand yards away from
          Marblehead.

11:42   One Japanese plane came in low despite antiaircraft fire,
          obviously to scan the *Marblehead* and check her condition.
          Whatever he saw, he left and did not return.

11:51   Captain Robinson was getting the hang of steering by en-
          gine now and was able to make a fairly straight course by
          keeping the front engine going and starting and stopping
          the starboard one. So the other ships need not fear a colli-
          sion. The men working to free the rudder reported prog-
          ress. They would free it, but it would take time.

12:02   Admiral Doorman sent a message to Admiral Glassford—
          maybe an afterthought. It said, "Send fighters."

12:27   The engagement was over. The Japanese were gone, and
          Marblehead was limping along, steering for Lombok Strait,
          en route to Tjilatjap. With a bit of luck, she would make it.

From *Houston* the battle had quite a different look. When the call
to action sounded, the pilots of the two float planes—which had returned to the ship after the Surabaya air raid—tried to man their
planes. But one plane was shattered by a blast from an antiaircraft
gun and could not fly. The other plane headed for the catapult. The antiaircraft gunners began firing 5-inch shells, and then every man could
see why the Japanese attack came from so high—the bombers were just
out of range of the antiaircraft.

Nine bombers came in on *Houston*. They did not waste any time,
but went right to work, and the sticks began to fall. Captain Rooks ordered the ship hard aport, and when the bombs fell they neatly straddled the ship, causing some damage from near misses but scoring not a
single direct hit. Those misses sent up huge geysers of water, and the
ship nosed deep into the columns, carrying water from stem to stern as
high as the quarterdeck.

The damage reports came in: the main antiaircraft director was out.
The second seaplane, caught in the catapult, was so badly damaged it
had to be jettisoned. But the ship was still all right.

Captain Rooks had learned by experience that the navy's antiaircraft
doctrine was wrong, so he headed for *Marblehead* as she was being
mauled to protect her with his ack-ack guns. As he did so, he caught

part of an attack that may have been meant for the stricken cruiser. One bomb hit *Houston* aft, a hole twelve feet wide was blown in the deck just forward of Turret No. 3, and fires broke out. One of the 8-inch guns inside the turret detonated, putting a tremendous scare into the men on deck. The turret itself was completely knocked out. That same bomb had passed through the searchlight platform on the mainmast, cut a gash in the leg of the mast, smashed through the radio shack, and finally exploded just above the main deck. The worst damage was in the turret and the handling room below—every man in those two spots was killed. Gunner's Mate Kunks, who was in the aft main battery magazine, may have saved the ship when he started the sprinkler system and dogged down doors to prevent the spread of fires.

Outside the turret, the after repair party was almost completely wiped out on the level just below the hole in the main deck. Only Lieutenant Francis Weiler, the officer in charge, was unhurt—he was not even scratched.

That was the only damage *Houston* received, but it was enough, for fifty men were killed aboard the ship that day.

That was the end of the action. Admiral Doorman had no stomach for his attack after two of the ships were damaged.

The mission was called off, and the ships of the Combined Striking Force headed home.

30

Rearguard Action in the Indies

Although twenty-six of her watertight compartments were flooded and she was still heavily down by the head, the men of *Marblehead* managed to keep the ship afloat, exercising what Admiral Hart later called "remarkable and praiseworthy" judgment. Had it not been for the quality of their seamanship, the admiral said, the ship almost certainly would have sunk, as *Tromp* feared she would.

It was 12:55 on February 4 when Admiral Doorman gave the signal to retire west, and the American destroyers *Stewart* and *Edwards* came up to give *Marblehead* the comfort of their close company.

Early in the afternoon the executive officer announced that the list that had been so pronounced was now reduced to 4 degrees to starboard, which was manageable. They had pumped twenty tons of water and greasy oil out of the main deck, and thus changed her buoyancy; they began jettisoning thousands of gallons of fuel oil, knowing that this reduced an already short supply. But it was oil or the ship.

Marblehead was still able to move nicely enough despite her crippled rudder. She was going along at 20 knots. At 2:15 in the afternoon Admiral Doorman ordered her to break away and head south to Lombok Strait, through which she would pass to Tjilatjap, and at 5:22 she entered the strait.

There was still a good deal of nervousness in the battered fleet. The Japanese had undeniable air control of the seas, and even now *Marblehead* was shadowed by a big flying boat. Captain Robinson did not know whether or not he could expect another attack before dark. Sunset was a welcome event, for it brought less danger of pursuit, and the Japanese submarines were notable in this campaign for their absence from the offensive line.

Just after midnight of February 4-5, Admiral Doorman and his Dutch contingent left the Americans and headed for Batavia. *Marblehead* continued, and before dawn was picked up by the destroyer *Pillsbury*, escorting the oiler *Pecos* to Tjilatjap, which had now been designated as the new operational American base. The bombing of Surabaya on the day before the Striking Force sailed had brought Admirals Hart, Glassford, and Purnell to that decision. Without sufficient air defense they could not risk remaining at Surabaya—despite its superior fuel and port facilities, and its excellent support system, including recreational activity for tired men. By contrast, Tjilatjap had only limited facilities and practically no recreation outlets. And the men would not soon forget the bars and clubs and girls of Surabaya.

Marblehead made her landfall on the starboard bow around dawn on February 6, and now finished the process of pumping out 300,000 gallons of fuel oil. This operation had created a tremendous slick trailing away behind her and pointing the way to aircraft. But it had also lightened her so that she drew only twenty feet forward and would have no trouble making port. She met her pilot and was towed into harbor by tugs.

Houston had preceded her and was already alongside the dock. Her wounded had been taken to the hospital, and her dead to the *Europeesche Begraafplaats* for temporary burial, until they could be taken home to America. Now *Marblehead* followed the same pattern. The officers and men who had died were buried—along with Yao Shao Ching, one of the Chinese mess attendants who had signed on in the days when *Marblehead* was on the Yangtze and the Asiatic Fleet was a way of life for Chinese and foreigners alike. Yao died like Commander Blessman, the senior aviator, doing his duty against the common enemy.

Communications being what they were in the Dutch East Indies, and Doorman being of a different naval tradition, Admiral Hart did not learn of the Striking Force commander's decision to abandon the attack until more than half a day had passed and the force had already been fragmented. Needless to say, Hart was furious; the Japanese were still milling about in the Makassar Strait and still could have been attacked by a pair of cruisers—even *Houston* might fight—and the destroyers. But Admiral Doorman was spooked by the ease with which the Japanese attacked from the air, and given no assurances of air protection, he refused to risk his ships.

There was still no assurance of air power. Aside from the refusal of British Air Chief Marshal Peirse to come to grips with naval problems in the ABDA command, there was a vast shortage of aircraft. The British had hurriedly shipped a hundred fine new Hurricane fighters to Southeast Asia, but these had already been almost totally dissipated in the Singapore and Malayan campaigns. The Dutch were losing their fighters and bombers to the Japanese air force. Thirty-six P-40 fighters had been brought to Java from Australia, but the Japanese had caught them on the ground several times, and in spite of improving dispersal habits, the planes were soon destroyed. The Japanese simply had too much power too close to the scene, while the Allies had little of anything.

Fuming at his headquarters in Lembang, Admiral Hart gave serious consideration to relieving Admiral Doorman of his command. Had Doorman been an American, he would have been almost immediately commanding a desk and not a flagship. But the strike against *Marblehead* and *Houston* had left the force without a sound American cruiser in which an American admiral could fly his flag. It was unthinkable that an admiral could operate out of a destroyer. The British had no suitable cruisers or admirals available at the moment, and so Hart would have to make do with Doorman no matter what he thought of him.

Further, the political considerations could not be ignored: The Dutch were already fretful because the East Indies were *their* islands, and the Americans and British had come in and were pushing them all over the place. Admiral Helfrich and the governor general both complained that Dutch officers were not getting assignments commensurate with their importance. So Doorman had to stay.

Admiral Hart did order Doorman to take his Dutch vessels to Tjilatjap. Then the admiral turned his attention to the situation of the whole ABDA command. All soon realized that it must falter before long by sheer pressure of events.

Field Marshal Wavell's basic concerns were Burma and Malaya, which were under attack by the Japanese. The enemy was rolling along in Malaya and very early had taken the whole peninsula, except for Singapore. The outlook was ominous as Wavell made two trips, one to Burma and one to Malaya, in this first week of February. When he returned he sent four fast ships to Malaya to bring three thousand Royal Air Force men down to Java, where they could fight again rather than become prisoners, as they might if they remained.

Meanwhile, Admiral Glassford was doing as best he could as commander of American naval forces in the Southwest Pacific. He was, in fact, reduced to almost the level of a naval district commander by

Tommy Hart's maneuvering. Glassford learned on February 4 of the damage to *Marblehead* and *Houston*, and next day he sent the fleet surgeon to Tjilatjap to supervise care of the wounded, and the fleet matériel officer to look over the ships.

The report was gloomy: *Houston*'s after battery was knocked out, but she was seaworthy and could still fight at half strength. As for *Marblehead*, she was in need of extensive repairs. Her berthing facilities were almost totally destroyed, the inside of the ship was full of oil residue, the galley was wrecked, and the structural damage to the bow and the havoc caused by those two direct hits must be repaired. The closest place for major repairs in the command was Trincomalee, the British base in Ceylon, and Hart decided to send her there.

The Japanese were making themselves felt in the Dutch East Indies more and more as the new year progressed. Forty miles south of Soembawa Island, in the eastern end of the island chain, the American destroyer *Paul Jones* was caught by Japanese planes and attacked for two hours, emerging unscathed through the skill of her commander. Almost every day now there was a raid on Surabaya as the Japanese softened the area up for invasion. They raided on February 5 and again on Sunday, the eighth.

That day Admiral Hart flew down to Tjilatjap to have a long, hard talk with Admiral Doorman. He found the Dutch admiral to be in poor condition. Doorman was still visibly shaken by the results of the bombing of February 4, and still unwilling to go into daylight action with the preponderance of Japanese air power against him.

Hart argued that they could not sit there and wait for the Japanese to eat them up. The enemy was moving against southern Celebes, and here was an opportunity to stop them.

Dragging his feet all the way, Admiral Doorman finally agreed to write up an attack order, and did so, calling for a foray into Lombok Strait, between Bali and Lombok islands, by *De Ruyter*, *Tromp*, four Dutch destroyers, and six American destroyers, to strike the enemy forces there and drive them back.

Half satisfied at least, Admiral Hart got into his plane and went back to Lembang.

But the attack never came off. The Japanese appeared at Makassar, near the southwest tip of Celebes, and this event so disconcerted Doorman that he did nothing.

All around the ABDA command, territory was falling fast to the relentless enemy. On February 15 the unbelievable happened: Singapore surrendered to the Japanese, and Britain's mighty base in Asia became but a memory.

For a week events had been moving so rapidly that the Allied command could hardly keep up with them. The fall of Singapore freed thousands of Japanese troops and dozens of ships to advance the timetable for the occupation of the Dutch East Indies. The Japanese had occupied the west coast of Borneo early in the game. On the east coast of Borneo, they held Tarakan, taken in early January. Since January 24 they had occupied Balikpapan, halfway down the island. Now they launched an amphibious invasion against Banjermasin, which would give them another airfield at the southern tip of Borneo, within easy striking distance, across the Java Sea, of Surabaya. At the same time a large Japanese force was heading for Sumatra, aiming to capture its capital, Palembang, the greatest oil center of the Indies.

In fact, as the submarines and other intelligence sections reported, the Japanese were moving in multiple directions—from the west, against Sumatra; from the east against Timor and Bali. Thus Java, the center of Dutch power in the Indies, would soon be under attack, and while Tjilatjap was at the moment beyond the range of Japanese aircraft, one or more new invasions would put an end to the safety of that haven. The Americans would then have no option but to remove their last base—and the logical place to move was Australia.

That week, as Admiral Hart considered the prospects, his naval force was augmented by the British cruiser *Exeter* and the Australian cruiser *Hobart*. True, the *Exeter* was old, and the *Hobart* was a light ship, but in effect they replaced *Marblehead* and the damage done to *Houston*. Doorman, with three Dutch cruisers, two British cruisers, four Dutch destroyers, and six American destroyers, still had something to fight with.

Politically, the situation was delicate. *Houston* had been sent off as a troop transport convoy ship, a fact that did not help the American position. The destroyers, the PBY aircraft tenders, and the American submarines still gave the United States a big voice in affairs. But the Dutch were quick to point out that American submarines were not very effective, American air power in the Indies was virtually nonexistent, and the only fighting ships left were a half-dozen old destroyers. The Dutch and British commanded the largest ships.

As these points were considered in Lembang, Vice-Admiral J. Ozawa of the Imperial Japanese Navy was moving out of Camranh Bay, in French Indochina, carriers, cruisers, destroyers, and other fighting and transport ships in three sections to invade the south. Included among his forces were troops no longer needed around Singapore. And among his prize targets was Palembang.

By February 11, Admiral Hart decided he knew what was happening, and he considered ordering the Striking Force out to meet the threat. But he hesitated. The Dutch were not eager to make such a commitment, and he was persuaded to wait. He did wait twenty-four hours, then ordered the Striking Force into the water west of Borneo to stop that Palembang invasion.

Admiral Doorman and his little flotilla set off from southern Java on February 13, threaded their way through Sunda Strait, and steamed for Banka Island, off Sumatra's northeast coast. His aim was to attack Japanese transports assembling inshore from Banka Island for the invasion of Sumatra and the capture of Palembang, fifty miles inland.

On learning that the Allied force was heading for Banka Island, Admiral Ozawa called his transports back—so Doorman found nothing. He lost destroyer *Van Ghent* when she went aground in a narrow strait. Destroyer *Banckert* took off the crew.

Then on February 15 the Striking Force was found by Japanese spotter planes. Once again it was a case of bombs hurtling seaward and ships maneuvering desperately to evade them. For eight hours the Allied ships were attacked by waves of Japanese bombers. This time the ships maneuvered so successfully that none were lost or seriously damaged, although two American destroyers, *Barker* and *Bulmer*, were damaged by near misses. But once again Doorman realized the futility of trying to fight his ships against unopposed air power. He turned his ships around and made for southern Java.

Next day the Japanese invaded Sumatra and quickly took Palembang. It was a thrust that gave the enemy possession not only of the rich oilfields but of another airfield, one in easy striking distance of Batavia, on the northwest coast of Java.

Meanwhile, the ABDA command was shuddering, and back in Washington Admiral King was unhappy at the failure of the Striking Force to secure a victory. All the reasons for the failure were there, but reasons were no substitute for success.

Thus King was in no position to argue very forcefully in the political battle that was fought in Washington in February. The Dutch were still complaining that they should have the major responsibility and authority for the defense of their East Indies territory. The attrition of American ships strengthened that argument.

In the second week of February, President Roosevelt, Secretary of the Navy Knox, and Admiral King saw that there was virtually nothing to be gained from this rearguard action in the East Indies. Appraised of the worsening military situation, King recognized that the defense line must now be moved back to that ultimate point, Australia, and that nothing before it could be saved, just as nothing after it must be lost under any circumstances.

On February 12 the Allied combined chiefs of staff in Washington, which included the American and British top officers of army, navy and air forces, ordered Field Marshal Wavell to give the Dutch Admiral Helfrich the operational command he wanted. Under these conditions, Admiral Tommy Hart could not stay. Already he was in conflict with Washington over Secretary Knox's determination that Glassford should have the fleet. Hart had little faith in the Dutch method of fighting this war, or in the Dutch assessment of the military situation as it developed.

So on February 14, as ordered, Admiral Hart turned over his ABDA naval command to Admiral Helfrich. He then went down to Surabaya and officially made Admiral Glassford the senior American officer in the area. Then Tommy Hart took a plane for Washington. His role was ended.

Admiral Glassford was in every sense commander of the U.S. Asiatic Fleet.

The submarines were the first to sense the change in attitude toward the war when Admiral Helfrich took over as commander of the Allied forces in the Dutch East Indies. All through this campaign Admiral Hart had been arguing with Admiral Helfrich about the disposition of submarines. The Dutch system was to use them close in as defensive weapons—to seek out enemy shipping as it attacked or came near the home territory, and then to hit it.

The American tactic was to find the enemy concentrations at their points of origin, trail them as they moved, and then send submarines to hit them long before they reached their objective.

Captain Wilkes's submarines were making many contacts while shadowing the Japanese capital ships and invasion forces. Sometimes they were lucky, sometimes they were not. *Sculpin*, for example, had early word of the movement of Japanese vessels that resulted in the landing at Makassar on February 8, but the transmission was never picked up, probably because of atmospheric interference.

On February 16 all this changed. Admiral Helfrich recalled the sub-

marines from their scouting missions, drawing them in to cover Timor
and Bali against Japanese attack. This change was greeted dolefully by
Captain Wilkes and the submariners, for it was against all they had
learned and practiced. The result of it was to uncover the entire length
of Makassar Strait so that the Japanese could send a major naval force
through undetected and unchallenged.

At about this time Washington had reports that indicated a very
rapid enemy movement against Timor, and so advised the ABDA command. Until this time the Americans had been making every move
from one base to another reluctantly. Tjilatjap, they knew, was their
last foothold as a base in the Dutch East Indies, and it could be maintained only so long as it remained beyond the reach of enemy bombers.
But now, as the Japanese moved relentlessly forward, Tjilatjap's days
were obviously numbered; and fleet orders began to reflect it. The submarine tender *Holland* and the destroyer tender *Black Hawk* just arrived at Tjilatjap from Australia were now ordered to move back to Exmouth Gulf on the west coast of Australia.

The war was about to hit Australia for the first time.

31

Air Raid on Darwin

February 19 dawned a bright warm morning in Darwin, on Australia's northern coast. With the summer sun shining, cumulus clouds floated overhead, growing larger and more feathery as the day went on. A breeze of 10 knots was coming from the west.

Just before eight o'clock that morning, Lieutenant Commander E. Grant, captain of the aircraft tender *William B. Preston*, announced to his executive officer, Lieutenant Lester A. Wood, that he was going ashore to confer with the American naval advisor and local authorities about delivery of aviation gasoline needed to keep the PBYs flying. He took a boat and headed inshore.

For the next hour and a half life aboard the ship was routine. In the radio room the operators were keeping tabs on the war situation, taking and sending messages. Throughout the ship the officers and men were doing their daily routine jobs.

But the routine was soon to be interrupted. For Japanese Vice-Admiral N. Kondo and his striking force were heading into Australian waters. The admiral had two battleships and three heavy cruisers with him, plus four carriers under the command of Vice-Admiral C. Nagumo. The purpose was to smash the Allied base at Darwin, and to soften up that city. For if the war continued as it was going, who knew but that Australia might not be occupied, although this British commonwealth was really not included in the original Japanese plans.

That morning, as Darwin lay sleepily in the sun, nearly two hundred fifty Japanese warplanes—heavy bombers, medium bombers, dive bombers and fighters—headed toward the sprawling little city, and its port. Most were from the carriers, but some fifty were land-based bombers. The harbor was filled with ships—one reason it had attracted the attention of the Japanese in the past. The Australian hospital ship *Manunda* was anchored there, alongside the *Preston*. Destroyer *Peary* was there, having just returned from an escort mission. An Australian troopship was nearby, together with an Australian freighter. Two Australian sloops also occupied the harbor, plus two Australian transports and two American army transports, and a tanker, the *Benjamin Franklin*.

Aboard *William B. Preston*, the alarm came at 9:50 with a call to general quarters and air defense. This was what she had been waiting for. For weeks Lieutenant Commander Grant had been joshed by fellow fleet officers because of his fearful nature: He had kept *Preston*'s boilers going all day long, even at anchor, and the anchor chain short, so he could quickly get under way. Now, with the skipper ashore and the ship under the command of Executive Officer Wood, she was moving five minutes after the air raid alarm came in. From her anchorage in the lower end of the east arm of the harbor, she began to go northwest toward Walker Shoals.

Then in came the bombers.

Lieutenant Commander O'Beirne (of *Preston*) saw them first, right overhead, and he shouted. Lieutenant Wood ordered hard right rudder, and at 20 knots the ship sped away. The Japanese were not after her this time. They did not drop a single bomb.

At 20 knots, navigation in a crowded harbor was something of a feat, and Lieutenant Wood ordered the helm this way and that—starboard to miss a buoy on the port, and then two-thirds speed to give *Peary* a safe margin as she got under way.

At 10:10 *William B. Preston* was hit by a small bomb, estimated to be only 100 pounds. It struck the main deck on the port side and ignited fourteen 4-inch projectiles into a raging fire. The bomb and the exploding shells knocked out the steering, and Lieutenant Wood used the engines to avoid the hospital ship *Manunda*, which was five hundred yards ahead.

Across the way *Peary* was hit at just about this time; she blew up with a tremendous explosion and sank quickly, men still firing their .50-calibre machine guns at the attacking planes.

The men of *Preston* counted six 9-plane formations overhead. Most of the planes were hitting the docks and the town, but waves of dive bombers were directing their attention to the ships in the harbor, first to the transports. Two ships along the jetty, apparently loaded with ammunition, suddenly blew up. Two American transports were hit—*Tulagi* began to go down by the stern, while *Meigs* had a large fire aft (later in the action *Preston* stopped and picked seamen from *Meigs* out of the water). Even the hospital ship took a bomb—fortunately a dud—although her green stripe and red crosses were easily visible in the clear sky.

Three PBYs moored in the harbor were hit and began building with streams of black smoke. Their crews miraculously escaped death from the bombing and strafing by getting into their boats and heading for shore. Up above, some P-40s went into action against the Japanese, but they were too few and the Zeros too many. The PBY men in their boats watched as one P-40 was shot down and two Japanese fighters strafed the pilot as he parachuted toward the water.

One of the PBY men, Chief Radio Mate M.L. Anderson, saw the pilot hit the water in the distance and went up harbor after him in his boat. It took a long time, but he found and rescued the pilot. This was a remarkable feat—in the confusion that overcame Darwin that day, it was wondrous that anyone had gone after a single pilot.

Meanwhile Zeros and bombers flew low across the harbor, strafing ships, the burning PBYs, and men escaping their stricken vessels in small boats.

By one o'clock in the afternoon the attack was over, the bombers and fighters were leaving, and the only sounds were those of crackling fires and exploding ammunition and gasoline. The harbor was smoking. Eight ships had been lost and nine damaged. Only two vessels remained untouched—one was a ship in the floating drydock, and the other was the transport *Admiral Halstead*.

Behind the harbor, the town of Darwin was a smoking shambles, with wreckage everywhere and fires burning in the bright sunlight as the flimsy wooden buildings went up in flames.

While the Japanese assault was in progress, *William B. Preston*'s temporary captain, Lieutenant Wood, realized that carriers were obviously involved, and that another attack might be coming at any time. So he decided to abandon the harbor and move out to sea and around to the safety of western Australia. The ship began to thread her way out of the harbor, then turned and steamed away from the destruction, leaving behind her captain and the crews of the three PBYs who had by now gotten safely to shore.

But *Preston* was still not in the clear. Just before three o'clock that afternoon, as she steamed away from Darwin, a Kawanishi flying boat swooped to attack her one more time. The plane dropped half a dozen bombs; all missed, and then it flew away. Even for a Kawanishi, this pilot was a good long way from friendly territory, and he did not hang around.

As for *Preston*'s regular skipper, Captain Grant had been aboard a small boat alongside one of those ammunition ships when the Japanese bombed, and the ship blew up with a force that overturned his boat and very nearly drowned him. He managed to drag himself through the water to a mooring buoy in the harbor and to hang on there until low tide, when he could make his way to shore. He went back to wait for news of the ship and listened to the rumors: She was not visible in the harbor, so she had been sunk—at least that was the rumor circulating that afternoon.

It was the same with PBY No. 18. Of two PBYs that took off from Darwin on scouting missions just before the Japanese attack, PBY No. 18, under the command of Lieutenant Thomas H. Moorer, never checked in again that day, so the men of *Preston*, steaming westward, concluded that Moorer and his crew were lost. Actually, they were having an adventure of their own, beginning almost at the time of the bombing of Darwin.

Moorer had headed out that morning to follow his routine patrol up Ambon way. At 9:20 in the morning the crew spotted a big merchant ship steaming toward Darwin and dropped down to have a look. At that moment the PBY was fifty miles off Cape Von Dieman, on Melville Island, north of Darwin. As they crossed the merchant ship in the usual pattern, suddenly out of the sun swooped nine fighters and behind them Moorer saw a seventy-two-plane formation which was headed for Darwin at an altitude of eight thousand feet. The PBY was unlucky enough to have crossed the path of one of the attacking air groups.

It took just one pass by those thundering fighters to shoot the PBY down. The port engine began to flame and gasoline streamed back from both wings—the tanks were shot full of holes. The fire on the port side spread to the tail and the plane began to burn in the air. The wings and fuselage were full of bullet holes. Luckily none of the crew was killed, although several were wounded. The Japanese fighters then turned, ignored the ship below them, and rejoined the formation to go about their business of escorting the bombers to Darwin.

It would have been advantageous if Moorer could have turned the plane about, head upward, and land in the sea with a measure of control. But this was out of the question. He had gone down low to investigate the ship and was caught at about six hundred feet. Now he was losing altitude rapidly, the fire was gaining, and he was moving down-wind at 125 knots.

He looked back on the port side and saw the tail assembly beginning to melt from the heat of the fire. Ensign W.H. Mosley, the co-pilot, began handling the throttle of the starboard engine, which was still functioning, so Moorer could concentrate on getting the plane down.

He tried to get the wing floats down, but the mechanism had been wrecked by the fighters, and the floats would not move. So he must take her in on the big body pontoon without bouncing to port or starboard if he did not want to catch a wing—the air speed was still 125 knots.

All during the attack they had fought back. The port waist had been too hot to occupy, but on the starboard side crewman T.R. LeBaron had manned the machine gun every second there was something in his sights. Co-pilot Mosley was wounded in the head, but he continued to handle the throttle. Moorer was wounded in the hip but he continued to fly the plane.

Down they came, very hot, and bounced three times before the plane stopped. Radioman R.C. Thomas was trying to contact *Preston* to inform the tender of their plight, but Japanese bullets had knocked out the radio.

The waist was now so hot, with the tail burning fast, that LeBaron jumped out and over the side and began swimming forward. The other men of the crew tried to break out the rubber boats. The first was full of holes and would not float. But the second was all right and they managed to shove it out the hatch. Looking aft at the flames, they all had a sense of urgency.

Crewmen J.J. Ruzak, A.P. Fairchild, and J.C. Shuler had to do most of this work, for Moorer, Mosley, and Thomas were all wounded. Thomas had somehow broken his ankle. The other member of the crew, F.L. Follmer, was wounded in the knee.

They got out safely before the plane sank, and made their way toward the ship they had been approaching. She identified herself as the American freighter *Florence D.* and came to pick them up. When they got aboard, her captain said she had been chartered to run cargo between Surabaya and Corregidor to relieve the Americans fighting in the Philippines. She was now carrying ammunition.

Lieutenant Moorer and his crew were rescued and seemed safe. But it was an illusion. For at 2:30 in the afternoon, twenty-seven Japanese planes came into sight, and when they saw the ship they changed course to head for her. As they came in, Moorer recognized them as Japanese carrier dive bombers.

The bombers peeled off, one after the other, to make individual runs on the ship. One bomb hit very close to Lieutenant Moorer, and he jumped over the side. Moorer had told his crew to go into the water if they were attacked, for if the ammunition cargo was hit and exploded, everyone would go up with the ship. The bombing continued, and more and more men dropped into the sea.

In a moment, Moorer was not so sure his had been the right idea, for a 500-pound bomb missed the ship and struck in the midst of the men struggling in the water, just about where Shuler was swimming. The sea erupted in a gout of spray and a column of water topped by foam. Moorer and his men felt as though their insides were being torn out as the hammer blow struck them. Then the water tower subsided in a series of high waves that nearly drowned them all. The bombers, having pasted the ship and seeing it sinking, turned away toward their carriers and soon the sea was quiet again. Moorer began rounding up his men. He found some flotsam and clung to that and swam it around until he picked up all but Mosley, LeBaron, and Shuler. He knew what had happened to Shuler. A man does not swim in the path of a 500-pound bomb and live to tell the tale.

After the bombing, the crew of the *Florence D.* put two boats over the side. The ship had sunk, but her decks were still above water; she had gone down in shallow water to rest on the mud. The boats picked up Moorer and his survivors.

The captain of the *Florence D.* had been injured in the bombing attack, so Moorer took charge, assigning Ensign Mosley to one boat while he took command of the other himself. The ship's crew were mostly Orientals, and they were not at all happy with what had happened to them. But Moorer managed to calm them down, particularly when Ruzak took the stroke oar in his boat and began leading them in rowing. It was fortunate that they got away, for the Japanese came back —or more Japanese planes came over—and strafed the *Florence D.* Seeing this attack, the Filipinos and others of the crew began to panic. Again Moorer managed to calm them as the enemy went away.

They had twenty-three men in one boat and seventeen in the other. They had no blankets, very little water, no medical supplies of any use, and the only food was canned milk and crackers. This might have to get them to civilization. Counting noses and comparing, Moorer learned that only Shuler was missing from his air crew. All the rest were safe, and so were all the steamer's crew except for three men.

By five o'clock in the afternoon they were organized, and they left the vicinity of the ship, setting a course for the southeast to reach the Australian coast. They were not far off and sighted land well before dark. Also before dark, a Lockheed Hudson passed over and blinked at them. Moorer knew this was an Australian patrol plane, but the Filipinos of the freighter crew thought it was the Japanese come back, and tried to jump out of the boats. It was all he could do to restrain them. He could not threaten or use force, because in jumping off the ship he had lost his pistol. Somehow, he managed to restore order.

They moved in toward land and waited for favorable surf and tide. High tide came at midnight, and they rowed in through the foaming surf to safety. They were on an uninhabited part of Bathurst Island, across a narrow strait from Melville Island.

They slept a little then. At eight o'clock on the morning of February 20, Lieutenant Moorer decided to take a party and walk around the island to the other side, where he knew that a mission was once located. He told Thomas, Ruzak, and LeBaron to remain with the four wounded crewmen. He tried to persuade the captain and most of the others to stay too, but they were afraid of being marooned and would not. So the group set out on the long trek.

The younger Filipinos forged on ahead, and the older men and the slightly wounded dropped back. Lieutenant Moorer was not only wounded but he was now reduced to a pair of shorts as his only clothing, and he had lost his shoes, so walking on the many detours they had to make around headlands became torture.

They reached a stream, the only one they saw, but the water looked so brackish and unpleasant that Moorer advised against drinking it. They went on under a baking sun. At the end of fifteen miles, Moorer decided they would never make the whole journey and that they must return to the others and the supplies to await rescue. He headed back. Some of the Filipinos had stopped at the stream and drank from it, and they suffered no ill effects, so everyone had water here, and then they headed back to the boats, to drink canned milk and eat crackers and wait.

On February 21, late in the afternoon, a Royal Australian Air Force plane flew over. Moorer wrote in big letters in the sand that they were marooned and needed food and water and rescue. The plane wagged its wings and flew off. That evening it came back, dropped food and water, and told the men that they might expect rescue soon, perhaps the next day.

Next morning, a rescue party arrived in the H.M.A.S. *Warranam-*

bool, a coastal patrol boat command, led by Lieutenant E.J. Barron. The water was too shallow on the beach for Barron to come in far, but he stood offshore and sent a sailboat in through the surf. The boat picked up the wounded first and headed back to the ship. Just then a shadow fell over them, and they heard the noise of an airplane. It was another of those ever-present Kawanishi flying boats, and it attacked the ship and boat with 100-pound bombs, but it did not hit anything.

The only firepower on the *Warranambool* consisted of .30-calibre machine guns, and they were not very effective, although the men fired at the big flying boat as it flew by. But as the sailboat headed back to the beach, Captain Barron moved his position and covered his ship and the boat with a smokescreen that effectively hid their actions from the Japanese. After a while, the Kawanishi pilot became discouraged and flew away.

The boat then rescued the remaining navy men and some of the freighter's crew, and promised to send other rescue vessels for the remainder of the ship's crew. By one o'clock on the morning of February 23 all personnel were safe and sound on the mainland, and next morning Lieutenant Moorer reported to Captain Collins, the American naval advisor at Darwin.

Although the town was badly burned and disorganized, Collins found them food and lodging at the Darwin Hotel and got in touch with *William B. Preston.*

Moorer and his crew were reporting for duty again.

32

The Juggernaut Rolls On

The fall of Singapore on February 15 was the key to all that occurred in the last two weeks of February 1942, for the huge Japanese forces on land and sea that had been concentrating around the bastion were suddenly freed to attack the Dutch East Indies—weeks before the Japanese high command had so expected. So from northeast and from northwest the Japanese were able to mount several invasion forces with covering battleships, cruisers, and aircraft carriers to add to the build-up of land-based airplanes they had been accruing each time they took a field farther south. The smashing attack on Darwin on February 19 was an indication of Japanese air strength.

To face the Japanese juggernaut, the Americans and Dutch had few ships and little air power. Admiral Doorman, commander of the Combined Striking Force, had already learned what it was like to be attacked in daylight by unopposed Japanese air power. Admiral Glassford, commander of the American naval forces, was just as worried over enemy dominance of the skies. But the British had the only significant air power in the area, and they would not commit it to support naval actions in the Dutch and American sectors. That was the way it was, and there was no use lamenting—the naval forces would have to fight with what they had.

In the third week of February, the enemy was moving everywhere, it seemed. Timor was under attack, seaplanes and aircraft carriers roamed the seas around the islands, and Japanese battleships, cruisers, and destroyers protected the transports that set out for the invasions. The squeeze was on Java from two directions.

For some time Glassford had been expecting an attack on Bali, which would give the Japanese another airfield and another base snuggled right up against the eastern end of Java. These expectations proved correct, and on February 18 a Japanese invasion force was in Badung Strait, along the southeast coast of Bali. It was led by Admiral Kubo in the cruiser *Nagara*, supported by seven destroyers. The Japanese began their landings that same night.

All these things—the strike on Darwin, the invasion of Timor, and the assault on Bali—were part of the same basic operation preparing for the invasion of Java.

The Japanese plan was nearing its final stages—months ahead of schedule. The timetable called for occupation of Malaya, the Philippines, Borneo, Celebes, Ambon, Timor, Bali, Sumatra, and Java in that order—and with the landings on Bali all but the last were nearly accomplished. Of course there was fighting, but the Japanese forces had almost unlimitable resources behind them (or so it seemed to the badly outnumbered Westerners). And as for air power, the Japanese did not have to depend on just the eight carriers in the area, for their Eleventh Air Fleet, a land-based air command, had moved its headquarters and its planes down from Formosa to Kendari, in southern Celebes, in the first days of February, when that place was secured.

The Allies learned on February 17 that a Japanese invasion force was headed toward Bali, and they made plans to attack it. At this time Admiral Doorman's forces were scattered at various ports in the Dutch East Indies, and so he ordered the ships to rendezvous at the scene of operations. His plan was to strike the Japanese in three waves.

The flagship *De Ruyter*, the cruiser *Java*, five Dutch destroyers, and two American destroyers were at Tjilatjap and would move out and strike first. They would be followed by cruiser *Tromp*, which was at Surabaya, and four other American destroyers, which were at Ratai Bay in Sumatra. The third attack would be made by Dutch torpedo boats.

Trouble began almost immediately. The harbor at Tjilatjap was narrow, so narrow that Admiral Glassford had ordered his ships earlier to stay in harbor under air attack instead of seeking the open sea, as was doctrine. The reason for Glassford's odd order was his fear that a warship would be sunk in the neck of Tjilatjap Harbor and function precisely as a cork in a bottle.

The ships sailed from Tjilatjap on the night of February 18 and the Dutch destroyer *Kortenaer* ran aground in the bottleneck. The other ships got around her, but she was lost to the operation.

At ten o'clock on the night of February 19 the column moved into Badung Strait, steaming about three miles off the Bali shore, the *De Ruyter* ahead, *Java* behind her, and the destroyers strung out at the end. But with the landings completed, most of the enemy vessels had already departed. There were only three Japanese ships at the scene—the transport *Sasago Maru* and the destroyers *Asashio* and *Oshio*.

Java fired the first shot, and then the Japanese, with searchlights and star shells, attempted to find out who and what was attacking them. The Dutch destroyer *Piet Hein* charged in, laying a smokescreen, firing torpedoes and guns, the American destroyers followed. *Java* or one of the destroyers hit the transport and damaged that ship, and one of the American destroyers, *John D. Ford* or *Pope*, managed to put a torpedo into her. Then the destroyer *Asashio* began firing torpedoes and guns at *Piet Hein*, hit her badly, and she sank.

Asashio came after *Ford*, which laid a smokescreen and ran, heading for the northern entrance of Badung Strait. Then *Ford* and *Pope* got into a fire fight with the two Japanese destroyers for a few moments, without any serious damage. The Americans fired several torpedoes at the Japanese ships, but did not hit them. They then circled and retired to the south, as *Oshio* and *Asashio*, confused by the smokescreen, began shooting at each other.

The cruisers and destroyers all then retired and it was time for the second group to attack.

In the second wave, the American destroyers went first—*Stewart, Parrott, John D. Edwards,* and *Pillsbury*. The cruiser *Tromp* followed them in as they steamed into the strait after one o'clock in the morning.

In the anchorage at Sanur on the Bali coast, the destroyers *Oshio* and *Asashio* were now circling, and the Americans fired fifteen torpedoes at them without effect. The Japanese ships rushed out, firing themselves, and the Americans let more torpedoes go—but none hit. A Japanese shell ricocheted off the water and killed one man and wounded the executive officer of *Stewart*. Another shell made a direct hit on the destroyer's steering compartment. *Pillsbury* nearly ran into *Parrott* and then fell out of the formation and the fight.

Tromp came up and exchanged fire with the two Japanese destroyers, her blue searchlight making her a good target. She made hits on *Oshio*, but the destroyers hit her, too. Then Admiral Kubo, who was too far away to get into this action, ordered another pair of destroyers to abandon a transport they were escorting in dangerous water and turn and fight with their fellows. Thus destroyers *Michishio* and *Arashio* came into the fight, attacking *Stewart* and *Edwards*. Guns were firing and torpedoes were launched, *Michishio* received heavy fire from *Pillsbury* and then *Edwards*. The Japanese destroyer went dead in the water and was left to sink, although prematurely, as she was saved later in the day. Then the American destroyers moved out into Lombok Strait, at the eastern end of Bali, and were off, *Parrott* experienced a narrow escape when she scraped bottom and nearly got stuck, but managed to churn herself off.

The Allied ships then retired, and the Japanese began to pull themselves together. The third Allied wave of Dutch torpedo boats sped through Badung Strait and reported they saw nothing. The Battle of Badung Strait was over. It wasn't much of a battle. The prize being hardly worth the effort—a single transport guarded by two tough destroyers. Even if it had gone perfectly, it would not have interrupted the Japanese plans.

The Japanese juggernaut rolled on. In the last two weeks of February the Americans and British were making ready to move out from Java— the fall of the island had become inevitable. However, the Dutch had a different attitude. This country was part of the Dutch Empire—there were generations of Dutchmen in Java, and the idea of sacrificing all this to the Japanese was so unthinkable that the civil authorities and Admiral Helfrich simply refused to contemplate it. But the American fleet auxiliaries and the American military emphasis were already being moved back to northwest Australia, outside the Japanese bombing zone, which could extend no further than Darwin, unless carriers were brought into play.

Nor was there much left of the Asiatic Fleet. Cruiser *Houston* was still afloat, even with her ruined rear turret, and there was aircraft tender *Langley*, as well as the destroyers, submarines, and service ships. But that was it. Cruisers *Boise* and *Marblehead* were long gone. Patrol Wing 10, the PBY force, was considerably weakened by the loss of four more bombers in the Darwin raid. Now, after the Badung Strait affair, *Stewart* came back to Surabaya for repair work, and careless placement of her keel in the floating drydock caused her to slip when she was lifted, roll over to port, and suffer far more damage than she ever had at sea. In fact, she was so badly hurt as to be considered wrecked. She was not to be used again in the East Indian defense.

The war situation was now changing so rapidly that Admiral Glassford could scarcely keep up with it. Trying to do so kept him running between Batavia, Lembang, Tjilatjap, and Surabaya for conferences. On February 19 Glassford sent the freighter *Collingsworth* to Colombo, Ceylon, and the United States with a load of precious tin—it might be the last out of the Indies for a long, long time. On February 21, 22, and 23, events moved so quickly that orders issued by the various ABDA

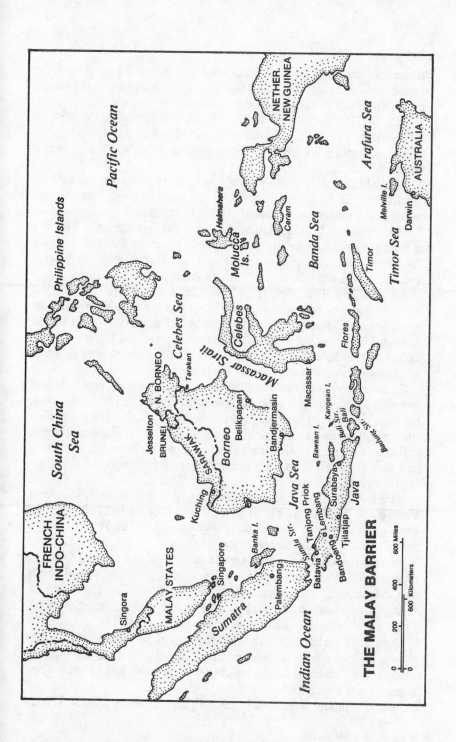

THE MALAY BARRIER

commands contradicted each other—and sometimes the previous order of the same command. It was a sign of confusion and the rapid roll-up of the Allied positions everywhere.

Admiral Helfrich, as commander of all sea forces in the defense effort, cabled London asking the combined chiefs of staff for help. The Allies could still hold, he said, if they got the planes and the ships and the men.

Admiral Glassford, ordered by his superiors to give every bit of help possible to the Dutch, was doing all he could. Nevertheless, he was moving his secondary forces back before it was too late.

Field Marshal Wavell, ABDA Supreme Commander, was sure the end had come. On February 23 he cabled Winston Churchill, warning the prime minister that the defense of the Malay Barrier had broken, and that it was simply a matter of days—perhaps hours—before the Japanese took Java. They already had everything else. There was no point in sending any more matériel to Java, he warned, and as for himself, he would stay if Churchill wished. The implication was very clear that if he stayed he was going to spend the rest of the war in a Japanese prison camp. As the American submarines had already warned, vast Japanese invasion forces were at sea, heading for Java.

Farthest away was Vice-Admiral Ozawa's main attack group. It had assembled in the quiet waters of Camranh Bay, on the Indochina coast, far from the prying eyes (the Japanese thought) of the Allies. On February 18, Admiral Ozawa raised the signal aboard his flagship *Chokai*, and the force set out—fifty-six transports guarded by carriers, cruisers, and destroyers. The armada numbered more than ninety ships, including the covering group.

Next day Admiral Nishimura headed away from Jolo, in the southern Philippines, with 41 transports covered by a smaller but still powerful force of 23 warships. And in the background Admiral Kondo hovered with 6 carriers, and 24 other warships.

To face this assault the Allies could muster only 16 fighting ships, 11 of them destroyers, and once again, on February 19, the lack of charts and unfamiliarity with these waters had its effect. The American submarine S-37 went aground at Lembongan Island in Badung Strait. Luckily she was able to pull herself off the reef.

During the next few days the Dutch prepared for the major sea battle they knew to be coming. Admiral Helfrich ordered all submarines, including the American boats, to cluster in around Java. Dutch ships mined Benoa Bay in Bali.

At about this time Japanese "marker" submarines appeared off Java.

The Japanese use of submarines was even more cautious and restrictive than the Dutch. Their first appearance usually marked the coming of the fleet a few days or hours later, for they were sent out ahead to spy out the territory.

As tensions rose, operations command for the Asiatic Fleet was moved to Bandoeng to be right with Admiral Helfrich. Surabaya was untenable. Tjilatjap soon would be. At Tjilatjap Commander Wilkes made ready to evacuate the submarine command, as ordered. On February 23 he moved the staff and headquarters personnel by submarine to Australia. Tenders *Holland* and *Black Hawk* were on their way to Exmouth Gulf in western Australia.

In fact, the American force in these waters was growing smaller every day. Destroyer *Whipple* was off for repairs after collision with a Dutch ship. Destroyer *Edsall* was damaged by a depth charge that had blown up under her stern. *Pillsbury* and *Parrott* were badly mauled in that attack on the Japanese invaders of Bali, and virtually out of ammunition, so they were withdrawn. *Bulmer* and *Barker* were on their way to Australia with the tenders, and *Pope* was under repair at Surabaya. So the American contingent of the Striking Force consisted only of destroyers *Ford, Edwards, Paul Jones,* and *Alden.*

On February 25 the Japanese landed a small force on Bataan Island, 150 miles north of Surabaya, to set up a radio station. The force was discovered by S-38, which surfaced and shelled the Japanese invaders. From other reports by submarines, coastwatchers, and the shredded fragments of Patrol Wing 10, Glassford learned that the Japanese were making a three-pronged drive on Java.

For a week everyone at ABDA had known that Field Marshal Wavell was planning to move the British out of the command and retreat to India to set up a new defense line. The Dutch asked Admiral Glassford what the American position was going to be. Glassford replied that his orders were to fight with the Dutch to defend the Netherlands East Indies and that he had no other orders. Of course this did not mean much, since not only was the air power virtually confined to the British but the troops were British and Dutch. The American contingent was reduced to a handful of battered ships. But it was odd that the American army air force *did* withdraw. Its commander in the ABDA command, General Lewis H. Brereton, flew to India on January 24, and some of the American air force planes also got away. Others did not make it in time to escape the Japanese.

The British withdrawal and the departure of the American air force were entirely realistic, given the disparity in strength that existed between the Allied and Japanese forces and the inability of the Western powers to supply the Southwest Pacific front in the early days of 1942. But the Dutch could not see it that way; Holland itself was occupied by the Germans, and they had determined to go down fighting. At least the British and American naval forces were still with them, and now they obtained full command of the Allied forces. For on February 25 the ABDA command was hastily dissolved as Wavell flew to India. Admiral Helfrich became commander of all forces in the area.

Admiral Glassford stuck with Helfrich, but he continued to make plans for the future. He had to find a new headquarters so that when the inevitable came in a few days he would have somewhere to go. On February 25, he sent Admiral Purnell flying off to Broome, on Australia's northwest coast, to survey the situation. Tjilatjap headquarters was abandoned that day, and the personnel were sent off to Australia in transports. A handful of officers and men remained but as far as operations were concerned, Asiatic Fleet had nothing left but its command post in Java and its commander.

On February 25 Admiral Doorman and the Striking Force were anchored in Surabaya, waiting, while the reports of the coming of the enemy flashed over their radios from many sources. *Houston* was tied up outboard of *De Ruyter*, and the Dutch cruiser *Java* was nearby. Seven Dutch and American destroyers completed the force at Surabaya, but reinforcements were on the way. From Tanjong Priok, near Batavia, Commodore Collins of the Royal Navy was dispatching five warships, previously on convoy duty, to join the Allied forces in this last big battle. They were the British cruiser *Exeter* and destroyers *Electra*, *Jupiter*, and *Encounter*, and the Australian cruiser *Perth*.

At dawn that day a formation of Japanese two-engined Bettys appeared above Surabaya and air raid warnings sounded on the ships. There were nine planes, but none scored a hit. They bombed the harbor installations and set fire to a warehouse. They did not come down low because *Houston* was firing her antiaircraft guns all during the attack. This was most fortunate as the ack-ack guns of the old Dutch ships could not reach the high altitude of the Japanese planes.

After the raid, *Houston* moved out into the stream so the ships would not be clustered in case dive bombers arrived on the scene. Another raid took place that afternoon, but again it was high-level and again ineffectual.

At dusk, Admiral Doorman ordered the force out for a night sweep in an attempt to locate the enemy. His refusal to move in the daylight hours was absolute, and nothing Helfrich or anyone else could say would change his mind. Admiral Helfrich and Admiral Glassford talked over the possibility of replacing him with Commodore Collins, for whom both had a high regard, but for reasons that were almost purely political, Helfrich said he could not do it. Doorman had to stay on.

The night sweep accomplished nothing. The Japanese were coming but they had not yet gotten that far south. So the ships returned to anchor at Surabaya on the morning of February 26. During that day they had to fight off more high-altitude air raids by the Japanese.

Around four o'clock in the afternoon, the men of the *Houston*, virtually exhausted from fending off three air raids, were cheered by the sight of newly arrived Allied ships. Into harbor came cruisers *Exeter* and *Perth* and the three British destroyers. *Exeter* was indeed famous among naval men, for she had been involved earlier in the war in tracking down and successfully attacking the German pocket battleship *Admiral Graf Spee* off the Uruguayan coast. The Americans and the Dutch were encouraged, and the odds they faced did not seem quite so unfavorable. It was no secret that Doorman was gearing up for battle, or that ABDA had been dissolved, or that Wavell and most of the other senior commanders had already left the island. Whatever boost in morale the men of the fleet could gain, they certainly needed it this day.

The Japanese juggernaut was on its way.

33

Disaster in the Java Sea

Hardly had *Exeter* anchored in Surabaya Harbor, when Admiral Doorman's staff sent word to all ships that they must be ready to move against the Japanese. For ominous news had come from Admiral Helfrich: Thirty transports were steaming for landings on Java, guarded by at least two cruisers and four destroyers. Doorman was to attack and pursue until he had "demolished" the Japanese force.

Strong words—reminiscent of the Spartans. Admiral Doorman had, in effect, been told to come home with his shield or on it. And there was no mistaking the urgency in the minds of either the sender or the man who received that fateful order.

That afternoon Lieutenant Thomas Payne, an aviator on the *Houston*, took the last operational plane of the cruiser off into the swamps to conceal it from the attacking Japanese. As darkness fell, and it became apparent that they were going to hit the enemy that night, Captain Rooks ordered Payne to taxi the plane over to the Dutch seadrome and stay there with it. Since it would be a night engagement, the spotter plane would be of no use in the fight, and there was no need to sacrifice it or let it become a fire hazard.

The Striking Force moved out that night and steamed north, east, and west, searching all night for the elusive enemy. The ships found nothing. Next morning, while still at sea, they were attacked by enemy bombers, but once again the guns of *Houston* kept the planes high and they did not hit any of the ships. By now, the men of the force were nearly exhausted from the strain of several days of high tension and readiness. They were literally living on their nerves. Admiral Doorman headed back for Surabaya.

They had failed to find the enemy. A stark fact that revealed one of the Allies' crucial weaknesses: lack of air support. Had they been able to send out search planes in the daylight hours, they would have found the Japanese. But the Dutch air force was now reduced to little more than a handful of Brewster Buffaloes at Surabaya, and they did not have the range for a thorough search.

Helfrich then issued a direct order telling Doorman to head out to sea again and find the enemy. Doorman disregarded the order and continued his course. But at 2:30 that afternoon, as he approached Surabaya Harbor, Doorman received a message he could not disregard: The enemy had been found—one force twenty miles west of Bawean Island and another sixty-five miles northwest of the island. Doorman was to attack.

Once again the Striking Force turned around. And now steaming to meet Doorman on the afternoon of February 27 came Admiral Takagi with heavy cruisers *Nachi* and *Haguro*, Admirals Nishimura and Tanaka in light cruisers *Naka* and *Jintsu*, and a supporting force of some fifteen destroyers. The Japanese transports were diverted to the west while the enemy fighting ships moved to destroy the defenders.

Several hundred miles farther to the west, another Allied force that could have strengthened Doorman's fleet was moving, through some extraordinary mixup of priorities, away from the battle area. It consisted of the old Australian cruiser *Hobart* and four British ships, cruisers *Danae* and *Dragon* and destroyers *Scout* and *Tenedos*, which had been detached from convoy duty to help the Dutch. But Admiral Helfrich had kept this flotilla at Batavia as a westward watchdog, and now, with that city under air attack, the ships were steaming for Tjilatjap. They would never make the battle, and in the end they would retreat to Ceylon without fighting the Japanese.

Admiral Doorman's Striking Force soon reached a point only fifty miles from the Japanese—the moment of decision had come. He headed straight for the enemy in a battle line, with the British destroyers in the lead, followed by cruisers *De Ruyter, Exeter, Houston, Perth,* and *Java,* with the Dutch and American destroyers on the port and to the rear.

They sorely missed Lieutenant Payne and his spotter plane that day! For this was to be no night attack, but a full daylight battle, and while the Japanese knew where the Allied force was and what it was composed of, Doorman was "blind." He pleaded with Admiral Helfrich for air cover of some kind, but Helfrich had to make a difficult decision. He had his handful of Brewster Buffaloes and a few dive bombers left. He had used the fighters to cover the dive bombers in a fruitless raid on the Japanese transports—there was nothing left for Doorman.

The Japanese float planes, spotters from the naval ships, appeared over the Striking Force about four o'clock. A few minutes later the destroyer *Electra* caught sight of the enemy crossing the force's bows from right to left. Doorman called for flank speed, the cruisers moved up to 26 knots, and the Dutch destroyers fell behind.

Soon the spotters in the foretop of *Houston* identified the enemy ships. They did it themselves because the communications between the ships left much to be desired: Admiral Doorman issued his orders in Dutch from *De Ruyter* over a voice radio. Aboard the American, Australian, and British ships Dutch liaison officers translated the orders into English. The British used a different system of signal flags, which only added to the confusion. *Houston's* men watched for themselves, and they soon identified two Nachi-class cruisers with their pagoda-like superstructure, ten 8-inch guns, and torpedo tubes.

Admiral Doorman changed course to the left, to parallel the enemy, and the British destroyers, which were then caught in the middle, turned about and took position on the far side of the Allied cruisers.

The Japanese began firing. In the Allied ships the first signs of the shooting were sheets of copper flame erupting along the enemy ship sides—then the smoke.

Those first salvoes were 2,000 yards short, but the Japanese kept on firing as the range closed. Meanwhile Admiral Tanaka led the destroyer squadron up against the British destroyers until they came to 18,000 yards, and then issued the order to fire. *Electra* was straddled by the first two salvoes.

Doorman's problem was to get his three light cruisers, *De Ruyter*, *Perth*, and *Java*, with their 6-inch guns and inferior range, into action without letting the enemy cross his T—which would allow them to shoot at his whole column of ships. He swung in to port to close the gap, and heavy cruisers *Exeter* and *Houston* began firing with their 8-inch guns. Although *Houston's* No. 3 turret was silent—it had been knocked out permanently in the battle near Bali on February 4—the remaining 8-inchers of her two forward turrets were blazing away.

From her gaff, *Exeter* flew a beautiful white British battle ensign. In the wardroom, the mess attendants had scarcely put away the tea setting—just before the sighting of the enemy Captain O.L. Gordon was about to sit down to tea. Now, as her guns began firing, she was having difficulty because she could not bring her after turret to bear on the enemy. If Doorman did not get his ships in close soon, and let the guns of the light cruisers begin to speak, the whole Allied fleet would be in deadly peril.

As the range closed, *Houston* kept pumping out shells, five or six salvoes a minute. On the fifth salvo a fuse box failed in No. 1 turret, putting the automatic rammer out of action. The men began ramming the shells and powder bags home by hand, although they would not and probably could not have done it in peacetime. *Houston* was firing shells with a deep red dye in them intended to mark the range—the huge red water columns from shells exploding in the sea frightened some of the Japanese, who did not understand the purpose of the dye.

With her sixth salvo, *Houston* got a straddle on a cruiser, and on the tenth her officers thought she had a hit—but Japanese war diaries deny it. Soon *Houston*'s men thought their target was aflame—but again the Japanese reports do not so indicate.

De Ruyter took a shell in the auxiliary engine room. Luckily this 8-inch projectile failed to explode, and a few moments later Admiral Doorman turned his column to the right in order to close the range. As things now stood, cruiser *Perth* was completely out of the battle, for her 6-inch guns would not reach the enemy. Perhaps moving in would help her and the other light cruisers.

Admiral Takagi saw the Allied maneuver and immediately decided to launch a torpedo attack. The Japanese cruisers and destroyers moved into position to launch, then began firing their missiles. Not one of these was effective—the range was too great.

But the Japanese destroyers did pull one effective trick: As they came in on their torpedo runs they laid a smokescreen which obliterated the Allied view of the Japanese cruisers. The Japanese cruisers enjoyed the services of three spotter planes, and could continue to fire effectively. The Allies could not.

The battle continued. Shortly after five o'clock that afternoon, Admiral Tanaka launched a new torpedo attack, and Admiral Takagi opened the range so his fire superiority would tell. The Japanese were worried. They had been fighting for an hour, and no major damage had been done. In another hour darkness would fall with that total blackout of the tropics. And the Japanese did not want a night fight when the daylight was so obviously to their advantage.

Exeter had already been the major target of the enemy ships and had suffered several near misses, one of which struck near her stern and flooded several compartments. Other Allied ships were hit: *Houston* took a pair of duds and *Java* was struck, but not seriously. The Japanese were not hurt, but the Allied ships were not either. The Japanese determined to close on the enemy.

As the Japanese destroyers headed in, *De Ruyter* and the other light cruisers fired on them, and destroyer *Tokitsukaze* was hit hard and threw up thick clouds of white smoke and steam. Yet she went on, and managed to fire her eight torpedoes. One by one the eight Japanese destroyers in the attack charged in and fired, until sixty-four torpedoes were speeding toward the Allied fleet.

At about this time a little flight of Dutch dive bombers arrived on the scene, escorted by Brewster fighters, which had been sent by Admiral Helfrich to attack the Japanese transports. Had the commander taken a few moments to polish off those Japanese spotter planes, the story of the Java Sea battle might have been changed. But he had his mission, and the danger of being jumped by a large number of Zeros was so great that he dare not risk the delay.

It was 5:07 when *Exeter* received a direct hit by an armor-piercing shell from cruiser *Haguro*. The shell struck the shield of the starboard No. 2 4-inch gun, killing four men of the gun crew. It then coursed through No. 1 boiler room ventilator and entered B boiler room, where it exploded, broke the boiler open, and destroyed steam lines, so that the ship immediately started to lose power. Six of the cruiser's eight boilers were knocked out. Captain Gordon watched the indicator go down until the vessel was making only 11 knots.

With this loss of speed, *Exeter* could not stay in the column, so the captain turned the ship to port and hauled out of the battle line. When he did so, Captain Rooks in *Houston*, who was just behind, thought there had been some change in the battle plan and that *De Ruyter* was moving them in another direction. Communications were so bad in this affair that Rooks can hardly be blamed for any conclusions to which he might jump.

Rooks turned hard aport, too, and behind him Captain Waller of *Perth* did the same, and behind him so did Captain Van Staelen of *Java*.

This point maneuver confused the Japanese, but it also confused Admiral Doorman and left the Allied battle force in considerable disarray. Six minutes went by and then Doorman turned his flagship around to rejoin the others.

Just then—at 5:15—the Dutch destroyer *Kortenaer* fell a victim to that swarm of torpedoes launched by the enemy destroyers. One of the fish struck her amidships, and blew the middle out of her, and her two ends folded down into the sea like a pair of shears. The stern went up with the ship's doctor sitting on top of it, dressed in life belt and steel helmet over his khaki uniform. Then it flipped over, giving the doctor and others a chance to slide off before it disappeared beneath the waves. From the guts of the ship, life rafts drifted up, and the survivors were able to put them together and climb aboard. They experienced difficulty because the breakup of the ship had left the surface of the sea coated with stinking black oil that got into their mouths and eyes and weighted down their clothes.

When Admiral Takagi saw Admiral Doorman turn to follow his errant cruisers and bring them into line again, he lost all caution, for he believed the Allies were running away. So he set out in hot pursuit. The cruisers and destroyers launched another torpedo attack. Japanese destroyer *Asagumo* was hit by a shell from an Allied gun, and she went dead in the water for a time, but then the engine was started again and she escaped the action.

At 5:20 Admiral Doorman ran up a signal—"All ships follow me"— and headed northeast, coming up around *Exeter*, which was obviously in trouble, and putting the line of ships between *Exeter* and the enemy, giving the British cruiser a chance to get away.

"What is your damage?" asked the admiral, as the flagship steamed by the *Exeter*. And when he learned that most of *Exeter*'s boilers had been knocked out and she could make only 15 knots, he ordered Captain Gordon to take the ship off to the safety of Surabaya.

Meanwhile, hurried by the gathering dusk that meant the spotter planes would shortly be of little use, Japanese cruisers *Nachi* and *Haguro* were firing vigorously at the Allied cruisers. Japanese light cruisers and destroyers prepared to launch another torpedo attack, and the British destroyer *Electra* turned toward the enemy to protect her damaged cruiser.

Followed by the other two British destroyers, *Encounter* and *Jupiter*, the *Electra* headed toward the enemy and soon saw rushing toward her the Japanese cruiser *Jintsu* and her accompanying destroyers. The cruiser began firing at *Electra*. First several near misses of 5- and 6-inch shells that shook the destroyer from one end to the other. Then the Japanese found the range. The first shell hit below the bridge. A succession of shells followed, knocking out communications and steam lines. Then, with a sudden screech of steam, the ship slowed in the water and came to a halt, her engines dead. A Japanese destroyer came charging at her. *Electra* fired a spread of torpedoes—and they all missed. Other Japanese destroyers and *Jintsu* came back and commenced firing at the sinking ship. Her men fired back, using local control when the gun sys-

tem was shot out; a turret was hit; B turret was burned out. The searchlight platform was blown off. The ship began settling.

A fire started amidships, which stopped the supply of ammunition to
X and Y turrets. They stopped firing and then one of them blew up.
The ship began to list.

Commander May, the captain, knew the end was near and gave the
order to prepare to abandon ship. A boat got away—and was hit by a
Japanese shell. A raft was put over and was sunk by another shell. Now
the men began jumping over the side and swimming away from the
ship so the suction would not take them under. Commander May
stood on his bridge and watched them and waved before going down
with his ship.

At this point, with the battlefield darkened by the gathering dusk
and by smoke from gunfire, ship fires, and smokescreens, the destroyers
Encounter and *Jupiter* emerged from the smoke to see *Electra* being
battered to death by *Jintsu* and her superior force of Japanese destroyers. The Japanese ships then ducked into the smoke, and so did
the Allied vessels as they moved to protect *Exeter*'s retreat. As the Japanese came out of the smoke to search for *Exeter*, destroyers *Encounter*
and *Jupiter* joined Dutch destroyer *Witte de With* to screen the injured cruiser. *Witte de With* suffered a huge shock when one of her
depth charges came loose, dropped over the side, and very nearly blew
off her stern. But she shook herself and survived, and then went off, ordered by Admiral Doorman to escort *Exeter* back to Surabaya.

Now Admiral Doorman's cruiser strength was reduced from five to
four, but of the remaining cruisers—*De Ruyter, Perth, Houston,* and
Java—the only one with 8-inch guns to match the Japanese was *Houston,* and with her after turret gone, she had only six 8-inchers able to
fire. *De Ruyter* wore her "Follow Me" flag, the others got into line, and
the remaining six destroyers spread out to cover them.

They went into the smoke, and came out on the Japanese side to
take on *Nachi* and *Haguro.* The Japanese cruisers straddled *Houston.*
That ship was in trouble. Captain Rooks had just learned that he had
less than fifty rounds of ammunition left for each of his 8-inch guns. To
make matters worse—although he had shells and powder—everything
had to be brought forward from the after magazines because the forward magazines were empty.

Houston began fighting like a wounded thing, which indeed she was,
her crew nearly exhausted after many nights of wakefulness at battle stations, and the condition of the men of the black gang coaling her fires
was even more desperate due to the heat.

The confusion of tongues and practices continued. *De Ruyter* signaled the U.S. destroyers to counterattack—and they had just digested that signal when the flagship canceled it and told them to make smoke. They had just gotten that straight when they received a new signal— "Cover My Retirement"—which indicated that Admiral Doorman was about to make a desperate move.

The destroyers then turned and headed toward the Japanese, smoke pouring from those old four stacks—and at fourteen thousand yards they fired torpedoes from their starboard sides, then swung around and fired from port. They moved wide then in a circle and came back.

Houston was moving in a strange way, changing course to bring her forward turrets to bear, and she was hit twice by dud shells. One ruptured several fuel tanks. Another went through the bow, and opened up forward compartments to water. But she fought on.

One of the destroyers made a hit on the Japanese destroyer *Asagumo*, and put her out of action for a little while. But the Japanese were feeling the power of victory, and Admiral Takagi ordered the transports to stop lying doggo and to head in for the beaches of Java. As far as he was concerned, the Allied Striking Force was nearly finished.

But Doorman had only changed his target. He was now looking for the convoys—for the ships full of troops that were trying to land on his beloved Java. As he ran up his confusing changes of orders, he was radioing Admiral Helfrich for information about the troop transports and where to go after them.

Admiral Takagi wondered if perhaps Doorman might try an all-out move against the transports, and he sent cruiser *Jintsu* and her destroyer squadron to make a great loop that would carry them to the southeast of the convoy. Admiral Takagi was on the other side of the transports, and so the convoy was protected from both directions that Doorman might take to reach the ships.

Doorman sensed that the transports were in the northwest, and headed in that direction, the other ships tagging behind him, with all communications lost and without knowing where they were going or why. Doorman's intuition was right—he was heading directly for the enemy convoy.

But he had no air intelligence, and those Japanese float planes were still up there, now dropping flares to illuminate the Allied ships. In one flare the two fleets caught sight of one another, and soon they opened fire. The range was too great for the American shells to hit anything— the Japanese fired torpedoes but the Americans swung into them and all missed.

Doorman now headed south to break off contact with the enemy and steam along the Java coast, still hoping to locate the transports. Soon the Allied ships were in the shallow waters of the coast. At nine o'clock at night, Doorman was moving westward in the darkness parallel to the coast and finding nothing.

But as they moved, either Japanese submarines were shadowing them or they were coming into stray mines, for at 9:25 that night *Jupiter* either struck a mine or was hit by a torpedo. She was kept afloat for four hours, but then she went down, and her men headed for the Java coast in life boats and rafts. Some made it.

At about this time, Commander Binford, the leader of the American destroyer division, decided Doorman was leading them into danger by going in so close to shore, and he opted to break away and go into Surabaya to replenish his low fuel supply. So at that moment the Striking Force was reduced to the four cruisers and the British destroyer *Encounter*. Less than an hour later, the ships came upon the survivors of *Kortenaer* in life rafts, and *Perth* ordered *Encounter* to stop and pick them up. That night the four Allied cruisers moved along without any destroyer support at all. The battle seemed to be over.

Admiral Doorman and his cruisers were now a hundred miles northwest of Surabaya, heading westward along the coast to find that convoy of transports that threatened his people and his land.

Admiral Takagi was now moving on a converging course. His spotter planes had run out of fuel and the night was to neither side's advantage as they steamed along. But at one o'clock the two forces came so close that they saw each other simultaneously. The Japanese ships came into view in the bright moonlight, far off to port of the Allied column of cruisers.

Takagi altered course 180 degrees. Both sides began firing without effect. But the Japanese kept coming straight for the Allied ships, until the range had dropped to eight thousand yards. Then the Japanese cruisers launched twelve torpedoes—Japanese cruisers still used torpedoes, unlike western cruisers. And this night the torpedoes were the key, for one struck *De Ruyter* aft, and in moments the whole stern of the cruiser was blazing high. The flames found the signal locker, and rockets began bursting in the air like the Fourth of July on the Chicago waterfront. The ship's company was driven forward, and *Perth*, behind her, had to dodge to keep from striking the flagship and running her down, while *Houston* had to dodge *Perth*.

These maneuvers may have saved those two ships, for behind *Hous-*

ton came another violent explosion, and *Java* began to burn, hit by another Japanese torpedo.

In a few minutes, *De Ruyter* and *Java* were both stopped dead in the water, burning furiously. Aboard the flagship the 40-mm. ammunition began to explode in the flames, and the order was given to abandon ship. Doorman, still able to reach his captains, ordered them to leave the scene—not to risk their ships against the Japanese force in the light of the flames—and to go on to protect Batavia.

Then there were more explosions aboard both Dutch ships, and as *Houston* and *Perth* raced off into the night and the safety of the darkness, the two gallant vessels went down, taking officers, men, and the admiral who wanted to fight at night.

34

NERK NERK NERK NERK

Admiral Karel Doorman was dead, and those who had said he was less than gallant began to change their words, perhaps to suggest that he was misguided and stubborn—but ungallant, never. His last lonely act in the pyre of his ship had been to send away those who might possibly have saved him so that they would be sure to save themselves. And if he had once said that his action in refusing daytime battle without air cover would cause him to go down in history as an ignoble character, that prediction could no longer be true—for he had fought most of his last battle in daylight, and with utmost valor.

But the Striking Force he had led was now so weakened as to be unable to come to grips with the powerful Japanese enemy. Not that the cruisers with their handful of guns could do much under any circumstances against what Japan had to offer—but now there were only *Houston*, with her handful of guns; one badly battered British cruiser, the *Exeter*; the smaller cruiser *Perth*; and a clutch of destroyers.

In fact, Captain Waller of *Perth* was the senior officer present and he led the *Houston* out of the dangerous waters toward Tanjong Priok, outside Batavia, where they arrived next morning. When Admiral Helfrich visited his headquarters, he learned of the death of Admiral Doorman, and the death of Dutch hopes that the forces of the sea would save them. It was a dreadful blow to a collapsing defense.

The news continued to trickle in, indicating the extent of the disaster and its repercussions. Late that night, U.S. submarine S-38 came to the place where the British destroyer *Electra* had gone down, and, attracted by the blinking white lights of life rafts, the submarine surfaced. Destroyer *Encounter* passed nearby and frightened her down to the bottom, but she persisted, surfaced, and picked up fifty-six survivors from the sea.

Seaman Benjamin Roberts, who was hurt and exhausted, stayed in the water until the last, directing the rescuers to his mates. "Leave me," said Roberts. "I can't make it. Get the rest." But they saved him anyhow, and he survived to join the other rescued men who were let off at the Surabaya lightship. There were now fifty-five of them—one man, Seaman Frederick Castle, had died of his burns and wounds on the submarine.

While the Americans transported their British cousins to a place where they hoped these brave men would be safe, they learned a little about the history of *Electra*—and in learning they were exposed to a view of what their own war at sea might be like.

For *Electra* had been in the thick of British naval action from the beginning of the war. In September 1939 when the Nazis began their campaign of conquest and opened the submarine war with the sinking of the liner *Athenia* in the North Atlantic, destroyer *Electra* had rescued survivors of that unfortunate vessel.

In the struggle for Norway, *Electra* was the first British man-of-war to reach Harstad, in the Narvik region, and she fought the Germans in the withdrawal from that area. *Electra* was with battleship *Warspite* on that fateful trip that led to the second Battle of Narvik.

Electra was along when mighty battleship *Hood* fell victim to the German dreadnought *Bismarck*, in the North Atlantic in May 1941, and she rescued *Hood* survivors. *Electra* was also there when battleship *Prince of Wales* smashed *Bismarck* two days later, and she proudly escorted that battleship home.

Electra was on the first convoy in World War II on the perilous route to Archangel, on Russia's White Sea. *Electra* brought *Prince of Wales* to Singapore in December 1941. She was there when *Prince of Wales* and *Repulse* were sunk by Japanese bombers in the opening days of the Pacific war, and she rescued 740 survivors of those vessels.

Electra had participated in the evacuation of Singapore and the last hours of that great base in January 1942.

Brave *Electra* had seen it all. The Americans heard her proud story and were so impressed as to put it into S-38's official papers, to be sure that others, right up to Admiral King in Washington, would know about her and the part she played in the Battle of the Java Sea.

For the Allied defenders of the Dutch East Indies, defeat in the Java Sea was not the only tragedy on February 27, 1942. While the ships of the Striking Force played out their drama in waters north of Java on that day, another debacle was taking place south of the island in the Indian Ocean. There the American aircraft tender *Langley* met her doom in a gallant attempt to supply the Allies' most pressing need—air power.

In many ways *Langley* typified the U.S. Asiatic Fleet, with its complement of old or outmoded ships. She had been built as a collier around 1910. In her youth she had been converted into a carrier with a flight deck superimposed over her upper works. Then as the art and science of carrier construction passed the old *Langley* by, she was relegated to the Asiatic Fleet and demoted into an auxiliary because she could not keep up on fleet maneuvers.

Her duty after she escaped from Manila and went to Australia was to move fighter planes about for the U.S. Army, which was the only American force in the area to have any sizable number of planes. So on February 22 *Langley* was sitting in Fremantle Harbor on the western coast of Australia, preparing for a convoy. She was deck-loaded with thirty-two P-40 fighter planes. Next to her in harbor sat the freighter *Sea Witch*, carrying another twenty-seven fighters. The difference was that *Langley's* planes were all assembled and ready to fly, and she had thirty-three pilots and twelve enlisted men as passengers, while *Sea Witch's* planes were still in crates. The steamers *Duntroon* and *Katoomba* made up the rest of this convoy, and they were to be escorted by the Australian cruiser *Phoenix*.

The plan called for *Langley* and *Sea Witch* to stay with the convoy until nearing Cocos Island, far to the southwest of Java, and then to double back northeastward to Tjilatjap. They were unlikely to meet any Japanese ships that far afield of the East Indies archipelago, and their angle of approach would protect them further.

That was the plan. It was changed. When Admiral Helfrich assumed control of all the forces in the area, one of his first actions was to order *Langley* and *Sea Witch* to peel off from the convoy early and travel as directly as possible to Tjilatjap.

From the beginning it was a precarious enterprise, for there was no airfield at Tjilatjap and no time to build one. Yet it was the only open Java port at which the planes might arrive safely. Surabaya was still functioning, but that city and port were bombed every day, starting at about nine o'clock in the morning. Surabaya was a dangerous proposition. So men at Tjilatjap got to work with axes, picks, and shovels to fix a strip for takeoff and to clear the trees from the road leading to the strip so the planes could be hauled there from the port. Men in this instance meant Dutch and American sailors, because most of the Javanese in Tjilatjap had already sensed the coming of the Japanese and had

fled to the hills, either to get away or to disassociate themselves from
the Westerners.

The work proceeded at the port, and the ships steamed ahead, coming to that last haven.

On they came without trouble, just as Admiral Helfrich had hoped.
In the interim, Helfrich consulted Admiral Glassford—after the fact—
and Admiral Glassford agreed with the decision. It was a desperate
plan, but they were now desperate men, and Glassford was in process of
moving the headquarters of the Asiatic Fleet. There was small hope
that this one act could change affairs—but there was no recourse as long
as there was any hope at all.

On February 23 *Langley* was rerouted to go it alone at flank speed,
while *Sea Witch*—under revised orders—stayed with the convoy, and
eventually made it safely to Tjilatjap.

At three o'clock on the afternoon of February 26, as *Langley* steamed
along, two Dutch PBYs located her. They reported that the Dutch
minesweeper *Willem Van der Zaan* was at sea about twenty miles to
the west, coming to escort *Langley* in. This was apparently Admiral
Helfrich's idea.

But Commander R.P. McConnell, the captain of *Langley* after Captain Felix Stump was relieved to go to headquarters, had information
from Admiral Glassford that the U.S. destroyers *Whipple* and *Edsall*
would come and get him. True, that had been the plan, but *Whipple*
and *Edsall* had seen so much action in the last few hours that neither
one of them was fit for the service—a fact that had not gotten to
Langley. Since Commander McConnell much preferred the safety of
the fast destroyers to the company of a 10-knot Dutch tub, he decided
to leave the Dutchman behind and went ahead on a zigzag pattern at
13 knots, looking forward to 0600 on February 27, when he expected
the two American destroyers to materialize.

After dark that night the confusion about the escorts seemed to get
straightened out. *Langley* was to accept the Dutch escort, Glassford
said by radio. So *Langley* dutifully steamed back to find the Dutchman
and the two PBYs. This turn of events was not to be a subject of
debate—there was no time.

That night *Langley* saw lights, turned hard right to avoid whatever
they were, ran into a nearby rain squall, came out, and continued the
backtrack. At 7:20 in the morning, she encountered the PBYs again,
and, of all unexpected ships, *Edsall* and *Whipple! Edsall* was fishing for
a submarine, so *Whipple* and *Langley* executed a big twelve-mile circle

to stay clear of those proceedings. Then *Edsall* joined up and the two destroyers stood off the bows of the carrier tender to screen her.

At nine o'clock in the morning, the men of *Langley* saw what they dreaded—one of those lazy-looking Kawanishi flying boats, which meant their course and speed and destination would be known to the enemy in a matter of minutes. In about two hours, or maybe less, they could expect an air attack.

Commander McConnell sent that message to Admiral Glassford and asked for fighter protection, just as Admiral Doorman was asking for fighter protection that day from the Java Sea. Glassford had none, as all knew, and Admiral Helfrich had to make the decision about the handful of Brewster Buffaloes whose presence was wanted in so many places. He decided to use them in an attack on the Java Sea transports. So there would be no fighter protection for *Langley*, and here she was, an aircraft ferry—a prime target for the Japanese. Everyone *knew* she must get a strike.

At 11:40 it came. Commander McConnell caused the alarms to be sounded, the air defense bugle to blow, and the ship went to general quarters, while the radio began to sputter the bad news.

NERK NERK NERK NERK NERK went the call—which interpreted Air Raid Air Raid Air Raid. . . .

The Japanese twin-engined Bettys came in, so clean and graceful with their brown and green wings and fuselage, and the blood-red circle of the Rising Sun on wingtips and tail.

Every man who raised his head could count them in the clear blue sky with its light cover of cumulus clouds. Nine planes, nine enemies who were soon going to begin pouring the rain of hell down upon them. Now the planes sailed overhead, just looking.

Langley was zigzagging on a pattern of her own. The planes were at about fifteen thousand feet. The captain was on the signal bridge, communicating by voice tube to the officer of the deck below him on the navigating bridge.

"Commence firing," he ordered.

Out of the radio shack came Radioman Charles A. Snay to see what was happening so he could give the word to his operators and they could put it on the air waves.

NERK NERK NERK went the radio.

Langley being attacked by sixteen aircraft.

"Full right rudder," shouted the captain as he looked up.

Down below the engine gang responded.

Up above the Japanese opened their bomb bays and dropped, and the first salvo of bombs struck off the port bow, just a hundred feet away—right where *Langley* would have been steaming had the captain not turned 90 degrees when he did.

NERK NERK NERK went the radio.

Zigzag went the *Langley* as she turned and turned again, the warm bright sea slapping her bows on one side and the other.

Up above, the Japanese flight commander was slow and patient. He had all the time in the world. There were no Allied Brewster fighters in sight, and if any showed up, the gunners of the Bettys could shoot them down with ridiculous ease, for these old Allied planes were of the early 1930s, not the 1940s. The Japanese flight droned along, each man following the leader and waiting.

They approached again, and when they were overhead, Captain McConnell swung the ship hard again at 90 degrees, and *Langley* moved out from under the point where the Japanese would have aimed—except that no bombs were dropped.

The planes moved lazily away, and circled, and came back for another smooth approach.

NERK NERK NERK went the radio.

Out there somewhere people were listening, but no one could help.

On the third approach, the very intelligent Japanese air commander above seemed to have caught Commander McConnell's rhythm, and he guessed correctly. For as the planes came to the dropping point, Commander McConnell had to decide—port or starboard—and he opted for starboard and swung the ship. But this time the Japanese had swung right with him. They dropped their bombs, which came screaming down, seven of them.

Two bombs straddled the ship. Shrapnel punched holes in the sides that let the water come rushing in, sending the pitter-patter noise along the hull that all below could hear.

But they heard more:

Bomb No. 1 smashed the aft motorboat and started fires in two other motorboats and fires on deck.

Bomb No. 2 set fire to planes on the flight deck and to other boats and rafts.

Bomb No. 3 smashed into the port after elevator and wrecked more planes and started more fires. The planes burned, but they did not explode, for the men of *Langley* had had the good sense to drain the gasoline from the tanks before the attack.

Bomb No. 4 struck near the port stack supports and smashed more planes on deck.

Bomb No. 5 struck starboard aft on the flight deck, wrecked the staff officers' quarters, and exploded on the lower deck, starting fires.

NERK NERK NERK said the radio.

Then silence.

Back on the air, the operator explained!

Got a hit that put us out for a few minutes . . . lost local control . . . transmitter went out but I plugged in batteries and am back now. . . .

Those monitoring *Langley*'s radio might think things were well under control, but the opposite was the case.

On deck the fire mains were out, the starboard main broken beyond repair. The side of the ship was pierced and she was taking water heavily. Soon she had a list of 10 degrees to port, and it increased. The captain ordered the wrecked planes on the port side of the flight deck pushed overboard to lighten her and help her balance.

The gyro compass broke down, and the steering control was moved aft, then moved back again. The telephones were out and the engine room was flooding.

The Japanese planes came back, slow and graceful, and they strafed the carrier, paying special attention to planes on deck. Cannon holes appeared in the planes and in the superstructure and in the flight deck.

NERK NERK NERK

Langley being attacked by . . .

On the bridge Commander McConnell ordered counterflooding to starboard to counteract the growing list to port. The orders were carried out, but the water was gaining so fast on the port side that counterflooding made no appreciable difference. *Langley* was dropping lower in the water.

In the radio room Radioman Snay tried to contact the bridge but found the telephone dead. He left his assistants and announced that he was going to the bridge for information.

Through the voice tube the engineering officer reported to the bridge that water was four feet deep in the port motor pit.

NERK NERK NERK

The Japs are now working close to our spread . . .

On the bridge Commander McConnell made a difficult decision.

"Prepare to abandon ship. Pass the word."

The order meant only that the officer of the deck and the divisional officers were to check the condition of the boats, examine the rafts, and alert the men to danger. But some seamen on the main deck, greenhorns in their first battle, heard that word "abandon" and panicked. Men began tumbling over the side.

Luckily *Edsall* saw what was happening, and came up behind, circling back and forth, picking the frightened seamen out of the water.

NERK NERK NERK

We are all okay so far. . . . Mama said there would be days like this . . . she must have known. . . .

Suddenly the comforting rumble of the engines ceased and from the engine room came the word: Engines stopped. Fire rooms flooding.

NERK NERK NERK

Hits on the flight deck and on planes. One on the well deck one on fo'c'sle. Gas fumes on the well deck. . . .

NERK

On the bridge Captain McConnell was estimating their chances. *Langley* was not nearly sunk, and she could probably be kept afloat. But what did that mean? There were no tugs to bring her to Tjilatjap. Could a destroyer tow her? And what about the Japanese? They would certainly be back. Tjilatjap was fifty miles away. Could they make it in time? And were there enough undamaged planes left to make it worth while?

NERK NERK NERK

Jap planes were . . . too high for our guns. We have a decided list. . . . Power off on ship AC to batteries. . . .

The captain's decision was a difficult one, but in the interest of his crew he came to the conclusion that *Langley* should be abandoned and sunk, for the mission was a failure. The Japanese would certainly come back and get them. Nor could *Langley*, in her present condition, negotiate the shallow entrance to Tjilatjap harbor. The flooding forward had brought her down too deep.

NERK NERK NERK

The Japs are jamming us as much as possible. . . . We are securing soon . . . the ship is listing . . . shot to hell. . . .

From the bridge came the order: ABANDON SHIP.

NERK NERK NERK Signing off. . . .

And the radio went silent.

On deck two boats were lowered, and the wounded were carefully placed in one motor launch. But as it went down, one end of the launch fell into the water, spilling out many of the occupants. No one had noticed that shrapnel had destroyed the launching supports on that end.

Soon the officers were supervising the dropping of seven life rafts and two balsa rafts, and men were going over the side. When only the captain and the executive officer were left, they made a last check for confused or wounded men, found none, and took to the boats themselves, leaving *Langley* forlorn and silent in the water.

Captain McConnell went to the *Whipple*. The exec got into No. 4 motor launch and went out to pick up survivors. *Edsall* was doing the same and so was her motor whaleboat.

All but sixteen of *Langley*'s complement were saved.

The captain went over it in his mind: The electric decoding machine had been thrown overboard. All code books and secret papers had been thrown overboard. The navigator's compartment had been checked and all marked charts and papers that might in any way help the enemy had been jettisoned.

He conferred with Lieutenant Commander E.S. Karpe of *Whipple*. They must sink her, and it was to be *Whipple*'s unpleasant task.

Captain Karpe gave the orders. The men of the destroyer manned their 4-inch guns and sent nine shells into *Langley* at the waterline, followed by two torpedoes. The old carrier began to take more water, and her profile lowered in the water.

She sank.

35

The Last of the Houston

On the morning of February 28 the atmosphere at Tjilatjap was tense. The sinking of *Langley* was known, and so was the break-up of the ABDA command and the departure of nearly all the brass hats except Admiral Glassford, who was sticking tight to Admiral Helfrich in Batavia, as his orders required. But this last American base in Java was finished. This day the port offices were closed, and the American personnel were ordered to find transportation and get to Australia. The end of the American presence in Java was very near.

During the long night S-37, patrolling in the Java Sea, had come upon one of *De Ruyter*'s boats which held some sixty survivors, crowded together in the small area. Among them were two Americans, and the submarine took them off. But the little S-boat could not possibly carry the Dutch castaways. She could and did give them five days' rations from her slender stores, but that was all she could spare, plus prayers for their safety. And then the Dutchmen had to be left to an unknown fate at the mercy of the sea and the Japanese, who controlled it.

This same day—almost the last of the Java operations—the American submarines were ordered withdrawn from the coastal patrols Admiral Helfrich had set up, and all ships of the Asiatic Fleet except submarines were ordered out of waters north of Java. This sea was indeed being ceded to the enemy.

S-39 went out on one last rescue mission. Australian Rear Admiral A.M. Spooner and a stray air marshal were supposed to have escaped from Singapore to the tiny island of Chebia, north of Banka Island, off Sumatra, where they were hiding awaiting rescue. S-39 was sent to do the job. She reached Chebia this day and found the village where the men were supposed to be, but it was burned out, and not a soul was on the island. Either the men had escaped or the Japanese had found them.

At Surabaya, Commander Binford of American Destroyer Division 58 hurried ashore on the morning of February 28 and telephoned Admiral Glassford at headquarters in Bandoeng. What next? was his question. Where should the four remaining American destroyers under his command go? Glassford did not immediately have an answer. He wanted to know the condition of the ships. The commander told him they were almost out of ammunition, badly beaten up, half broken down, and nearly out of torpedoes. It was certainly apparent to Glassford that they were hardly in condition to fight—and fight for what? Java obviously could not be saved. The Japanese landing forces were already in action, and there was no air and no sea power to stop them.

At two o'clock in the afternoon, not having heard from Bandoeng, the destroyer commander called again, and this time Admiral Glassford gave him specific instructions. He was to take destroyers *Alden, John D. Edwards, Paul Jones,* and *John D. Ford* to Australia, to Exmouth Gulf, there to rearm them and await orders.

That same day Admiral Purnell arrived at Exmouth Gulf and found the place impossible for naval operations, with tides, currents, and general conditions all unsuitable. He issued instructions to move everything out to Fremantle, nearly a thousand miles south, and left for that port himself the same day.

Not knowing of this change in plans—but no matter, they would soon find out—the four destroyers set out. They negotiated the east entrance to Surabaya Harbor cautiously, passed the lightship, and, then speeding to 22 knots, headed for Bali Strait, where they would hug the Java shore and hope they would not run into a handful of Japanese battleships. That night they did run into Japanese warships—three fast destroyers—but they escaped a major fight and at 27 knots headed for Australia. They made it safely.

One more American destroyer of the Asiatic Fleet remained in Javan waters that day—*Pope.* She was lucky enough to have a full load of torpedoes. She and the British destroyer *Encounter* were ordered to escort crippled cruiser *Exeter* from Surabaya to Ceylon for repairs.

That left a third convoy of ships of the Striking Force still in Japanese waters. It consisted of cruisers *Houston* and *Perth* and the Dutch destroyer *Evertsen,* lying at Batavia's base of Tandjong Priok.

Houston was in very rough shape this day. Her rear turret was still out; a major dockyard repair would be needed to make it usable again.

During the Battle of the Java Sea her turrets Nos. 1 and 2 had each fired 101 salvos of ammunition or a total of more than six hundred shells. The concussion from this firing had torn down everything on the upper decks that was not fastened securely. Drawers were knocked out of place, clothes fell off their hangers in the lockers. Radios and books were knocked to the floor all over the ship.

The admiral's cabin, where President Roosevelt had stayed from time to time, was a shambles, wrecked by repeated concussions, so that even the soundproofing was torn from the bulkheads. The glass windows of the bridge were shattered. Fire hoses were leaking along the decks and making the passageways sloppy underfoot. Many plates were sprung from concussions and near misses, and the ship was steadily taking water. Even so, when Captain Rooks was asked for an appraisal of her seaworthiness, the captain told Admiral Glassford that *Houston* was ready, willing, and able to fight. And so she was—battered and with a crew that was nearly exhausted but yet unbowed.

The days just passed had taken their toll—half the time had been spent at battle stations, and some of the men now were under sedation for exhaustion. Among the black gang, the doctors were treating some seventy cases of heat exhaustion. Every man who could be spared and who could work was still moving ammunition from turret No. 3 up forward. The job was not finished until late in the afternoon of February 28, after nearly twenty-two hours of constant labor.

During the morning hours the men got some relaxation if they were off watch, but the officers had almost none, because hour after hour the lookouts reported Japanese planes just above the horizon. The enemy was out there watching and waiting for *Houston* and *Perth* to make their move.

Houston and *Perth* had planned to refuel at Tandjong Priok, but the Dutch port authorities would give *Houston* nothing and gave *Perth* only three hundred tons of fuel, which might possibly take her to Australia. They were saving what they had left, the authorities said, for ships of the Dutch Royal Navy.

Pilot Thomas Payne, who had taxied his seaplane away from *Houston* at Surabaya as she set out for the Battle of the Java Sea the day before, now flew in from that place and landed out in the harbor, then taxied in slowly so he would not be shot at by his friends.

Captain Rooks went ashore in the afternoon and conferred with Admiral Glassford. The admiral had been talking to Admiral Helfrich that afternoon, and Helfrich wanted the cruisers to go to Surabaya. There they would get into a fight, he hoped, for Helfrich was still thinking about saving Java from Japanese invasion, even though all others knew it was far too late. Glassford might have refused to send the American ship, but his orders were still to help the Dutch. Instead he used persuasion, and the final decision was to send *Houston* and *Perth* to Tjilatjap.

While ashore, Captain Rooks and Captain Waller of *Perth* were informed by the British authorities that Sunda Strait, between Java and Sumatra, was open. A reconnaissance plane had reported at three o'clock in the afternoon that no Japanese surface units were in the area. That plane somehow had managed to miss a force of sixty transports that were just ready to land troops on Saint Nicholas Point at the northern entrance to the strait. Admiral Kurita was there with his Western Attack Force, and not far away lurked another guardian force built around the carrier *Ryujo* and four heavy cruisers, ready to take on any Allied ships that might come along. There were light cruisers and a whole squadron of destroyers to cover the landing, too.

If *Houston* and *Perth* steamed into Sunda Strait they would run the gamut of this whole series of forces. Major General Schilling, the commander of the Royal Netherlands Army, knew of the coming of this invasion force, but so confused were affairs in Java by this day that he did not know that *Houston* and *Perth* were in harbor, nor that they planned to go on; and neither Admiral Helfrich nor Admiral Glassford had the information about the landings. The whole interservice structure was breaking down with the collapse of the ABDA command.

Captain Rooks and Captain Waller went back to their ships that afternoon, with their instructions. Somehow the rumor had started that *Houston*'s men were headed for San Francisco and a long leave. That rumor was greeted with cheers, and morale on the ship went up because of it.

They waited then. The captains had hoped to sail at 6:30 in the evening. The pilot who had been promised for that hour did not show up. He never did show up in fact, and *Perth* led out an hour later, to pick the way through the minefield.

The plan had been for *Evertsen* to accompany the cruisers, but her skipper had not been so informed. As the two cruisers passed by her on the way out of the harbor, Captain Waller sent for a message. The captain of the Dutch destroyer agreed that he would like to follow, but said his boilers were down. It would be an hour before he could tag along after them.

Outside, the ships moved up to 28 knots and headed for Sunda Strait, with *Perth* in the lead.

Just before eleven o'clock that night the Japanese destroyer *Fubuki* spotted the Allied ships and raised the alarm. For a moment there was real concern in the Japanese force, because the amphibious landing was under way, and this was the vital hour, when a really strong attack might knock the whole thing into a cocked hat.

But soon *Fubuki* discovered that there were only two ships in this convoy, and *Houston* and *Perth* had still not seen the blacked-out Japanese destroyer that zigzagged along, keeping an eye on them and informing the Japanese fleet of their position.

At 11:25 Captain Rooks was on the bridge of *Houston*, with Lieutenant Harold S. Hamlin, Jr., the officer of the deck. They watched *Perth* carefully so they could respond quickly to that ship's movements. The ship was alert; turrets Nos. 1 and 2 were manned and powder trains were in motion. Star shells were laid out for the boat deck antiaircraft guns. If they did encounter the enemy, at least they would be able to see what they were doing.

The sea was calm. There was no wind, and a full moon gleamed down on the mountains of western Java. Saint Nicholas Point light came into view—a sign of the entrance to Sunda Strait. Then they saw the vague silhouette of ships—Captain Rooks decided instantly that these were not ordinary Dutch patrol craft. He immediately ordered general quarters.

Captain Waller's ship challenged the nearest vessel with a blinker light, and the other made a reply with a strange green lamp. They now were certain that it was Japanese. *Perth* opened up with a salvo from her No. 1 turret and changed course, turning hard to starboard, which had her moving north. *Houston* fired a salvo and turned after her.

The Japanese destroyer fired back. She sent nine torpedoes at the two ships, but all missed because of the radical Allied maneuver. The Japanese also sent up a flare that not only illuminated the area but warned their comrades that action against an enemy had begun.

Indeed it had. The torpedoes that missed *Perth* and *Houston* traveled hot and fast, and hit several of the Japanese transports that were landing their men inshore. So the Allies won a round without scoring a hit.

Houston began firing star shells, and there before her to port was a cluster of Japanese warships. The cruisers swung north into the passage between Panjang Island and Saint Nicholas Point to escape the trap. But now a heavy cruiser and ten destroyers lay between them and the point, and two other cruisers and several destroyers were making way to engage them.

Houston and *Perth* began firing at everything they saw, and with the great number of Japanese ships milling about they were never out of targets. One after another they scored hits on transport ships. The *Sakura Maru* sank. Three other transports were hurt and ran onto the beach. One of these ships carried General K. Imamura, the leader of the army expedition, and he went over the side. He clung to a bit of driftwood for twenty minutes until he was rescued. Meanwhile, the ship lost most of its deck-loaded cargo, which fell overboard.

From the bridge of *Houston*, the sight was blinding, confusing, and amazing all at once. No matter where one turned there were targets illuminated by the star shells of the ships. The water was literally churning with Japanese torpedoes, and each time one missed, there was a very good chance that it would end its journey against the hull of another Japanese ship—many torpedoes did just that. Destroyers kept rushing in to illuminate the two Allied cruisers with searchlights for the benefit of their heavy cruisers farther off. The skilled gunners of *Houston* shot out those searchlights time and again. One enemy destroyer was hit point blank by a salvo from *Houston* and went careening off, smoking and afire. The port 5-inch guns of *Houston* found the range of another destroyer and tore off her bridge.

The fight went on and on. For fifty minutes the men of *Houston* watched the Japanese firing, often at their own ships, and not one shell touched the cruiser. Fifty charmed minutes in the maelstrom of battle! There was one flurry: A salvo of heavy shells passed completely through the wardroom—from starboard to port—without exploding.

But this luck could not last. Not with all those ships shooting at the two Allied vessels. First was *Perth*'s agony. She was hit by four torpedoes almost simultaneously, and at the same time the gunners of one of those big cruisers found her. She sank very quickly.

Now all those Japanese cruiser and destroyer guns were concentrated on *Houston*, and the Japanese destroyers came in like angry terriers to send their torpedoes at the ship.

First she took a shell in the forecastle that started a fire in the forward paint locker.

That was not too serious. But the flames made an aiming point for the enemy, and the Japanese gunners began hitting the forecastle repeatedly.

Three Japanese destroyers, moving together, crossed the wake of *Houston*, three thousand yards astern. They could have been blasted by turret No. 3, but that turret was out. The three, in concert, launched torpedoes.

Commander Maher, the gunnery officer, spotted the wakes and

warned Captain Rooks, on the bridge. The captain maneuvered, and torpedoes flanked the ship. The captain had sailed between them!

But it could not last. Suddenly a torpedo crashed into the port side. The explosion killed every man in the after engine room and smashed machinery below. *Houston's* speed was immediately reduced to 23 knots. Smoke and steam spewed out of broken lines and ventilators over the gun deck, driving the men away from their guns.

The 5-inch gun director was knocked out, and the men had to fire by local control. They kept going, getting back to the guns when the first gush of steam ended. Power was knocked out of the shell hoists, so the ammunition had to be brought up by hand. When men tried to go below, they found their way blocked by debris. The gunners were reduced to firing star shells.

A second torpedo, a moment later, caught *Houston* just beneath the communications deck on the starboard side. As she trembled with the blow, the Japanese cruisers suddenly seemed to find the range simultaneously, and the ship shuddered again and again under the impact of 8-inch shells. No. 2 turret blew up with a roar, sending high columns of flame into the air. The heat became so intense that it drove everyone off the bridge. Communications throughout the ship were now totally disrupted.

Half a dozen men stumbled out of the wreckage of No. 2 turret, led by Ensign C.D. Smith, the turret officer. But there was nothing they could do for either their dead companions or the gun. This explosion flooded the magazine and now No. 1 turret was put out of action because she had no more ammunition. The 5-inch guns, the pompoms, and the .50-calibre machine guns were all she had left with which to fight.

Japanese torpedo boats raced in. The pompom gunners got one of them and watched it explode. But another came in and launched a torpedo that hit *Houston* forward of the quarterdeck. The ship began taking water by the hundreds of tons through the holes smashed by three torpedoes and many 8-inch shells. She took a strong list to starboard, and her speed fell off so that her captain could no longer maneuver to miss the enemy fire.

Captain Rooks looked around him on the bridge and summoned his marine bugler.

"Sound Abandon Ship," he ordered.

The bugle call echoed along the sides of the ship. Men still died as they sought to get off, for the Japanese kept up their hail of fire, and the shells struck and exploded smashing the cruiser to bits.

Captain Rooks stood at the head of the ladder on the communications deck, wishing godspeed to the men as they left the ship, shaking hands and pressing arms. It was obvious to all that he had no intention of leaving the *Houston*. The communications officer struggled to destroy his secret papers and equipment. He came back from a radio shack that had been destroyed by the Japanese and he found the captain lying on the deck, nearly unconscious, downed by fragments from a Japanese shell. The captain died in Ensign Levett's arms.

Commander David Roberts, the executive officer, and Commander John Hollowell, the navigator, went back to the boat deck to see if they could get some boats launched, to give the men a better chance for life. They were not seen again.

As the ship lost its speed it became an easy target for the Japanese, and more torpedoes plowed into the hull, more shells raked and sifted the wreckage of the decks, hurling high the bodies of men already dead.

The Japanese destroyers now held her in their searchlights and came near, attacking with machine guns and light antiaircraft guns. Men jumped over the side and swam away, fearful of being caught as the ship went down, and the Japanese machine gunned them in the water. Finally a torpedo ended her anguish. The ship rolled, and the air caught the American ensign, which straightened out and showed the full stars and stripes just before the *Houston* sank into the waters of the Sunda Strait.

Of the thousand men aboard, not quite four hundred were picked up by the Japanese and sent to prison along with their cousins from the cruiser *Perth*. Oddly enough, they were also joined by the men of *Evertsen*, for that destroyer had followed the cruisers to Sunda Strait, far behind, and had managed to arrive just as the Japanese were celebrating the death of *Houston*. It took just a few minutes to destroy *Evertsen*.

The Striking Force was down to nearly nothing now, and so was the fighting contingent of the Asiatic Fleet.

36

The Pecos *Adventure*

On the day that *Langley* was diverted from her original course in a desperate gamble by Admiral Helfrich, the oiler *Pecos* was setting out from Tjilatjap along with the destroyer *Parrott*. They were bound for Colombo on a mission for Admiral Glassford, and so *Pecos* was in the area when *Langley* was sunk. And nothing could be more logical than that she would be called upon to pick up the survivors of *Langley* from destroyers *Whipple* and *Edsall*. That meant nearly all the officers, airmen, and crew, since few lives had been lost.

At one o'clock in the afternoon *Pecos* was traveling southwest toward Cocos Island. Her course was immediately altered to take her eastward toward Christmas Island, for this British outpost was deemed the most likely place to transfer the survivors with least trouble and least chance of interference from the Japanese.

The vessels moved to the northwest tip of Christmas Island, and *Parrott* went off about her own business. There was so much work for the handful of destroyers still in operation that they always had two or three jobs piled up. *Parrott* steamed away, and *Pecos* waited for *Whipple* and *Edsall* to come up with the men of the carrier.

Commander E.M. Crouch, the senior officer and leader of Destroyer Division 57, made arrangements by radio with the British to send pilot E. Craig out in a boat to bring the *Pecos* in safely, and Lieutenant Commander T.A. Donovan of the *Langley* went ashore to join Craig in the boat and help direct Lieutenant Commander E.P. Abernathy, the captain of the oiler.

At ten o'clock on the morning of February 28, *Pecos* was ready to come in, and Craig and Donovan went out in a light boat to greet and pilot her. Just then, three Japanese bombers arrived on the scene, and in the excitement as the pilot boat came up to *Pecos*, her propeller caught in a trailing line and fouled. Pilot Craig caught a Jacob's ladder and hoisted himself up to the deck of the oiler. When last seen, Lieutenant Commander Donovan was floating away in the pilot boat, trying desperately to clear the propeller so he could start the engine. After that, the men of *Pecos* and the destroyers were too busy with the Japanese planes to pay any further attention to his plight. The Japanese planes circled, came back, and dropped a stick of seven bombs on the three ships. Luckily, not one hit. Then the ships were saved from further attack by the approach of a rain squall which hid them from the Japanese. When the squall blew over, the enemy planes were gone.

It was obvious, however, that Christmas Island was not a safe place for the transfer of the survivors of *Langley*, so the vessels moved away at 12 knots, *Pecos*'s top speed. They headed south, and at eleven o'clock that night turned toward Exmouth Gulf, supposedly the new base of the Asiatic Fleet. There was no chance to move people that night, for the wind whistled along at 26 knots. But around dawn the wind died down, and at 4:45 on the morning of March 1 the captains in radio consultation decided it would be safe to try to make the exchange.

Pecos reduced her speed to only a knot or so—just enough to make steerageway—and turned 180 degrees to the wind, creating a lee of sorts. Her 40-foot launch was put over the side, and after five trips to *Whipple* and three to *Edsall*, the survivors were all on the deck of the *Pecos*. The destroyers, as nervous as greyhounds, signaled and were off on other missions ordered by Admiral Helfrich and Admiral Glassford on this fateful day.

By 8:15 the two destroyers had disappeared over the horizon at high speed, and *Pecos* was plugging along at her 12 knots on a course of 160 degrees, planning to pass 130 miles west of the western tip of Australia and then head into Fremantle to drop the survivors. This city had medical and housing facilities that Exmouth Gulf would not have.

At ten o'clock their trials began in the form of a single-engined Japanese plane with nonretractable landing gear. The plane circled the oiler as if to identify her, and then went away. But Commander Abernathy knew that it was only a question of an hour or two until something else happened. Although he could not know it, the Japanese carrier *Soryu* was not far away, and the plane's radioed message was picked up and brought to the air commander.

At 11:45 that morning the first wave of dive bombers appeared over *Pecos* and began tracking her. The bombers came down out of the sun, and dropped. All three of these first bombs missed, but each bomber carried a pair of missiles, and they came back. Three more bombers joined them, and *Pecos* underwent twelve attacks in all in that first wave. One bomb struck just aft of the No. 1 3-inch gun, killing and wounding several men.

It was remarkable that so few of the bombs hit the slow oiler, but Captain Abernathy used the same tactics as those employed by other fighting ships—as the bombers reached their point of drop, he turned hard right or hard left, and it was simply luck in a guessing game that helped him win this round.

As they all knew, when they realized they were under attack by carrier planes, there would be other rounds. The carrier had the entire day to harry them—there were no Allied carriers within thousands of miles, and there was precious few land-based Allied aircraft anywhere in the region.

An hour after the first attack, a second wave of six bombers appeared. By this time *Pecos* was suffering from her wounds. The one hit scored in the first round had put a 15-foot hole in the main deck and damaged several oil tanks. It had wrecked the power and oil and fire lines forward, but the crew had managed to put out the fires. There were dead and wounded men on the decks, and the boom of the mainmast was knocked loose, which gave the ship a reckless appearance, suggesting worse damage than she had in fact suffered from this blow. Actually, the most dangerous wound inflicted on the first round had come from a near miss to port, forward, which had ruptured plates which caused flooding and given the ship an 8-degree list to port. This list was quickly corrected by counterflooding—the watertight compartments held.

The second wave of bombers was disastrously accurate. Those six planes scored four direct hits on *Pecos*. One bomb went through the No. 1 motor launch and exploded forward of the bridge, blowing out the side of the ship to the waterline for some twenty feet. Several men on the bridge and members of antiaircraft control unit were killed or wounded.

The second bomb knocked out the radio antenna, putting *Pecos* out of touch with the world. It crashed below and broke bulkheads and plating. Soon the tanker was listing 15 degrees to port. The captain ordered the port anchor let go to lighten the load, and pumped oil out of some forward compartments to help compensate for the increased weight caused by the intake of water.

The third bomb knocked out the No. 1 5-inch gun, and killed and wounded most of its crew. The fourth bomb exploded on the main deck and destroyed several steam lines and more of the plating. A near miss aft killed more men of the gun crews with flying shrapnel.

Some of the men were lost inadvertently, because of the panic that overcame the ship's crew and the same lack of crisis discipline that had overtaken the men of *Langley*. The same men may have even been involved. As it became apparent that *Pecos* was sorely hurt, men began to panic, and although the ship was under way, they threw out life rafts and managed to disengage two of the boats. The boats were dropped over the side, but by the time the men jumped it was almost impossible for them to reach them and so many were needlessly drowned simply because of inexperience and fear. It took the combined efforts of Captain Abernathy and the officers of *Pecos* and *Langley* to put an end to the panic.

The third wave of bombers, which arrived just before three o'clock in the afternoon, did not score any direct hits. *Pecos* was lying low and sluggish in the water, with many holes in her hull, taking water steadily. Two near misses just off the starboard at bridge level killed and wounded more men and seemed to make her sit even lower.

Then, about 3:40, one more near miss to port made the captain realize that she was doomed. The two remaining whale boats were hoisted over the side and four life rafts were pushed over. The captain ordered the ship abandoned, and men began to jump the very short distance from deck to water.

The men who could get off did so. Some wounded could not escape, nor could some who were trapped below decks. *Pecos* pointed her bow down and her stern into the air and plunged to the bottom of the sea.

During the period when the radio was operative, the steamer *Mount Vernon* had been contacted and had altered course toward *Pecos*. Soon *Whipple* reappeared and began rescuing survivors, who were taken to the *Mount Vernon* when she reached the scene. It was now around eight o'clock at night, and the rescue was screened from possible enemy action by darkness. But the same darkness made it impossible to see every man clinging to a bit of flotsam. So only 232 officers and men from both *Langley* and *Pecos* were rescued that night, whereas *Pecos* alone before the fight had carried 15 officers and 227 men of her own.

It was a sad and bedraggled gang of survivors who headed for Fremantle.

37

Retreat from Java

When the Allied naval commanders decided to send the crippled British cruiser *Exeter* to Ceylon for repairs, escorted by U.S. destroyer *Pope* and British destroyer *Encounter*, they debated which route the ships should take to reach the Indian Ocean.

They had to go through one strait or another, for they were lying at Surabaya, on the north coast of Java, and must move around to the south either through Sunda Strait, at the west end of the island, or through Bali or Lombok straits at the east end. Admiral Glassford suggested the Japanese probably had control of Sunda Strait, but Admiral Palliser, the British commander, thought it more likely they controlled Lombok Strait, while Bali Strait was too shallow and dangerous for a cruiser. So Admiral Palliser gave the fateful order: the convoy should proceed south via the western exit, Sunda Strait.

The three admirals had also detailed the Dutch destroyer *Witte de With* to this force, but through another of those confusions of divided command, the captain of *Witte de With* had granted shore leave to his men, and they were scattered all over Surabaya and beyond at the crucial moment. *Witte de With* was left behind—to be sunk by the Japanese a few days later.

So on that last day of February the three ships of the convoy set out through the Surabaya minefield. At four o'clock on the morning of March 1, they sighted and avoided a small convoy of Japanese ships. Captain O.L. Gordon of the *Exeter* knew that there was no point in winning a pyrrhic victory and losing these three ships if he could help it. He took as his orders the attainment of Ceylon. The little convoy headed on.

However there was just too much Japanese naval power in the waters of Java that day, and it was not long before the three Allied vessels were spotted. The first to see them was a plane from one of the cruisers *Nachi* or *Haguro*, and on learning of the presence of the Allied ships, the two heavy cruisers turned to shadow them. Admiral Takagi was ready for battle.

So was Admiral Takahashi, whose flagship *Ashigara* was leading cruiser *Myoko* and a pair of destroyers. Soon the battle was joined— *Nachi* opened fire on the Allied ships.

Pope and *Encounter* ran ahead on an easterly course to protect *Exeter*, and they made smoke as they went. But the Japanese had spotting planes that quickly nullified the effect of smoke. *Exeter*'s fire control system failed at this crucial moment, which meant that her shells were being wasted in salvoes fired wide of the mark.

The guns had begun roaring at 10:20 in the morning. Forty minutes later the three Allied ships were searching for rain squalls, hoping thus to escape what seemed to be certain destruction. But the Japanese were too many, and they closed in, engaging all three ships. Like the Japanese cruisers, *Exeter* was equipped with torpedoes, and she fired them, but to no avail. The range was too great, and to achieve a closer range would have risked suicide in the mouths of the guns of the heavy cruisers.

An hour after the opening of the battle, the Japanese found the range and put a shell into *Exeter*'s boiler rooms, causing the cruiser to lose power and knocking out the gun controls. The ship slowed to 4 knots, which made her a lifeless target for the Japanese cruisers. When they began straddling her, Captain Gordon ordered his men off the ship, and very shortly thereafter Japanese destroyers fired eighteen torpedoes at the sitting duck. One of them hit, and she exploded and went down very quickly.

Soon *Encounter* was hit and abandoned. *Pope* was about to experience the same treatment when a rain squall appeared ahead, and Commander W.C. Blinn headed toward it. Inside the weather blanket, the men tried to make repairs, while the officers on the bridge changed course and tried to outfox the enemy. They did for a time; when the ship emerged from the squall the Japanese were nowhere in sight. But again the arm of nemesis was long, and the power of the Japanese on this day was simply overwhelming. What the cruisers could not do, an airplane did: It caught sight of *Pope* and trailed her, sending the Japanese the information that this lone enemy was escaping their net.

The carrier *Ryujo* had been involved in the whole landing operation at Saint Nicholas Point, at the head of Sunda Strait, basically to provide protection for the landing troops, and now she was called upon to provide the kiss of death for *Pope*. Her planes took off after the destroyer. Six dive bombers arrived first, and the men of the destroyer fought them with everything they had. First the 3-inch gun aft failed, and then the other guns heated or ran out of ammunition. On the eleventh diving attack, the Japanese scored a near miss just off the No. 4 torpedo tube, which caved in the plating of the hull, wrecked the port engine shaft, and flooded many compartments. That was the beginning of the end.

When the dive bombers ran out of ammunition, they were followed by half a dozen high-flying level bombers from *Ryujo*. Captain Blinn managed to elude their attacks, but *Pope* continued to flood, and the damage control officer reported that she was not going to stay afloat much longer. So secret material was destroyed, demolition charges were set, and the motor whale boat was put over the side along with life rafts.

The men and the officers abandoned the ship, setting off charges. The Japanese helped at the last minute—a cruiser newly arrived on the scene began firing salvoes into the stopped destroyer. On the sixth salvo the cruiser's shells struck. *Pope* plunged to the bottom stern first.

The survivors made the mistake of firing on a Japanese plane that flew in low to look them over. Thereupon several Japanese planes came to strafe the men in the boats and in the water. But the men who were not killed managed to stay together until the Japanese rescued them several nights later.

Thus on March 1, the Striking Force that the Allies had assembled was no longer in existence, and all the ships of the Asiatic Fleet that had participated in it were gone—either en route to Australia or sunk in the waters around the Malay Barrier, which had proved to be no barrier at all. The Japanese landings on Java, begun shortly after *Houston* and *Perth* were sunk, were proceeding in full force.

That night Admirals Palliser and Glassford considered their situation, and listened to reports from various sources that indicated the Japanese were landing in strength on the island. Had they wished to fight now, there was nothing left to throw into the battle.

Even if they could round up a few vessels from Australia and other areas, by the time they arrived the whole island would be in the hands of the enemy—it would be needless sacrifice.

The two admirals decided they must face Admiral Helfrich with these opinions and proceeded to his headquarters. Admiral Palliser flatly argued that Admiral Helfrich release them from his order to fight to the last, for it would only mean death or imprisonment for all who had so far survived.

Admiral Helfrich, drawing himself up in dignity and indignation, replied:

> I must decline to accept your recommendation. I must continue resistance as long as I have ships that can fight. I have already ordered a greater concentration of submarines against the enemy in the Java Sea. The enemy will make another attempt to land tonight near Rembang. He may succeed tonight but I shall attack the next wave of transports.

It was gallant but foolish. The Japanese were already ashore and not fifty miles from Batavia. Palliser knew this. So did Admiral Glassford. Palliser spoke:

> Then I must say to you, as the senior British naval officer in this area, that my instructions from the Admiralty are to withdraw His Majesty's ships from Java when resistance will serve no further useful purpose. That time, in my judgment, has come. Therefore I feel it my duty to order His Majesty's ships to India at once, and this I propose to do.

Helfrich was aghast, even though he must have known that the end was near. Still, this was Dutch territory, and how could a man give up his homeland without fighting to the last for it?

He asked Palliser if he realized that he was under his, Helfrich's, orders. Palliser replied that of course he did, but that in this vital matter he could not do other than his duty as he saw it.

This reply kindled in Admiral Helfrich's mind the whole history of the joint defense and the strategy that had been involved, wherein British and Dutch ideas were often in conflict. He said:

> You know that I lent to the British when Malaya was threatened all of my fighting fleet—my cruisers, my destroyers, my submarines, my air—and all of it was placed at your disposal for your operation as you saw fit. In so doing we suffered grave losses. Furthermore you did not hold Malaya. Singapore is now in the hands of the enemy. You failed. I think the wisest course now is to let me continue to handle this situation and save Java.

But it was too late for recriminations to save the day, and even if Palliser had agreed with the Dutch assessment of the British effort in Malaya, the admiral could not do other than he was doing. It was all academic anyhow—there was nothing left with which to fight. Said Palliser:

I cannot alter my decision.

Helfrich asked for a one-hour delay while he consulted the governor general of the Dutch East Indies, but Palliser refused to delay his decision. Helfrich then turned to Admiral Glassford.

And you, Admiral Glassford, what do you intend to do?

Glassford, of course, had already sent most of his forces to Australia for safety. The port at Tjilatjap had been abandoned. The submarine headquarters had been moved to Australia. True, American ships were still in the waters around Java, but they were on the move. American submarines were still active, but, like the British, the Americans had lost about everything they could afford to lose here. Yet Glassford still had his orders, and they had not been changed. He said:

My instructions are to report to you for duty. Any order you give me will be obeyed at once. I wish to say to you, however, that I concur without reservation in the advice given you by your chief of staff [Palliser]. I am to retire to Australia by order of my commander in chief; if necessary, to abandon Java, but this is for you to decide.

Helfrich saw it all, finally. And he mustered his dignity.

Very well then, Admiral Palliser, you may give any orders you wish to His Majesty's ships. Admiral Glassford, you will *order* your ships to Australia.

Admiral Glassford left to do just that. He set out by car for Tjilatjap and arrived there late next evening. At the base he assembled the handful of Americans still holding on, and made arrangements for their evacuation. Two PBYs were still at Surabaya. They were ordered to Tjilatjap, and two more were called from Broome, Australia.

On March 2, a demolition party went to destroyer *Stewart*, lying toppled in her drydock ever since the Badung Strait affair, and set off some charges. They believed they had destroyed the useless ship, but they had not—the Japanese later repaired and used her throughout the war.

There were a handful of almost useless vessels in the harbor—old gunboats and merchant ships, and a few British corvettes. All were cleared out that day, and Admiral Palliser came down from Bandoeng to join Admiral Glassford aboard one of the PBYs that took them to Australia.

The defense of the Malay Barrier had ended in defeat.

When he arrived at Exmouth Gulf, on Australia's west coast, by PBY on March 2, Admiral Glassford concurred in Admiral Purnell's finding that it was not a proper place for a base. After a conference aboard the destroyer tender *Black Hawk* with the commanders of the two seaplane tenders *William B. Preston* and *Childs*, he left for Fremantle that same night.

His activities during the next few days included paying duty calls on other commanders and the civil authorities, establishing offices at Perth, a few miles from Fremantle, and solving the problem of his uniform. For Admiral Glassford's blues had been left behind in Java and he needed replacements. So short was the clothing supply, and so great the demand, that Admiral Glassford had to wind up with an inter-Allied compromise. He obtained a handsome set of blues—but they were made of Royal Air Force sky-blue wool!

He also began writing his report of command activities of the Asiatic Fleet, covering the period that began in China and ended with the last day in Java. It was a sad task, for the lonely ships of the far-off fleet had become even lonelier.

The Asiatic Fleet retreated from Java with no carriers, no cruisers, a handful of destroyers, 20-odd submarines, and a few service ships. By normal standards, the remnants could hardly qualify as a squadron. The condition of the ships made the appraisal even more doleful. The destroyers were a compendium of spit and sprung rivets, while the submarines were held together by tension and courage.

One by one the ships were accounted for. Tender *Otus* had been coming back to Tjilatjap from Ceylon; she was diverted in time to save her. Destroyer *Edsall* had been caught by the Japanese shortly after leaving *Pecos*—and she was sunk. *Pillsbury* was also sunk by the Japanese, and so was the gunboat *Ashville*, which had tried to make the dash from Tjilatjap.

But Commander Binford's destroyer group—*John D. Ford, Paul Jones, John D. Edwards,* and *Alden*—was safe in Australia. So were *Parrott* and *Whipple*. In fact, these six destroyers, the crippled cruiser *Marblehead*, and two gunboats were the only surface fighting ships of the old Asiatic Fleet to escape the Java campaign. Cruiser *Houston* and five destroyers had been lost, as well as aircraft tender *Langley* and other service ships. And the Dutch and British ships in the area had been virtually wiped out.

The Asiatic Fleet command had been severely reduced, and everything that Admiral Glassford learned, from Washington and from Melbourne and Sydney, indicated that it would be a long time before there would be any build-up. Except for the submarines and Patrol Wing 10's handful of PBYs, the fleet was now a ragtag operation.

The submarines would still fight on in Dutch East Indian waters. Commander Wilkes, their commander, was one of the last Americans to leave Java, on March 2, when he embarked in *Spearfish* for Fremantle. His submarines would henceforth report back to that port no matter where they might operate. Wilkes now had his priorities straightened out. Oil was the lifeblood of the Japanese economy and the Japanese fleet. Oil was available to the Japanese in the Dutch East Indies. So on March 6, Wilkes set as the priority of Asiatic Fleet submarines the destruction of Japanese supply lines between the East Indies and Japan proper—and particularly the oil supply lines that ran between Sumatra, Borneo, and Japan.

But by now the submarines were hunted as well as hunters, as the tale of *Perch* would show.

Perch was on patrol in the Java Sea, not far from the Japanese ship concentrations, where the hunting was bound to be good. But at two o'clock on the morning of March 2, on the surface, she was spotted by a Japanese destroyer, which came after her. She dived to 150 feet, but the enemy managed a damaging depth charge attack. She went down, the lights went out, the boat began to leak water, and the Japanese continued to attack. They attacked for hours, and many of the "ashcans" did vital damage to the submarine.

By three o'clock in the afternoon, the sounds of propellers had moved away and stayed away long enough for the captain to try to bring the boat up. She was stuck in the mud. Her periscopes were broken, her hatches were sprung and leaked water, many of the boat's motors were out, and the air was growing very foul. Finally, at 8:30 that evening, the crew managed to break the suction, get her out of the mud, and come to the surface.

All night long they ran for safety, but at five o'clock their luck ran out as three Japanese destroyers appeared on the scene. *Perch* dived. The hatches stuck, and immediately she began to take water, and the stern dropped so fast the captain thought he would never get her up again. She came up, slowly, ready to fight. She was ready except that her gun would not train and so was useless, and she was taking water badly. The captain decided to scuttle, and did so, the men coming up on deck and diving off into the water. The Japanese picked them up, roped them off on one section of deck, and gave them hardtack, tea and cigarettes. They were on their way to prison camp.

That was the lot of the lucky who were surprised by the Japanese and defeated. The lot of the unlucky submarine was to simply disappear, as *Shark* did.

In the Java Sea, after March 1 all ships were enemy, and the submarines of Asiatic Fleet began to score more heavily. *Seal* got two hits on a ship near Bali, and two more hits on an auxiliary. *Seawolf* ran into five ships in Badung Strait, sank a transport and a destroyer, and damaged three other ships. S-41 got a hit on a transport near Cape Mangkalihat, eastern Borneo. *Sailfish* claimed damage to a Kaga-class carrier in Lombok Strait. S-39 sank a tanker north of Sunda Strait. S-38 hit a light cruiser in that area, and *Salmon* also claimed hits on a light cruiser.

So even as the war ground along with apparent defeat for the Westerners everywhere they turned, the Japanese knew they were in for trouble from the submarines of the U.S. Asiatic Fleet.

38

The End of the Fleet

While the surviving ships of the Java campaign were gathering at Fremantle, that "other branch" of the Asiatic Fleet—the men and boats left in the Philippines—were playing a fighting role in the defense of Bataan and Corregidor.

This desperate rearguard operation displayed the Asiatic Fleet at its very best, and men who had been enjoying "the soft life" now faced up not only to reality but to living in crisis every moment for weeks and months at a time.

On March 1, a thousand men of the fleet were still on Bataan, overlooking the fortress of Corregidor. Most of them were at Mariveles, on the southern tip of the peninsula, which the navy had turned into a fortress. The vessels that remained were the China gunboats and a handful of PT boats, tugs, and other service ships. From the south, Admiral Glassford had radioed to Admiral Rockwell, much earlier, suggesting that he send them down to help in the defense of the Indies. But General MacArthur had stepped in, and in his forceful way had said that under no conditions would he let the boats go, for they were performing vital work around Bataan and Corregidor.

That statement was true enough, although by the beginning of March the activities of the surface craft were sharply restricted. The old submarine tender *Canopus* is a case in point. She had been bombed several times and hurt badly, with many of her men killed or wounded. She looked dreadful, with broken decks and fires still burning.

But much of that look was artful dodgery conducted by Commander E.L. Sackett, her skipper. After a few bad bombings he had pumped water in to give her a list, left the surface damage as it was and helped it along with a few fake additions. He also kept smudge pots full of oil rags burning to give an indication of fires. She looked like nothing more than an abandoned wreck, but the fact was that she was a busy factory, undertaking major repairs of the machinery on Bataan.

The other vessels afloat were all being used for night patrol work in close to Corregidor. In the daylight hours they hid in coves or in protected anchorages and hoped the Japanese would not attack them from the air. At night they were tigers—although they worked on the short leash of a diminishing fuel supply. Among them, this assortment of river gunboats, minesweepers, tugs, and the four PT boats still afloat managed to give the Japanese, with all their combined fleet, a very bad time, particularly if they approached the inshore waters of Bataan.

In the first week of March, with the collapse of the whole Java defense line and the growing feeling of entrapment indicated by the paucity of transportation out of the Philippines, General MacArthur began talking about going south. Already the American and Australian press were loudly discussing the need to have MacArthur regroup the whole Asian defense system from Australia. The merits of these arguments quite apart, Admiral Rockwell and the other naval authorities wished they had not been made quite so loudly, for in the second week of March, as if anticipating MacArthur's departure, the tempo of Japanese patrol work all around the Philippines stepped up remarkably.

Washington told MacArthur it would be all right to leave and turn command over to General Wainwright, who had been settled upon as the sacrificial lamb. The plan called for the general and his staff to go out by PBY, but in the end it was decided to use the PT boats as the surest and safest method of getting them away. MacArthur invited Admiral Rockwell to leave with him, along with a few members of his staff. In all, on March 11, some twenty-two passengers set out in the four PT boats, under the command of Lieutenant John D. Bulkeley, for the southern Philippines. It was a dangerous and difficult passage as they headed for Macajalar Bay on the northern coast of Mindanao. The boats got separated and came too close to major Japanese ships for comfort. But they made it. MacArthur and Rockwell were welcomed by General Sharp's army forces and put aboard a pair of B-17s for Australia, and on March 17, they arrived safely at Darwin.

The departure of Admiral Rockwell left Captain K.M. Hoeffel as the senior officer of the Asiatic Fleet in the Philippines. The situation of all the defenders was growing close to critical. They were short of food and losing weight every day. Medical supplies were getting low, and hundreds of men were suffering from fever. The only method of supply these days was by submarine, and inefficient and stopgap as it might be, that was the way it was done.

The struggle continued, with its daily bombings and the constant rollback of the Bataan line, all through the month of March. Five days after the evacuation of Admiral Rockwell, Lieutenant Champlin, his aide on loan to General Wainwright, and a number of other members of the staff were ordered out of the Philippines, along with army nurses and specialists. They would be taken out by Lieutenant Chapple, who brought the submarine *Permit* into the waters off Corregidor on March 16. As he waited, he went through the typical submarine drill of the times: He submerged and stayed quiet until dark, and then surfaced and made ready for action.

At about this time, Captain Hoeffel made a call to General Wainwright's headquarters and reached Lieutenant Champlin. "Pack up what you've got," the captain told the lieutenant. "And come to Corregidor at once. I'll see you at 1800."

Champlin did not know what he was wanted for. He was relatively happy on Bataan—risking his neck day and night under fire as he accompanied Wainwright on his visits to the troops. In fact, the general had already recommended Champlin for a pair of Silver Stars for deeds of valor, although Champlin did not know it then. He hated to leave in a way, so he went to Wainwright to ask if the general concurred in his return to Corregidor.

"Yes, Champ," said the general. "You're leaving tonight for Australia." He knew all about it; he agreed that Champlin was Rockwell's aide, not his, and belonged with the admiral. His last gesture was to give Champlin a letter and ask him to mail it when he got to Australia. Then Champlin left, tears in his eyes, and headed for safety, leaving one of the bravest men he had ever known, without being able to do anything further to help.

Clutching the Garand rifle the general had given him, Lieutenant Champlin headed down to Corregidor, and that night he was one of 111 people jammed into *Permit*, which had accommodation for half that number. They were depth-charged and spent thirty-six hours on the bottom off Verde Island, between Luzon and Mindero islands. The air grew so stale that the men began putting down lime to take up the carbon monoxide, and the captain feared that they might never surface again. They subsisted on Dutch stew—picked up earlier at Surabaya, and they slept on the "hot bunk" system, with bunks in continuous use. One officer occupied three lined-up chairs in the wardroom; another slept under the wardroom table.

As if conditions with all these people aboard were not bad enough, Lieutenant Chapple was given a combat mission—an assignment he accepted with complete aplomb. He traveled east to Tayabas Bay, in southern Luzon, to look over the shipping situation, took several shots at a destroyer and missed, was forced to dive for yet another depth-charging.

That was a hard night for the passengers. The submarine was clanging like a trolley car from the depth charge near misses. One charge settled below the boat and blew the bow up at an angle of 40 degrees. All the loose gear in the boat was knocked about, the lighting system failed for a time. When they finally reached Australia, the passengers knew they had been on a real voyage.

Back in the Philippines, the tempo of Japanese operations continued to pick up speed. With Java under occupation, Tokyo began pressing General Homma to get the Battle of Bataan finished so that the work of building the Greater East Asia CoProsperity Sphere could proceed. General Homma put the pressure on his commanders and on the navy. The Allied fighters on Bataan and Corregidor soon felt the intensity of the enemy action.

So did Commander Alan McCracken of the gunboat *Mindanao*, whose little flotilla of China river-gunboats was forced into ever-increasing evasion efforts. These three boats—*Mindanao, Oahu*, and *Luzon*—moved out east of Bataan every night. In February they had been in the south harbor anchorage of Manila Bay and they had patrolled bravely. In March they began to run out of fuel, and by the middle of the month they were taking turns just standing out at a point three miles east of Corregidor.

On the night of March 25 the three gunboats spotted nine Japanese boats, barges, and tugs coming out from Cavite, apparently bound for Corregidor to attack or infiltrate the lines. They ran in and attacked the boats, engaging them in a long fire fight without really knowing in the darkness what hits they had scored. Later they learned that the Japanese lost six small boats and tugs in this engagement, but it had to be broken off because in chasing the enemy the U.S. boats came up too close to Japanese field guns on the Bataan shore and were taken under fire.

Because of the serious difficulties in which every American found himself, camaraderie was the keynote among the navy men, and it even extended to the army. On March 30, *Mindanao* and *Oahu* were attacked from the air, and an army antiaircraft battery on Corregidor managed to shoot down one of the most persistent planes. So the cook of *Mindanao* searched around his galley and found a small store of mincemeat he had been saving up for a special occasion. That night the ship's boat delivered to the Corregidor ack-ack battery a dozen fresh-baked mince pies.

There were few such delicacies left on either Corregidor or Bataan. The reserves of canned tomatoes were growing smaller in Queen Tunnel. The supply of rice, the staple diet now, was also running out. And although Captain Wilkes would send submarines with supplies, the sixty tons or so that a submarine might bring in was hardly more than a drop in the bucket compared to the needs of the men of Bataan.

Swordfish was given the supply detail on April 1, and she sailed with forty tons of supplies from Fremantle for Corregidor. She was then scheduled to make a trip to Cebu Island to pick up another load of food and deliver it to Bataan. Then she would go home to Fremantle. In order to accomplish this supply mission, Lieutenant Commander C.C. Smith, her skipper, ordered all the torpedoes but eight off the boat, and reduced the ammunition virtually to zero. The ship's gun was left with only twenty-five rounds.

Smith set out then on a typical voyage. For several days, while outside Japanese waters, he was able to travel on the surface, watching carefully to be sure that these were still *not* Japanese waters. But on April 6, in Dutch East Indian waters, he dived at six o'clock in the morning and traveled submerged until six o'clock at night, when the sun was setting.

On April 7 he followed the same routine. But on the eighth, *Swordfish* encountered a Japanese submarine, which spotted her on the surface and came racing up, but then could not determine where she had dived. *Swordfish* was very near Ombai Strait, north of Timor Island, at this time, and she lay doggo on the bottom while the enemy submarine echo-ranged but did not find her. After this narrow escape, she surfaced at 10:30 that night and ran through the passage.

Next day *Swordfish* was still heading for Corregidor, but on April 10 her orders were changed. General Wainwright had evacuated Bataan on April 8, and those supplies, which had seemed so vital for the defense of the peninsula, were no longer vital. Smith was ordered to begin normal patrol operations in the Ambon area, between Celebes and New Guinea.

The operations were anything but normal. Smith spotted a few ships, but they were small ones, and with his limited supply of torpedoes he did not feel like wasting them. He was then ordered to scout the coast of Ceram Island, just north of Ambon and he did so. He could have shelled some installations there, but decided against it. He only had those twenty-five rounds, and they might be needed to defend the ship.

So *Swordfish* was out for thirty days on patrol, with her primary mission aborted. She did not fire a torpedo or shoot her gun before she came back to Fremantle on May 1.

Meanwhile attrition followed attrition in the Philippines. On the night of April 5 *Mindanao* and *Oahu* were on patrol east of Bataan when they ran into thirteen Japanese boats. These Japanese had 3-inch guns and .50-calibre machine guns, and one 3-inch shell started a fire in *Mindanao*'s pyrotechnics locker that made a grand display of fireworks above the ship. Captain McCracken pulled out of the fight, put out his fires, and then got back into the fray. They burned one Japanese boat that night, he was sure. They thought they had destroyed some others.

This fight caused the Japanese to scour every possible hiding place from the air with even more vigor in the next few days. *Mindanao* was also in on the evacuation of Bataan, picking up some sixty exhausted troops in her long boat, and keeping them safe until nightfall, when they could be delivered to Corregidor.

With the fall of Bataan, the Japanese naval and air activity in the waters around the peninsula was again increased.

On April 9 the minesweepers, gunboats, and tugs got the full attention of the squadrons of Japanese fighters and bombers that had been harrying the troops on Bataan until the evacuation. The ships were anchored three miles off the north shore of Corregidor at four o'clock that afternoon, when the Japanese shore batteries began to open up on them.

Lieutenant Commander T.W. Davison, the captain of *Finch*, was sitting in the little wardroom of minesweeper *Quail*, discussing with Captain Morrill what they were going to do next for excitement when the shelling began. He leaped out of his chair and scurried to his own ship as the shots began falling around them. All the ships got under way and zigzagged out into the center of Manila Bay for safety, the Japanese shore batteries adjusted their range and continued to drop shells among them.

Two of the fleet's tugs were sunk by the Japanese in that brief engagement, but the other vessels got away. Or at least they got out of range of the field guns. Then nine dive bombers began an attack, peeling off one after the other and screaming down to bombing range. Bombs began to land all around the ships, but they were all near misses, no hits. Minesweepers *Finch* and *Tanager* shot down one Japanese plane. *Luzon*, the old China river patrol flagship, took a shell in the admiral's quarters. All the ships were strafed by the low-flying Japanese who came in the teeth of the fire the ships threw up from their 3-inch guns and .50- and .30-calibre machine guns.

The battle continued without cease until seven o'clock, when the Japanese planes moved off in the gathering darkness and the guns stopped firing from the shore. But the Japanese won the fight, because by the end of the day the little ships were very nearly out of fuel, and they had expended large quantities of ammunition.

That night Captain Hoeffel ordered the gunboats and the smaller vessels abandoned. The crews of the three gunboats were sent to join the defenders of Fort Hughes on Caballo Island, just south of Corregidor. The crew of *Luzon* were to man the 14-inch naval battery at the top of the little island, those of *Mindanao* to go to Battery Craighill with its four 12-inch mortars, and those of *Oahu* to the antiaircraft batteries. The guns and salvageable items from the gunboats and other ships were to be removed and taken to the forts to continue the fight.

The officers and men did as they were told, but they also decided to make as much use of the ships as they could in the time left to them. They camouflaged the vessels, making them look deserted and half destroyed. And then, at night, they came aboard and worked the water evaporation plants and other machinery for the benefit of those ashore. But the deterioration from this point on was steady, caused by periodic Japanese bombing and the ravages of time without repairs.

From this point on the submarines that came in to Corregidor could no longer use the north channel between Bataan and the island. The Japanese had mined it. One of the sweepers, badly damaged as she was, was sent out to sweep a south channel through the minefield. They then settled down for the siege.

The bombings of the forts grew in intensity. After April 15 the Americans at Corregidor began to take heavy casualties, and the hospital in Malinta Tunnel became crowded. The Japanese were now operating day and night, taking advantage of the growing American weakness.

On April 8 the Americans evacuated Mariveles after destroying the installations there. The Dewey Dry Dock was blown up, along with minesweeper *Bittern*, which had been hit in an air raid so long ago. The tug *Napa* was destroyed rather than have it fall into the hands of the Japanese.

Canopus, the submarine tender, was backed out of her berth at Lilinbon Cove at four o'clock in the morning, and both anchors were set in such a fashion that she would block the cove. She was in twelve fathoms of water. Captain Sackett then supervised the scuttling. They opened the torpedo warhead locker and the forward magazine, then the flood valves forward and the main injection valve. Slowly she took a list, and then began to sink, but it was one o'clock in the afternoon before she finally went down.

The tunnels at Mariveles were blown up. The reluctant Filipino civilians were paid off and sent away with wishes for good luck—which they would need. And then Captain Sackett and his men set out for Corregidor in the two motor launches and the motorboat. Suddenly there was a tremendous explosion on the shore. It must have come from the gasoline storage facilities bottled up in the caves that had just been blown up. The explosion sank the motorboat, killed one man and wounded seven others, and nearly swamped the other little craft.

That was almost the end of the ships of the Asiatic Fleet in the Philippines. Down south, after taking General MacArthur and Admiral Rockwell to safety, the PT boats continued to operate for a while, until expended one by one. *PT-34* and Lieutenant Bulkeley's *PT-41* one night ran afoul of a Japanese cruiser off Negros Island, and fired some torpedoes at her. She responded with salvoes from her big guns and sent her destroyers after the presumptuous mosquitoes. During this fight, Lieutenant R.D. Kelly of *PT-34* thought he saw the cruiser turn into two PT-boat torpedoes. Her lights seemed to flicker and go out, and then he did not see her again.

PT-34 then had many other adventures trying to evade the Japanese and get to safety. She was chased and bombed and fought back with her machine guns until they were wrecked. In her last engagement she was beached when she could no longer fight, and abandoned after her dead and wounded were taken off. Later Lieutenant Kelly went back and burned her—an act symbolic of what was happening everywhere.

On April 27 Lieutenant Commander E.T. Neale of Patrol Wing 10 set out on one last daring mission to the Philippines. Leading two PBYs, he flew from Perth to Darwin, to General Sharp's area in Mindanao, and finally to Corregidor, to pick up more of the people the high officials had decided would be rescued from Japanese captivity. The two flying boats made Corregidor, picked up their passengers, including a number of army nurses, and came out. On the way home, Neale's plane was banged up in a landing and had to be repaired, an almost impossible job without reasonable facilities. And yet impossible or not, it was done, and the plane made it safely back to Australia. But the Japanese were moving fast. They captured the other plane and its passengers, just as they snared most of the stragglers and men who escaped into the jungles to fight on.

On May 4 minesweeper *Tanager* was hit by Japanese guns, and she exploded. On May 5, the Japanese bombed *Mindanao* and *Pigeon*, and both were destroyed. That left only minesweeper *Quail*, and she had been hit by three 6-inch shells and was in almost desperate condition. Two-thirds of her crew had been sent off to man Corregidor guns, and only a handful were left aboard.

On the night of May 5 the Japanese decided they would put an end to the troublesome American foothold on Corregidor and the little island forts nearby. At 8:30 that night the guns opened up. Commander J.H. Morrill of *Quail* was aboard the last vessel of the Asiatic Fleet in Philippine waters, and he watched in awe the scene of destruction that was spread before him. He estimated that the Japanese were using at least three hundred field pieces—perhaps twice as many. As the barrage grew in its intensity, a sheet of flame and smoke settled over Corregidor, and as the shells hit and tore away rock and shrubs, landslides cascaded down the steep slopes, until the beach was obliterated from view by clouds of dust so thick that searchlights from the "rock" peered through the murk like yellow cat's eyes.

From the frail decks of *Quail*, Commander Morrill and his men watched as the Japanese invaded the north shore of Corregidor, a landing timed by a green rocket. For when the rocket came up, the barrage suddenly ended, and the landing began. The silence was almost eerie—all that could be seen were a few machine-gun flashes, and all that could be heard were the sounds of those machine guns on Melinta Hill firing at the invaders.

The Japanese did not like those machine guns. At two o'clock in the morning the barrage of Melinta Hill opened up again for half an hour. The guns boomed and the flashes lit up the hill. Then another green rocket was fired and the barrage stopped. This time Melinta Hill was silent.

At 4:30 in the morning of May 6 Commander Morrill had a message from the land: He was to put the rest of his men ashore at Fort Hughes, on Caballo Island, for the defenses there were weak and they needed men to operate the antiaircraft guns.

So more men and officers went to Caballo Island that morning. Soon the Japanese attack on Corregidor began again, and this morning it seemed to be concentrated on Monkey Point. Then both dive and level bombers plastered Corregidor and Fort Hughes time and again. *Quail* seemed so small, so inoffensive and so nearly destroyed—perhaps so insignificant—that the Japanese did not seem even interested in hitting her.

At 10:30 that morning the order from Queen Tunnel was to scuttle all ships—the last message Commander Morrill was to receive from headquarters on Corregidor. He saw white flags on the island, dotting the hillsides here and there. But the Japanese kept right on firing. White flags were also up at Fort Frank on Carabao and Fort Drum on Fraile, two little islands south of Caballo, but guns and planes continued to hit those forts as well.

Commander Morrill went ashore at Fort Hughes and brought men to the dock to help him scuttle his ship. As they were ready to step into the ship's boat, it was sunk by a shell, and the captain and four men had to swim out two hundred yards to another moored boat. Then, under strafing from airplanes, they rowed over to *Quail* and began sinking her. More white flags could be seen above the forts. The Japanese continued to attack.

On May 6 the men of Fort Hughes spiked the cannon and began throwing away their rifles and handguns, and raising white flags. The Japanese ignored them. Over at Corregidor, they were now on Monkey Point.

Commander Morrill and his men left the scuttled *Quail* and took refuge in the deserted tug *Ranger*, which was beached near the Caballo shore. There they hid from the Japanese, for Commander Morrill was determined that he was not going to give up. He had a 36-foot naval launch at his disposal, and a pocket watch, and some small-scale charts of the Philippines and the Netherlands East Indies. He had some crewmen and would pick up some more.

He was going to try to escape.

39

The Last Heroes

As of May 6, 1942, the Asiatic Fleet had in fact ceased to exist, for all its ships were gone, and those which had managed to escape at various times and were now in Australian waters were rapidly being absorbed in a command that would eventually become "MacArthur's Navy," commanded in its later days of glory by Admiral Thomas F. Kincaid. Admiral Glassford had made his approach to Washington for supreme command of sea forces in Australia—just as MacArthur had the land forces command—and Glassford had been rebuffed. There would only be one supreme commander in Australia.

Henceforth, from that command would emanate the mainstream of Allied power in the Pacific war. For the fall of Corregidor was imminent. It took place shortly before midnight on May 6, when General Wainwright surrendered all forces in the Philippines to the Japanese. Although the enemy continued attacking some of the Allied positions, including the outlying forts, in the following days the battle for the Philippines was over.

But at Fort Hughes Commander Morrill did not wait for the surrender. He had a working unit of the Asiatic Fleet and he was going to fight until he reached Allied territory. So the morning of May 6 found Morrill and his men busy with their plans. They scoured the *Ranger* for clothes, guns, ammunition, and better charts. They found 450 gallons of diesel fuel aboard, and stowed that in their 36-foot boat.

When darkness fell, they took the boat in to Fort Hughes to consult with the rest of the crew of *Quail* and determine who wanted to come along. Some of the men who had been fighting the Japanese at those guns were too exhausted to make the journey, but Gunner Donald G.

Taylor and sixteen men opted to join Morrill and make the attempt to break out and fight their way to Australia.

At 10:15 that night they set off to leave the bay and the white flags that flew so forlornly on Corregidor as the Japanese continued to shoot at the exhausted Americans. They left none too soon. Fifteen minutes later the Japanese began laying down a barrage on Caballo Island, which meant Fort Hughes. Had they waited, it was very likely that their boat would have been sunk and the chance to escape lost.

The Americans moved slowly and cautiously in their boat, and they hid in a cove on the south shore of Manila Bay, across from Corregidor, as long as the lights of the barrage continued to flash. Not until a green rocket ended the firing did they move again. Then they headed out down the coast at 3 knots. At one o'clock on the morning of May 7 they spotted two destroyers patrolling near Fortune Island, south of the bay, and then another destroyer and a patrol boat. So it was back to the cove that night under cover of darkness, to hide and find another exit next day.

On May 8, five miles away from Fort Hughes, they watched the Japanese continue to bombard the forts throughout the long day. A pair of seaplanes came over, but the men of *Quail* had covered their boat with green fronds and branches, and the seaplanes dipped down to three hundred feet right above them and did not see them. They saw a pair of destroyers and a minesweeper and sixteen patrol boats stand into Corregidor, and then come out. They were sure the boats were taking out prisoners of war.

They would have left their cove on the night of the seventh except that one of the destroyers came in and anchored a few hundred yards from the boat and remained until dawn. So did they. They stayed in hiding until long after dark on May 8, and then got in their boat and headed south along the coast.

All night long they saw the lights and searchlights of Japanese destroyers and patrol boats, but they hugged the shore and were not seen. They passed Fortune Island again, still hugging the shore, and spotted three enemy patrol boats in the darkness between Fortune Island and the Lubang Islands, to the southwest. They waited until the boat nearest shore had turned, and then they scurried by, and no one saw them.

On May 9 the men of the fleet met daybreak off the southwest coast of Luzon Island. They had at least escaped the trap of Corregidor and Manila Bay. They did not know the shore, and so they stayed outside the reef that day, hoping no one saw them, painting their gray boat black to disguise it as anything but an American naval craft, and tearing off the taffrail to change it even more.

That night of May 9 they set out at eight o'clock to make the Verde Island passage between Luzon and Mindoro. Patrol boats again. Lots of them. Then the engine, which had not been used for months for sustained effort, broke down and they had to get under canvas and work with flashlights to get the engine going again before dawn.

At daylight on May 10, the eighteen men in their boat reached the Luzon village of Digas and met their first friends in days. But the villagers had bad news. There were small garrisons of Japanese all around the area, and the Americans must not stay. So the Filipinos gave them food and they headed for the Bondoc Peninsula, a southern arm of Luzon.

There, in the village of Bondoc, they secured a Manila newspaper, two days old, which told of Wainwright's surrender of Corregidor, but dated it at least two days before the Japanese stopped shooting at Corregidor. Morrill and his men were confused but not inclined to discover the facts by asking the Japanese.

On May 13 they shoved off into more open waters, entering the Sibuyan Sea and moving on past the southwest end of Masbate Island, in the central Philippines. They reached Cebu on May 15.

Between Cebu and Leyte they had a fright. They passed a tanker flying the Japanese merchant flag, and he came by only three thousand yards away. They all hid below except the helmsman, who looked more pirate than naval man, and they passed inspection, for the tanker went on, and no snooping Kawanishi flying boat came up to investigate them.

At one o'clock in the afternoon of May 15 they landed on the northwest coast of Leyte. From a Chinese storekeeper, they bought more diesel oil and some canned goods for their journey across the open sea. They also learned that the Japanese were on Leyte in strength and that American and Filipino units were surrendering to them. They must not stay. Even now, their friends told them, the Japanese may have learned from traitors that they were in the area.

That night, as if to emphasize the matter, a small power boat entered Tabango Bay, where they were moored, on the Leyte coast. Once it was inside the bay, the Americans sped off as silently as possible, headed for Surigao Strait between Leyte and Dinagat islands, and continued south.

Two and a half years later, some of the very Japanese who were patrolling these islands would go to their deaths here at the hands of Ad-

miral Kincaid's heirs to the Asiatic Fleet. But now it was Japanese
water and very dangerous.

May 17—Squalls. They reached Tandag on northeastern Mindanao. Got more provisions from another Chinese merchant. More oil.
More encouragement—but also the bad news that the Japanese were
coming here. They saw six patrol boats that night but they were protected inside a cove, and the Japanese went on by.

May 18—They left Port Lamon, cheered by Filipinos who increased
their fuel supplies and even swam out to the boat with a drum of diesel
fuel. But they had the feeling of urgency to be away, and that night
they were gone, heading farther south.

Now they were outside the zone of friendship—they were into the
East Indies, gone from Philippine waters. Whatever friendship forty
years of association had made up north could not be transferred here.

On May 24 they arrived at Fisang Island, north of Timor, and the
engine conked out. Should they go on by sail? The problem was a
burned-out bearing. But for sail they had no counterboard—the 36-
footer was never intended for sailing; she was a work boat with an engine. The natives of the Dutch East Indies were not interested in these
foreigners any more than they were interested in the Japanese. They
were strictly neutral in a struggle between people who meant nothing to
them.

The Americans must go on, that much they knew, for among people
like this they would be sure to be betrayed eventually. These islanders
would take neither United States nor Philippine currency. The only
way Morrill could secure some supplies was through barter for valua-
bles.

They managed to crank up the engine, although they did not get the
bearing fixed. They could limp along a little way. They made it to the
island of Keor, in the easternmost Dutch East Indies, where they saw a
lugger in the lagoon. They entered the harbor, and the lugger ran up
the Japanese flag—which sent their hearts into their mouths. But then,
when the lugger crew saw that the new arrivals were Americans, they
ran down the Japanese flag. Interesting, but not a good place to linger.

At Keor they met a schoolteacher who spoke a little English, and he
informed them with an air of great knowledge that the Japanese had already captured Tasmania and New Zealand and were moving on Australia. It was not very comforting information, but they had no way of
knowing whether or not it was true.

Here the men of *Quail* paused long enough for their mechanical wiz-
ard to fix the engine. They had to—they were about to set out across

the open sea for Australia, and they could not take chances on a break-down, or at least no more chances than they were already taking. So they ran the danger of detection and beached the boat, while the mechanics carved a new stern bearing for the propeller shaft from hardwood and installed it. It worked.

They said good-bye to the "friends" at Keor, whom they did not trust, and set out for nearby Molol Island, and then on May 31 for the long jump south to Melville Island, north of Darwin, Australia, which they reached on June 4. There they encountered their first real friends, Australian missionaries, and they had a good meal for the first time in months. The next day they moved on at a leisurely pace into Darwin, crossed the bar, and entered the harbor without a single bit of attention being paid them. They then made their way to land, to report to the only Americans in sight, some officers of an army air force unit.

They had sailed twenty-nine days, these men of the Asiatic Fleet, all of it in an open boat. They had traveled 2,060 miles without a sextant or decent charts, using a pocket watch as a chronometer. Commander Morrill had brought his men to base, and now he was looking for his fleet, ready to fight again.

In capsule, the story of Commander Morrill and his men was the story of the Asiatic Fleet. As Admiral King put it, theirs is the story of a "magnificent display of human courage under impossible conditions."

Let that be the fleet's requiem.

Bibliography

The material in this book comes from many sources. Besides the invaluable information provided by various branches of the U.S. Navy—its library, its history division, and the naval academy—and from interviews with many naval persons, I used material from *Proceedings*, the monthly publication of the U.S. Naval Institute, and from numerous books that have touched on the subjects covered. In addition, the book contains tales told to me during my own years in China.

Among material from the navy's history division, I drew extensively on the reports of two leading commanders of the Asiatic Fleet, Admirals W.A. Glassford and Thomas C. Hart. Glassford's three reports, official and unofficial, tell his whole story with the fleet, going back to the gunboat days on the Yangtze, including his escape in the *Luzon* from Shanghai to Manila Bay shortly before Pearl Harbor, through to the establishment in western Australia of the remnants of the fleet. Hart's two excellent reports cover his feelings and actions throughout the period of his command.

Outstanding among numerous navy narratives used are the four written by Lieutenant Malcolm M. Champlin, giving accounts of events at Bataan, Cavite, and Manila, and during his escape from Corregidor by submarine. Also especially useful were reports by Commander Thomas K. Bowers (land fighting in the Mariveles area), Commander Alan McCracken (adventures of the *Mindanao*, including the last days of the Bataan campaign), Commander J.H. Morrill (escape by launch to Australia), and Lieutenants J.B. Dawley and Thomas Moorer (PBY adventures).

Valuable information came from action reports of many fighting ships, including *Houston, Marblehead, Langley, William B. Preston,* and *Peary*. Among publications in *Proceedings*, I found the narrative of Cadet J.K. Taussig most useful in compiling the chapter on the Boxer

Rebellion. My own book *The Boxer Rebellion* and Robley D. Evans's *An Admiral's Log* were also vital to this chapter.

More than a score of other books provided me with important source material. Especially valuable were Hamilton Darby Perry's *The Panay Incident*, a complete account of that memorable affair; Kemp Tolley's *Yangtze Patrol*, with much colorful anecdotal material; and three books by Samuel Eliot Morison: *The Rising Sun in the Pacific, 1931-April 1942* (Volume 3 in his distinguished nine-volume *History of the United States Naval Operations in World War II*), *The Two-Ocean War*, and *Old Bruin*, dealing with Commodore Matthew D. Perry's career.

The following books are recommended for further reading:

Barker, Albert S. *Everyday Life in the Navy*. Boston: R.G. Badger, 1928.

Braisted, William Reynold. *The United States Navy in the Pacific, 1897-1909*. Austin: University of Texas Press, 1958; reprint, Westport, Conn.: Greenwood Press.

——*The United States Navy in the Pacific, 1909-1922*. Austin: University of Texas Press, 1971.

Coontz, Robert F. *From the Mississippi to the Sea*. Philadelphia: Dorrance, 1930.

D'Albas, Andrieu. *Death of a Navy*. Greenwich, Conn.: Devin-Adair, 1957.

Dewey, George. *Autobiography*. New York: Scribner's, 1913; reprints, New York: AMS Press, 1970; New York: Scholarly Reprints, 1971.

Dyer, George C. *On the Treadmill to Pearl Harbor, the Memoirs of Admiral James O. Richardson*. Washington, D.C.: U.S. Naval History Division, 1973.

Evans, Robley D. *An Admiral's Log*. New York: D. Appleton, 1910.

Hawks, Francis L., ed. *Narrative of the Expedition of an American Squadron in the China Seas and Japan, Performed in the Years 1852, 1853, and 1854, under the Command of M.C. Perry, U.S. Navy*. 3 vols. Washington, D.C.: A.O.P. Nicholson, 1856.

Hoyt, Edwin P. *The Boxer Rebellion*. New York: Abelard-Schuman, 1968.

——*The Last Cruise of the Emden*. New York: Macmillan, 1966.

——*The Army Without a Country*. New York: Macmillan, 1967.

Johnson, Robert E. *Thence Around Cape Horn*. New York: Naval Institute Press, 1964.

Knox, Dudley W. *A History of the United States Navy.* New York: Putnam's, 1948.

Mitchell, Donald W. *History of the Modern American Navy, from 1883 Through Pearl Harbor.* New York: Knopf, 1946.

Morison, Samuel Eliot. *The Rising Sun in the Pacific, 1931-April 1942.* Boston: Atlantic-Little Brown, 1948.

———*The Two-Ocean War.* Boston: Atlantic-Little Brown, 1963.

———*Old Bruin: Commodore Matthew C. Perry, 1794-1858.* Boston: Atlantic-Little Brown, 1967.

Perry, Hamilton Darby. *The Panay Incident.* New York: Macmillan, 1969.

Rodman, Hugh. *Yarns of a Kentucky Admiral.* Indianapolis: Bobbs-Merrill, 1928.

Sawyer, Frederick L. *Sons of Gunboats.* New York: Naval Institute Press, 1946.

Thomas, David A. *The Battle of the Java Sea.* New York: Stein and Day, 1969.

Tolley, Kemp. *Yangtze Patrol.* New York: Naval Institute Press, 1971.

———*The Cruiser of the Lanikai.* New York: Naval Institute Press, 1973.

Walworth, Arthur. *Black Ships Off Japan, the Story of Commodore Perry's Expedition.* New York: Knopf, 1946; reprint, Hamden, Conn.: Shoe String Press, 1966.

Wheeler, Gerald F. *Prelude to Pearl Harbor.* Columbia: University of Missouri Press, 1963 (also in paperback).

Wiley, Henry A. *An Admiral from Texas.* Garden City: Doubleday, 1934.

Winslow, Walter G. *Ghost of the Java Coast, the Saga of the USS Houston.* Satellite Beach, Fla.: Coral Reef Publications, 1974.

Index

H 12